W9-ARC-711

Structure and Creativity in Religion

Religion and Reason 14

Method and Theory
in the Study and Interpretation of Religion

GENERAL EDITOR

Jacques Waardenburg, *University of Utrecht*

BOARD OF ADVISERS

Th. P. van Baaren, *Groningen*
R. N. Bellah, *Berkeley*
E. Benz, *Marburg*
U. Bianchi, *Rome*
H. J. W. Drijvers, *Groningen*
W. Dupré, *Nijmegen*
S. N. Eisenstadt, *Jerusalem*
M. Eliade, *Chicago*
C. Geertz, *Princeton*
K. Goldammer, *Marburg*
P. Ricœur, *Paris* and *Chicago*
M. Rodinson, *Paris*
N. Smart, *Lancaster* and
Santa Barbara, Calif.
G. Widengren, *Stockholm*

MOUTON PUBLISHERS · THE HAGUE · PARIS · NEW YORK

Structure and Creativity in Religion

Hermeneutics in Mircea Eliade's Phenomenology and New Directions

DOUGLAS ALLEN

University of Maine

Foreword by
MIRCEA ELIADE

ST. JOSEPH'S UNIVERSITY   STX

BL43.E4A68
Structure and creativity in religion :

3 9353 00061 5714

BL
43
.E4
A68

175269

MOUTON PUBLISHERS · THE HAGUE · PARIS · NEW YORK

ISBN: 90–279–7594–9

Jacket design by Jurriaan Schrofer

© 1978, Mouton Publishers, The Hague, The Netherlands

Printed in Great Britain

To my parents, David and Frances
My first teachers
To my Vietnamese comrades
Some recent teachers

Foreword
by
MIRCEA ELIADE

It was with great interest that I read the manuscript of this work several years ago. I knew the author, a young philosophy professor, who was ardently pursuing both phenomenology and Indian thought but who was also showing a budding interest in problems concerning the history of religions. We discussed certain chapters at length and I personally profited a great deal from this dialogue. When I accepted Professor Douglas Allen's suggestion that I write this Foreword, I decided to return to and continue the discussion begun in our earlier meetings.

I now realize the brashness of this project. To be at all meaningful and to the point, the dialogue between an author and his critic must take into consideration all the problems posed by the author's work and all the objections raised by his critic — even at the risk of extending the author's commentaries to book length. For myself, I plan someday to dedicate an entire work to discussing the objections put forth by some of my critics, those who are responsible and acting in all good faith (for the others do not deserve the bother of a reply).

For the moment, I shall have to limit myself to a few observations of a rather general nature. In attempting to present what is essential in my methodology, Professor Allen has rightly stressed, firstly, the importance of the dialectic of the sacred and, secondly, the central role of religious symbolism.

As I have stated so many times, the sacred has shown itself to be an element in the structure of consciousness and not a stage in the history of this consciousness. A meaningful world — for man cannot live in a state of 'chaos' — is the result of a dialectical process which phenomenologists and historians of religion call the manifestation of the sacred. Human existence takes on meaning through the imitation of the paradigmatic models revealed by Supernatural Beings (godheads, mythical ancestors, civilizing heroes, and so forth). The imitation of transhuman models, that is to say, the ritual repetition of acts performed by these Supernatural Beings at the dawn of time, constitutes an essential feature of religious life. At the most primitive levels of culture, *to live as a human being* is itself *a religious act*; as eating, sexual activity and work are performed in accordance with models revealed by Supernatural Beings, they thus have a sacramental value. In other words, being — or rather becoming — a man means being 'religious'.

The dialectic of the sacred, then, preceded all the other dialectical movements which were later discovered by the mind and served as their model. Through the experience of the sacred, man grasped the difference between that which was revealed as real, powerful and meaningful and that which lacks these qualities, namely the chaotic and perilous course of things, their fortuitous and senseless appearing and disappearing. In the final analysis, the experience of the sacred opened the way for systematic thought.

This in itself should be sufficient to stimulate the interest of philosophers in the work of religious historians and phenomenologists, but there are other aspects of religious experience which are no less compelling. Hierophanies — that is, manifestations of the sacred expressed in symbols, myths and Supernatural Beings, etc. — are apprehended as structures, and these form a prereflective language calling for a particular hermeneutic. As a result of this hermeneutic labor, the materials at the disposal of the religious historian present a series of 'messages' awaiting decoding and comprehension. These 'messages' do not 'speak' to us only of a past long stilled but reveal existential situations of great moment to modern man.

Professor Allen has rightly stressed the importance I attach to symbols and to symbolic thought in the interpretation of the religious phenomenon. Indeed — to mention only a few of the most characteristic features — symbols are capable of revealing a mode of reality as a structure of the world not evident on the level of direct experience; their principal trait is their multivalence, the ability to express several things at once the connection of which is not evident on the level of direct experience; symbols are capable of revealing a perspective in which diverse realities are linked within a whole or even integrated in a 'system'. Of equal importance is the capacity symbols possess for expressing paradoxical situations or certain structures of ultimate reality which would otherwise be inexpressible (*e.g. coincidentia oppositorum*). Finally, the existential value of religious symbolism must be underscored, namely the fact that a symbol always aims at something real or at the very situation of human existence as such.

By way of conclusion, I must add that my understanding of religious symbolism was greatly enhanced by my stay in India. I feel I was extremely fortunate to have been able to go to India when I was scarcely twenty-one and to have stayed there for three years studying with Professor Surendranath Dasgupta at the University of Calcutta, especially fortunate to have had the chance to live in his Bhawanipore home, to visit most of the cities and the most important temples and, in particular, the chance to spend six months in a Hardwar *ashram* in the Himalayas. My encounter with this tradition-laden culture at an age when spiritual discoveries can still enrich and transform one's personality has had important consequences over and beyond my work as an Indian scholar. Indeed, the understanding of religious symbolism as it is lived at the level of the people has helped me to better grasp the symbolism still alive in my own tradition, that of an Eastern European people.

It has been in pursuing these initial discoveries through the course of the years that my interest has focused more and more on folklore and popular traditions — whether European or Asiatic —, on archaic religions, on mystics and on the shaman techniques for attaining ecstasy.

Having himself personal experience of Indian culture, Professor Allen has firmly grasped the importance of India in my intellectual formation. One more reason to express my gratitude for his attentive and sympathetic reading and consideration of my work.

Paris, August 1977   MIRCEA ELIADE

Author's Preface

Examination of the discipline of the History of Religions (*Religions-wissenschaft*), of which the phenomenology of religion will be viewed as one 'branch', reveals that the central contemporary problems are methodological in nature. Most of the nineteenth and twentieth century approaches to religious phenomena, while involving a vast accumulation of religious data, have tended to be methodologically uncritical, highly subjective and normative. My position is that if Mircea Eliade, who is considered the foremost contemporary phenomenologist of religion, represents a methodological improvement over previous approaches, this is because of an impressive hermeneutical framework which serves as the foundation for his phenomenological approach to religious phenomena.

Throughout our formulation of the nature of Eliade's phenomenological approach, our attempt to relate his phenomenology to various methodological problems and to concepts in phenomenological philosophy, and our suggestions for new directions in moving beyond his phenomenology, the reader will notice the crucial importance of concepts of 'structure' and 'creativity'. Structure is at the foundation of Eliade's methodology. Eliade will claim that religious experience has a specific religious structure; that in terms of the unique structure of sacralization, we may distinguish religious from nonreligious phenomena. He will attempt to interpret meaning through structure; to grasp the meaning of a particular religious phenomenon by reintegrating it within its structural system of symbolic associations.

In Eliade's phenomenology, creativity emerges not out of some void but from structure, not from nothingness but from what we do with structures that are in some sense 'given'. Creativity emerges when we can experience those fundamental structures of the world, those essential symbolic structures, and 'revalorize' them so that we 'burst open' the prevailing limiting ways of experiencing reality to reveal new universes of meaning. Not only will Eliade view the history of religious manifestations as a creative process, but he will criticize 'modern' society for its provincialism and will suggest possibilities for new creative breakthroughs and new philosophical anthropologies.

There are three distinguishable but interrelated parts to this study. In Part I, we examine the leading nineteenth and twentieth century approaches and arrive at some understanding of the present hermeneutical situation in the History of Religions. In order to understand Eliade's approach, it is necessary to comprehend the contributions and limitations of the evolutionists, functionalists, and other anthropologists; of the sociologists, psychologists, and phenomenologists; in short, of the various approaches which have defined the context within which Eliade interprets the meaning of religious phenomena. Chapters 1, 2, and 3 provide a brief but rather comprehensive introduction to the major approaches in the History of Religions.

In Part II, we formulate the key methodological notions which provide the foundation for Eliade's phenomenology: the dialectic of the sacred and the profane and the 'autonomous', universal, coherent, structural systems of symbolic associations. In terms of the interaction of these methodological notions, we can begin to determine on what basis Mircea Eliade distinguishes religious from nonreligious phenomena and interprets the meaning of a religious phenomenon. In contrast to the numerous interpreters of Eliade who have submitted that he has never been concerned with questions of methodology and is methodologically uncritical, we maintain that Eliade has an impressive methodological framework of interpretation. This is probably the first attempt to ground Eliade's methodology in his view of symbolism.

Part III presents the most controversial analysis in the book and at the same time offers the greatest possibilities for new directions and creative 'openings'. Here we go far beyond anything Mircea Eliade has ever written. We raise many methodological issues implicit in his approach and endeavor to modify his phenomenological approach to render it more adequate and to suggest many creative possibilities for future research.

Several sections of this book are revisions of previously published articles. I wish to thank the following journals for permission to use revisions of these articles: 'Mircea Eliade's Phenomenological Analysis of Religious Experience', *Journal of Religion* 52 (1972): 170–186; 'Givenness and Creativity', *Journal of Thought* 8 (1973): 270–78. An earlier version of one section in the book appeared as 'A Phenomenological Evaluation of Religious Mysticism', *Darshana International* 12 (1972): 71–78.

I would like to thank the University of Maine at Orono Faculty Research Funds Committee for a Faculty Summer Research Award, which was of great assistance in allowing me to revise the manuscript and get it into publishable form.

I would like to acknowledge a debt of gratitude to several persons who have assisted me in this research. I have been overwhelmed by the lively spirit, creativity, and dedication of Professor Mircea Eliade and by the personal interest he has shown toward my research during the past ten years. From the perspective of phenomenological philosophy and philosophy in general, Professor John J. Compton provided invaluable assistance: this complemented the suggestions of such Historians of Religion as Professors Charles H. Long and Winston L. King. During the earliest stages of this research, Ruth White provided great assistance. Finally, I wish to acknowledge the assistance of Ilze Petersons, whose understanding and sensitivity are reflected throughout this book.

Contents

Part Two: *Eliade's Phenomenology: Key Methodological Notions*

Part Three: *Eliade's Phenomenology and New Directions:*
          Some Methodological Issues and Conclusions

PART ONE

Methodological Approaches in
the History of Religions

Early Methodological Approaches

Introduction

Mircea Eliade identifies himself with the modern discipline originally known as *Allgemeine Religionswissenschaft*. The expression *Religionswissenschaft* was first used in 1867 by F. Max Müller in his *Chips from a German Workshop*.[1] By using the term *Religionswissenschaft*, Müller wanted to stress that this new discipline would be freed from the philosophy of religion and especially from theology. This discipline would be descriptive, scientific, and objective; it would avoid the normative and subjective nature of previous studies of religions.

The German term *Religionswissenschaft* has not been given a generally acceptable English equivalent. Scholars in the field refer to their discipline by such titles as 'the science of religions', 'the history of religions', 'comparative religion', 'the phenomenology (psychology, sociology, etc.) of religion', 'the study of world religions'.[2] What is at stake here is not simply a difficulty of translatability or a trivial question of personal preference. Many historians of religion have little if anything in common with various comparativists. Indeed, they may claim that the exponents of comparative religion are really theologians

1. 'It is true that the term "science of religions" had been sporadically used earlier (in 1852 by the Abbé Prosper Leblanc, in 1858 by Stiefelhagen, etc.), but not in the strict sense given it by Max Müller, which then passed into current usage.' Mircea Eliade, *The Sacred and the Profane*, p. 216. Cited hereafter as *The Sacred*.
2. For a study of the growth of this discipline and its nomenclature, see Louis Henry Jordan's *Comparative Religion: Its Genesis and Growth* (Edinburgh: T. and T. Clark, 1905). An excellent work on the development of this field is the first volume of Henri Pinard de la Boullaye's *L'Étude comparée des religions* (Paris: Beauchesne, 1922). See the two-volume work by Jacques Waardenburg, *Classical Approaches to the Study of Religion: Aims, Methods and Theories of Research* (The Hague and Paris: Mouton, 1973–74). Volume 1 consists of an Introduction ('View of a Hundred Years' Study of Religion') and an Anthology. Volume 2 contains what is probably the most comprehensive Bibliography available for the major scholars in the field from 1850 to 1950, with the exclusion of scholars who are still alive.

in disguise. Even when individuals refer to their work by the same term, it is sometimes difficult to discern much similarity in anything they are doing.

'Comparative religion' is the most popular term, but it has the disadvantage of having been employed repeatedly for normative purposes. Ever since about 1880, when 'comparative religion' came into common usage, most 'comparativists' have compared religions in order to determine their relative value and then to demonstrate the superiority of their own position.[3] As Huston Smith has written: 'Comparisons among things men hold dear always tend to be odious, those among religions most odious of all. . . . Comparative religion which takes such questions [of comparative worth] for its concern usually degenerates into competitive religion.'[4] Not only has the proponent of a particular religion conceived of comparative religion as a form of apologetics, but, in a similar polemical fashion, others have sought to demonstrate the 'primitiveness' and lack of value in all religion.

Scholars have attempted to eliminate some of this confusion by agreeing to an English title that would most adequately reflect the nature of *Allgemeine Religionswissenschaft*.

Thus, the world-wide organization of scholars in this field has recently adopted an official English title, 'The International Association for the Study of the History of Religions.' It is readily apparent that the term 'history of religions' has come to be regarded as a synonym for the 'general science of religions', and as such the nature of the discipline must be discussed in the total context of *Religionswissenschaft*.[5]

In this study we shall understand 'History of Religions' as referring to the entire discipline of *Religonswissenschaft*. This general study of religion has been classified in various ways; one of the best known classifications has been Joachim Wach's division of the field into four branches: history, phenomenology, psychology, and sociology of

3. W. Brede Kristensen, *The Meaning of Religion*, pp. 1–2.
4. Huston Smith, *The Religions of Man*, p. 15.
5. Joseph M. Kitagawa, 'The History of Religions in America', *The History of Religions: Essays in Methodology*, p. 15.

religion.[6] When we wish to refer to history 'proper', which will be viewed as one 'branch' of the 'History of Religions', we shall use the term 'history of religions'. When a scholar uses 'history of religions' while referring to the entire field of *Religionswissenschaft*, we shall insert '[History of Religions]' in the text. It will be our position that Mircea Eliade is a Historian of Religions, who specializes in that branch of the History of Religions known as 'the phenomenology of religion'.

Throughout this study, the terms *homo religiosus, premodern, traditional, archaic, and primitive*[7] will usually be used interchangeably. By *modern* and *nonreligious*, we refer to a characteristic attitude of contemporary Western society: 'Modern man's originality, his newness in comparison with traditional societies, lies precisely in his determination to regard himself as a purely historical being, in his wish to live in a basically desacralized cosmos.'[8] At this point, we shall simply indicate that the modern person denies that which is most characteristic of *homo religiosus*: the recognition of a 'transhuman', 'transhistorical', transcendent, absolute reality (the sacred), which manifests itself in the world and which allows us to know all that is ultimately meaningful, significant, and real.[9]

We shall now begin our sketch of methodological approaches in the History of Religions. By means of this historical sketch, we intend to lay the foundation for understanding the nature of the History of Religions as an academic discipline today. More specifically, we wish to see how Mircea Eliade deals with the central issues and problems

6. See Joachim Wach, *Sociology of Religion*, pp. 1–2; C. Jouco Bleeker, 'The Contribution of the Phenomenology of Religion to the Study of the History of Religions', *Problems and Methods of the History of Religions*, p. 40.

7. The term 'primitive' can be misleading since it immediately suggests certain pejorative meanings (naive, simple, etc.) which often interfere with our attempt to describe these cultures as objectively as possible. In addition, it will often be necessary to distinguish differences in the attitudes of various 'premodern' cultures. For example, 'primitive' ('pre-literate', 'archaic') is properly applied to the Paleolithic hunters and food gatherers, although it does not describe such cultures as Upaniṣadic India. See Mircea Eliade, *The Myth of the Eternal Return*, p. 3; Mircea Eliade, *From Primitives to Zen*, p. vi.

8. Mircea Eliade, *Rites and Symbols of Initiation*, p. ix. This book was first published as *Birth and Rebirth* (New York: Harper & Brothers, 1958).

9. See *The Sacred*, pp. 202–203.

emerging from past approaches to religious phenomena and whether his phenomenological approach can be evaluated as a methodological improvement.

Our presentation will generally adhere to some sort of chronological order. When it seems advantageous, both to bring greater coherence to the multitude of facts and to stress crucial issues, we shall not hesitate to violate this 'horizontal' format by introducing a 'thematic' principle of organization.

The History of Religions: Its Prehistory

Although the History of Religions as an autonomous discipline only began in the nineteenth century, investigations into the nature of religion are well documented as early as ancient Greece. Sometimes theories arose from the natural curiosity aroused by exposure to 'exotic' cultures of hitherto unknown peoples; usually theories arose from apologetic and theological needs when different religions came into contact with each other.

Charles J. Adams submits that 'The two situations most evocative of theories on the nature of religion have been those where rival religious systems confronted one another directly and those of crisis and breakdown within an established religious community.'[10] The emergence of rationalism in Europe, as evidenced in the re-examination of religion by the Enlightenment, illustrates the second 'situation'. It appears that the creation of the History of Religions was largely a product of the thought of the Enlightenment.

Often the Enlightenment is characterized as rejecting religion in the light of scientific and intellectual progress. Certainly this is the strongest current in French Encyclopaedism: *homo religiosus* is the 'slave of superstition', still imprisoned by the 'yoke of religion'. One recalls Diderot's image of the 'Hydra of religion': Deism had cut off a dozen heads, but from the one head it had spared all the others would grow once again; all forms of religion must be completely rejected.

Ernst Cassirer has shown that this characterization of the Enlight-

10. Charles J. Adams, *A Reader's Guide to the Great Religions*, p. 28.

enment is extremely misleading. It is true that the authority of revelation was undermined, but most thinkers accepted the deistic notion of reason and proclaimed a new form of religion. For many, 'the fundamental objective is not the dissolution of religion but its "transcendental" justification and foundation'. In undermining the importance of revelation and appealing to 'the inviolable, eternal laws of reason', the Enlightenment thinkers usually emphasized the notion of *religio naturalis*, a universal religious quality underlying all particular religious manifestations and known through reason.[11]

However, if the later Historians of Religions accepted this notion of *religio naturalis* and the sufficiency of reason in understanding religion, it should be noted that it was in terms of the normative judgments of reason that religious forms were characteristically ascribed to the earliest 'prescientific' stages of cultural development. Indeed, when phenomenologists of religion, such as Rudolf Otto, G. van der Leeuw, and Mircea Eliade, insist upon the complexity and the *sui generis* character of the religious, they are reacting against what they consider a 'rationalistic bias' inherited from the Enlightenment.

If it is true that the History of Religions grew out of the scientific and rational attitude of the Enlightenment,[12] it is equally true that such a field could have begun only after being supplied with a body of empirical data: documents were submitted on primitive cultures; the field of Orientalism began to flourish; Indo-European philology and comparative linguistics were established.

We can now formulate the major problem which led to the birth of the History of Religions. Since scholars no longer had recourse to the norms of revelation and traditional religious authority, how were they to understand and evaluate this multitude of recently accumulated 'religious data'? The direction the new discipline took in dealing with this problem can largely be seen in the cultural context of the period: 'it

11. Ernst Cassirer, *The Philosophy of the Enlightenment*, pp. 134 ff. See Kitagawa, 'The History of Religions in America', pp. 17–18.

12. Although almost all scholars seem to agree that the History of Religions was largely a child of the Enlightenment, we should note that there are a few Historians of Religions who place greater emphasis upon the contributions of Romanticism. See Kees W. Bolle, Introduction to Jan de Vries's *The Study of Religion*, p. xx; Jan de Vries, *The Study of Religion*, pp. 39–58; Gerardus van der Leeuw, *Religion in Essence and Manifestation*, vol. 2, pp. 691–694.

is remarkable to note that the beginnings of Comparative Religions took place during the middle of the nineteenth century at the very height of the materialistic and positivistic propaganda.'[13]

Such a cultural context can be witnessed in Auguste Comte's *Cours de philosophie positive*, in which Comte formulated his theory of 'the law of the three stages', with the theological as the 'lowest' state of development. 'This Positivism treats religion as a dated point of view, a primitive structure in the evolution of man.'[14] The positivist tended to regard religion in the modern world as 'merely a survival from man's primitive past, and doomed to disappear in an era of science and general enlightenment'.[15]

The positivistic and materialistic viewpoint was combined with a belief in evolutionism. In 1859 Darwin's *Origin of Species* appeared, and scholars began to look for other forms of evolution, including the evolution of religion. Characteristic of the thought of this age was Herbert Spencer's belief in a 'unilinear evolution' and 'progress by evolution'.[16] Evolution was seen as the gradual progression from what was simple and homogeneous into what was complex and heterogeneous. Significantly, Spencer believed that this entire process of 'cosmic evolution' could be accounted for by the physicists' laws of matter and motion. His 'progress by evolution' even came to be viewed as 'something religiously profound, that here was a new cosmic conception based upon the operation of Natural Law'.[17]

It was during this period that the modern discipline of *Religionswissenschaft* had its beginnings. There were two major 'groups' in its early stages: Max Müller and other philologists and Sir Edward B. Tylor and other ethnologists. *Essays in Comparative Mythology*, which some

13. Mircea Eliade, 'The Quest for the "Origins" of Religion', *History of Religions* 4, no. 1 (1964): 156–157. With slight modifications, this article is reproduced as chapter 3 in Eliade's *The Quest: History and Meaning in Religion*.

14. De Vries, *The Study of Religion*, p. 63. In his later writings, Comte does introduce his new 'Religion of Humanity', which seems to contrast sharply with his earlier 'positive philosophy'. It is Comte's positivism, not his 'Religion of Humanity', which most influenced nineteenth century Historians of Religions.

15. Gerhard Lenski, *The Religious Factor*, p. 3.

16. In 1855 Spencer published his *Principles of Psychology* and two years later, in *Progress, Its Law and Cause*, he extended his evolutionary theory to encompass all aspects of the cosmos.

17. Homer W. Smith, *Man and His Gods*, pp. 354–356.

consider the first important book in the History of Religions, was published in 1856 by Müller. In 1871 Tylor published his monumental *Primitive Culture*, in which he tried to explain the origin and evolution of religion.

Mircea Eliade, in concentrating on the nineteenth century obsession with determining 'origins' (of language, the Indo-Aryan races, culture, art, religion, etc.), offers an explanation for this 'synchronicity' between a materialistic and positivistic attitude and the great interest in archaic and Oriental religions:

> One could say that the anxious search for the origins of Life and Mind; the fascination in the 'mysteries of Nature'; the urge to penetrate and decipher the inner structures of Matter — all these longings and drives denote a sort of nostalgia for the primordial, for the original, universal *matrix*. Matter, Substance, represents the *absolute origin*, the beginning of all things: Cosmos, Life, Mind. . . . Through science, man will come to know matter ever more correctly and master it ever more completely. There will be no end to this progressive perfectibility. One can unravel from this enthusiastic confidence in science, scientific education, and industry a kind of religious, messianic optimism: man, at last, will be free, happy, rich, and powerful.
>
> Optimism matched perfectly well with materialism, positivism, and the belief in an unlimited evolution.[18]

This then was the cultural context within which the autonomous, 'scientific' study of religion began and flourished: the 'positivistic' approach to the documents of religions; the attempt to arrive at the origin and first forms of religion; the search for the 'laws of evolution' of religion; a tremendous enthusiasm and confidence in the unlimited possibilities that scientific progress in this field would yield.

PHILOLOGY AND COMPARATIVE MYTHOLOGY

The first significant group in the History of Religions was composed of philologists; through the scientific analysis of language, they

18. Eliade, 'The Quest for the "Origins" of Religion', p. 158.

believed it possible to comprehend the nature of religion. These philologists formulated 'naturistic' explanations of religion which maintained that the gods were no more than personified natural phenomena, such as the sun, the moon, and the rivers.

The leading proponent of 'the nature-myth school' was Max Müller, for whom the 'key' to deciphering the essence of religion was 'comparative mythology', and this in turn could only be understood by a method of philological analysis. More specifically, the 'key' for Müller was solar mythology. Other comparative philologists emphasized the storm-clouds (Kuhn), the wind (Schwartz), and the sky (Preller).[19]

Max Müller seems to endorse a traditional empiricist epistemological analysis: all human thought, language, and knowledge is derived from sense experience. Hence, the religious 'intuition of the divine' or idea of 'the Infinite' is based upon sensations arising from forces of external nature on human beings. More specifically, Max Müller submitted that it was the 'intangible' natural phenomena, such as the sun or the wind, which provided human beings with the idea of the infinite.

> His thesis was that the infinite, once the idea had arisen, could only be thought of in metaphor and symbol, which could only be taken from what seemed majestic in the known world, such as the heavenly bodies, or rather their attributes. But these attributes then lost their original metaphorical sense and achieved autonomy by becoming personified as deities in their own right.[20]

Religion arose when what was originally only a name (*nomen*), metaphorically expressing the naturalistic forces, through the 'illusion' of myth was given the status of a god (*numen*). 'Whenever any word, that was at first used metaphorically, is used without a clear conception of the steps that led from its original to its metaphorical meaning, there is danger of mythology; whenever those steps are

19. For a detailed account of the formulation of Müller's view and his controversies with Andrew Lang, see Richard M. Dorson's 'The Eclipse of Solar Mythology', *Myth: A Symposium*, pp. 15–38.

20. E. E. Evans-Pritchard, *Theories of Primitive Religion*, p. 21.

forgotten and artificial steps put in their place, we have mythology, or, if I may say so, we have diseased language.'[21]

Thus the whole supernatural world arose from the limitations, ambiguity, and 'illusion' of language;[22] myth is described as a 'pathological' condition, a 'disease of language'. It follows, according to Max Müller, 'that the only way we can discover the meaning of the religion of early man is by philological and etymological research, which restores to the names of gods and the stories told about them their original sense'.[23]

For example, at first it seems that the Greek myth of Daphne makes little sense: Apollo, a solar deity, chases Daphne, who escapes his embraces when she is transformed by the Earth into a laurel tree. Müller resorts to philological analysis and submits that the Greek name for laurel can be traced back to the Sanskrit name for the dawn. Now the original meaning of the myth becomes comprehensible: the sun chasing away the dawn which finally disappears in the bosom of Mother Earth.

Although the above analysis suffices to reveal how strongly Max Müller was influenced by the cultural and intellectual setting of nineteenth century Europe — the detached, rational, scientific approach to the religious data; the concern for origins; the negative evaluation of religion — there is another side to this scholar, which is evidenced in his admiration for Oriental spirituality.[24]

21. Max Müller, *Lectures on the Science of Language*, pp. 375–376. William A. Lessa and Evon Z. Vogt, *Reader in Comparative Religion: An Anthropological Approach*, p. 11, describe this birth of religion and its gods through a 'disease of language' in the following terms: '. . . the forces of nature were transformed by man from abstract forces to personal agents, that is, spirits. . . . Natural phenomena came to be compared to human acts, and expressions originally used for human acts came to be applied to natural objects. . . . After this had been done, spirits had to be invented to account for the acts attributed to them by their names, and so arose pantheons of gods. . . . Thus religion is really a fabric of errors. The supernatural world was composed of beings created out of nothing.'

22. Ernst Cassirer emphasizes the point that language for Müller is 'inherently metaphorical', and it is the 'inherent ambiguity', resulting from its inability to describe things unequivocally, that best explains the origin of myth and the birth of the gods. See *Language and Myth*, pp. 3–4, 85–86; *An Essay on Man*, pp. 109–110.

23. Evans-Pritchard, *Theories of Primitive Religion*, p. 22.

24. Müller was especially fond of Vedānta, which he described as 'a system in which human speculation seems to me to have reached its very acme' and which he com-

Probably more than any other European scholar, Max Müller made Indian spirituality available to the West. His *Sacred Books of the East* represents a landmark in the History of Religions. This renowned Sanskritist felt that he had discovered in the Ṛg Veda the primordial form of religion.[25] In his philological analysis, Müller often attempted to understand an Indo-European religious form by tracing it back to its Aryan, Vedic, 'original' manifestation. In 1891, he claimed that 'the most important discovery which has been made during the nineteenth century with respect to the ancient history of mankind . . . was this simple equation: Sanskrit Dyaus-pitar = Greek Zeus pater = Latin Jupiter = Old Norse Tyr'. So important was this finding, according to Müller, than 'Ancient history has become as completely changed by that one discovery as astronomy was by the Copernican heresy.'[26]

Although Müller certainly overstated the role of comparative mythology in understanding religious phenomena, all Historians of Religions recognize that myth is one of the essential features of any religion; that the interpreter cannot understand a religious tradition without understanding its myths. It is therefore imperative that we avoid a common misunderstanding, which we can observe by distinguishing two general interpretations about the nature of myth.[27]

---

pared favorably with the philosophical systems of Plato, Kant, and Hegel. See Müller's *The Six Systems of Indian Philosophy*, pp. v–xvii, 183, and 193.

25. We may note that Müller's concern for origins and primordial forms was not accompanied by the common nineteenth century formulation of a unilinear, 'progressive' evolutionary account of the development of religion. In his *Chips from a German Workshop*, vol. l, p. 48, Müller writes that 'we shall learn that religions in their most ancient form, or in the minds of their authors, are generally free from many of the blemishes that attach to them in later times'.

26. Max Müller, 'The Lesson of Jupiter', *Anthropological Religion*, p. 82.

27. Several excellent sources for comparing various interpretations of myth are *Daedalus* 88, no. 2 (1959); Thomas J. J. Altizer, William A. Beardslee, J. Harvey Young, eds., *Truth, Myth, and Symbol; The Monist* 50, no. 4 (1966); Thomas A. Sebeok, ed., *Myth: A Symposium*; Joseph J. Kockelmans, 'On Myth and Its Relationship to Hermeneutics', *Cultural Hermeneutics* 1 (1973): 47–86; Perry C. Cohen, 'Theories of Myth', *Man*, n.s. 4 (1969): 337–353; G. S. Kirk, *Myth: Its Meaning and Functions in Ancient and Other Cultures*.

There is the view of the nineteenth century, which we have seen in 'comparative mythology'[28] and which is probably accepted by most contemporary philosophers: to say that something is 'merely' a myth is to point out that it is a 'fiction' or 'illusion', an 'unreal' and uncritical 'invention' of the imagination, and as such is distinguished from and even opposed to 'reality'.

Yet for archaic societies and for cultures in which myth is 'living', myth means 'true story' in the sense of 'sacred tradition, primordial revelation, exemplary model'. This second view is given the following formulation by Eliade:

> Myth narrates a sacred history; it relates an event that took place in primordial Time, the fabled time of the 'beginnings'. In other words, myth tells how, through the deeds of Supernatural Beings, a reality came into existence. . . . In short, myths describe the various and sometimes dramatic breakthroughs of the sacred (or the 'supernatural') into the World . . . the myth is regarded as a sacred story, and hence a 'true history', because it always deals with *realities*.[29]

Because of this equivocation in our contemporary usage, it is absolutely essential that we distinguish these two views of myth in all that follows: we must not confuse the latter, which claims to be descriptive and phenomenological, with the former, which is clearly evaluative. Many scholars have assumed the normative view and then have had very little patience in trying to understand just what the myth meant for the people who believed it.

28. It is interesting to note the opposite approaches taken by Romanticism and 'comparative mythology'. Romanticism extolled mythology as grasping what is concrete and living, whereas language, 'a faded mythology', only preserved things in an abstract and formal manner. Ernst Cassirer (*Language and Myth*, p. 85) points out that since 'comparative mythology' in the second half of the nineteenth century 'adopted the methodological principle of basing mythological comparisons on linguistic comparisons, the factual primacy of verbal concepts over mythic ones seemed to them to be implied in their procedure'. Eliade strongly opposes this latter tendency, which he takes to be a reductionism of the autonomous structure and function of the myth, and, as we shall see, he is even criticized for being 'a romantic'.

29. Mircea Eliade, *Myth and Reality*, pp. 5–6. In 'Archaic Myth and Historical Man', *McCormick Quarterly* 18 (1965): 24, Eliade states that 'the foremost function of myth is to reveal the exemplary models for all human rites and all significant human activities'. See Raffaele Pettazzoni, 'The Truth of Myth', *Essays on the History of Religions*, pp. 11–23.

ETHNOLOGY

Modern anthropology

Shortly after the birth of the 'science' of philology and comparative mythology, 'modern anthropology' began to take shape. Its first significant group was composed of British anthropologists: Tylor, Lang, Robertson Smith, Marett, Frazer, etc. Impressed by Darwinian evolution, these ethnologists tended to combine their 'positivistic' approach to the 'religious facts' with a view of historical and cultural evolutionism. Naturally they were preoccupied with the question of 'origins' or 'first forms', which would serve as the foundation of this evolutionary process.

As we read these anthropologists— and the philologists, as well— we are impressed both by their desire to accumulate empirical data, amass documentary evidence, and analyze the specific facts; and at the same time by their efforts to frame the most imaginative schemes and arrive at highly speculative theories.

With respect to the question of origins and genesis, where one finds the most imaginative hypotheses formulated, several approaches can be delineated.[30] According to the so-called 'comparative' method, 'evidences' from societies throughout the world were removed from their particular contexts and arranged in a sequential scheme; in each case the ethnologist had a 'preconceived plan' which enabled the anthropologist to order his or her data in this particular manner. Another method was based on discovering cultural 'survivals'; existing survivals rendered intelligible the history of the past. Other methods were based on a 'principle of the psychic unity of mankind— human nature is basically uniform, therefore similar results have come independently from the same causes'. Thus, what the evolutionists discovered in contemporary primitive cultures revealed to them the nature of human beings at the origin of culture.

Now it is evident why these cultural anthropologists, in their search for origins and evolutions, devoted so much time to religion and thought that they had defined the nature of religion. 'The study of the

30. Lessa and Vogt, pp. 9–10.

religion of early man and contemporary primitives was considered important because the nature of religion was understood to be identical with its origin.'[31] By analyzing primitive cultures, one could understand the nature of religion; or, what amounted to the same thing, by analyzing 'religious data', one was able to understand the earliest stages of culture. And then, from this 'primordial' stage of religion, one could discover human progression through 'higher' stages of cultural evolution.

Animism

In 1871, E. B. Tylor published his *Primitive Culture*, in which he tried to explain the origin of religion and the nature of its development.

> The first requisite in a systematic study of the religions of the lower races is to lay down a rudimentary definition of religion. . . . It seems best. . . simply to claim, as a minimum definition of religion, the belief in Spiritual Beings. . . . I purpose here, under the name of Animism, to investigate the deep-lying doctrine of Spiritual Beings. . . .[32]

'Animism', as the 'minimum definition of religion' and the explanation of its 'origin', is the belief that all of Nature is animated, that it has a soul.

Tylor then attempts to explain how archaic persons created this universal notion of the soul in terms of a 'savage biology' and a 'rational primitive philosophy'.

> It seems as though thinking men, as yet at a low level of culture, were deeply impressed by two groups of biological problems. In the first place, what is it that makes the difference between a living body and a dead one; what causes waking, sleep, trance, disease, death? In the second place, what are those human shapes which appear in dreams and visions?[33]

Reflecting upon these phenomena, the 'ancient savage philosopher'

31. Charles H. Long, *Alpha: The Myths of Creation*, p. 2.
32. Edward B. Tylor, *Primitive Culture*, vol. 1, pp. 424–425.
33. *Ibid.*, p. 428.

probably made several 'obvious inferences' and reached the following conclusion: these phenomena could be understood in terms of the presence or the absence of some 'unsubstantial' entity, the 'personal soul or spirit'.

The primitive then extended this idea of the soul to animals, to plants, and even to inanimate objects. 'The soul, being detachable from whatever it lodged in, could be thought of as independent of its material home, whence arose the idea of spiritual beings, whose supposed existence constituted Tylor's minimum definition of religion.'[34] From this initial stage of animism, Tylor described the unilinear evolution of religion through polytheism and finally to the monotheism of more 'civilized' cultures.

We may note two features in Tylor's account which will characterize most of the early methodological approaches. First, his explanation of the origin and nature of religion seems highly 'rational': primitive animism arose from empirical observations and from logical deductions based upon these facts of nature. 'They are doctrines answering in the most forcible way to the plain evidence of men's senses, as interpreted by a fairly consistent and rational primitive philosophy.'[35]

Secondly, in using this highly rational basis of interpretation, Tylor takes a rather 'negative' view regarding the nature of religion: the primitive confuses that which is merely subjective with objective reality; animism rests upon a 'psychological delusion and mistaken logical inference'.[36]

We shall now delineate several 'pre-animistic' approaches, which are usually viewed as reactions against the animism of E. B. Tylor. Modern Historians of Religions, in emphasizing the complexity of their religious data, are certainly indebted to these scholars for their 'discoveries': mana, taboo, magic, etc. However, the point we wish to make is that from the phenomenological perspective of Mircea Eliade, these approaches may have accumulated new facts and introduced

34. Evans-Pritchard, p. 25.
35. Tylor, p. 429.
36. *Ibid.*, pp. 428 ff. We shall see that Mircea Eliade's phenomenological approach reacts against both of these methodological tendencies. See David Bidney, 'The Concept of Value in Modern Anthropology', *Anthropology Today*, pp. 684–687.

new religious types, but they did not radically alter the basic hermeneutical situation of a Tylor. These 'pre-animistic' approaches shared most of Tylor's methodological assumptions and underlying theories: a 'rationalistic' and 'positivistic' approach to the religious facts; a belief in a unilinear evolutionary scheme; a 'negative' view of religion in which *homo religiosus* was placed at the 'origin' of the evolutionary process.

Evolutionary pre-animism

Major criticisms of Tylor were first presented by anthropologists who found that their data on primitive cultures in Melanesia and Polynesia did not support his theory of animism.

> The Melanesian mind is entirely possessed by the belief in a supernatural power or influence, called almost universally 'mana'. This is what works to effect everything which is beyond the ordinary power of men . . . this power, though itself impersonal, is always connected with some person who directs it; all spirits have it, ghosts generally, some men. If a stone is found to have a supernatural power, it is because a spirit has associated itself with it.

This power or force, according to Codrington, was not physical but supernatural, was not fixed in anything but could be conveyed in almost anything. If a person is a successful warrior, if a yam grows very large, if a canoe is swift, it is not because of any 'natural' conditions but because each is influenced by or possesses mana.[37]

Not long after Codrington wrote about this concept in Melanesia, anthropologists began to find similar concepts of a dynamic, impersonal, supernatural power all over the world. There were the Polynesian mana, the Sioux *Wakanda*, the Algonquin *manitou*, the Iroquois *orenda*, the Crow *maxpe*, the *hasina* of Madagascar, the *baraka* of Morocco, and countless other exemplifications of this seemingly ubiquitous concept. Georges Dumézil, in criticizing this generation of scholars, indicates the extreme to which this search for variations of the concept of mana led: 'elle est présente partout où l'on peut parler de

---

37. R. H. Codrington, *The Melanesians*, pp. 118–120.

religion, et des mots précieux comme sacer et numen, hagnos et thambos, brahman, tao, la "Grâce" même du christianisme, en sont des variations ou des dérivés. Une génération de chercheurs s'est consacrée à établir cette uniformité.'[38]

From this concept of mana and its related terms, there developed the theory of 'dynamism' or 'pre-animism'. In 1900, the British anthropologist R. R. Marett published his article 'Preanimistic Religion', which was republished in *The Threshold of Religion*. According to Marett, Preuss, and many others, the primordial and universal stage of religion was to be identified with the human belief in and emotional reaction to this impersonal and dynamic power. Although this force is often an attribute of a soul or spirit, it is not itself a spirit; the primordial religious experience need not presuppose the existence of a soul. In short, the first form of religion is not an animistic but a pre-animistic conception.[39]

Marett stressed an essential aspect of this pre-animistic concept which Codrington had previously observed: mana, *orenda*, etc., do not in themselves possess any moral dimension. They can be used for good or bad purposes.[40] What is essential at this first stage of religion is that this force is regarded as that which is 'real', successful, creative, perfect — that which above everything else truly 'is'.

During the first two decades of the twentieth century, this theory of dynamism was believed to have refuted Tylor's theory of animism and was widely accepted. Even today one finds scholars, although usually not Historians of Religions or ethnologists, subscribing to the view that the concept of mana represents the universal, primordial form of religion.

There are several decisive criticisms of the pre-animistic theory of mana.[41] This notion is not a universal idea and hence cannot be taken as the first stage of all religions. In fact, mana is not even a pan-

38. Georges Dumézil, Preface to Mircea Eliade's *Traité d'histoire des religions*, p. 5.
39. R. R. Marett, 'The Conception of Mana', *The Threshold of Religion*, pp. 99 ff.
40. Codrington, p. 118; Marett, pp. 112 ff.
41. H. Ian Hogbin, 'Mana', *Oceania* 6 (1936): 241–274; A. M. Hocart, 'Mana', *Man* 14 (1914): 97–101; Paul Radin, 'Religion of the North American Indians', *Journal of American Folklore* 27 (1914): 335–373. See Mircea Eliade, *Myths, Dreams and Mysteries*, pp. 126–131; Eliade, *Patterns in Comparative Religion*, pp. 19–23. Cited hereafter as *Patterns*.

Melanesian concept. In their effort to uncover 'uniformities', the pre-animistic theorists generalized too quickly and were insensitive to the various differences signified by these pre-animistic concepts.

Research by Hocart, Radin, Hogbin, Capell, and many others (and even Codrington's original distinctions) render the description of mana as 'strictly impersonal' extremely doubtful. 'How can mana be impersonal if it is always attached to personal beings?' (Hocart). The Indian doesn't make the opposition between personal and impersonal; his or her concern 'is, in the first place, the question of "real existence" ' (Radin).

> It follows that the question must be put in ontological terms: that which exists, what is real on the one hand, and that which does not exist on the other— not in terms of the personal or impersonal, nor of the corporeal or non-corporeal, concepts which, for the consciousness of the 'primitives', have none of the precision they have acquired in more highly evolved cultures. Anything filled with mana exists on the ontological plane and is therefore efficacious, fecund, fertile.[42]

A concept sometimes associated with mana is taboo (tabu). Marett submitted 'the taboo-mana formula' as the 'minimum definition of religion'.[43] It is not difficult to understand why taboo would be associated with mana: if things that are manifestations of the sacred are manifestations of an extraordinary and supernatural power, then they are not only to be venerated but also to be feared. Where mana exists we inevitably find taboo. 'The reverse, of course, does not always hold true, for much taboo stems from contexts not associated with mana.'[44]

In Polynesian the opposite of taboo is *noa*, 'free'. Taboo (tabu) signifies that some person, place, or thing is 'forbidden', because contact with it is dangerous. As distinguished from our everyday usage, involving negative societal mores ('Miscegenation is taboo' for

---

42. Eliade, *Myths, Dreams and Mysteries*, p. 129.
43. R. R. Marett, 'The Taboo-mana Formula as a Minimum Definition of Religion', *Archiv für Religionswissenschaft*, vol. 12 (1909). Significant works dealing with taboo include those by A. Gennep, Frazer, French, E. S. Handy, R. Lehmann, Radcliffe-Brown, H. Webster, and F. Steiner.
44. Lessa and Vogt, p. 203.

most Americans), the Polynesian and religious interdictory usage always involves a sacred or supernatural power.

Frazer thought of taboo as a kind of 'negative sympathetic magic': 'harmful consequences are averted when certain acts are not performed.' Sociologists have usually interpreted its function in terms of stabilizing a cohesive social structure in a particular society. For Freud, it helped to explain the origin of religion.

It would seem that taboo has played an important part in the interpretation of religion primarily because its interdictory connotation was 'thought to provide an understanding for the separation of the sacred from the profane — a separation which lies at the heart of every religion'.[45]

> ... the elements of the taboo itself are always the same: certain things, or persons, or places belong in some way to a different order of being, and therefore any contact with them will produce an upheaval at the ontological level which might well prove fatal. You will find the fear of such an upheaval — ever present because of this difference in the order of being between what is profane and what is hierophany or kratophany. . . .[46]

This 'negative' aspect in the dialectic of all religious manifestations, this 'ambiguity' of the sacred, this sacred-profane dichotomy which lies at the heart of all religion will be seen as an essential part of Eliade's phenomenological analysis of the religious.

Another pre-animistic hypothesis assumed that there had been a stage of magic which preceded religion.[47] Sir James Frazer had read *Wald- und Feldkulte* (*Cults of Forest and Field*, 1875–77) in which W. Mann- hardt formulated his hypothesis of the 'demons of vegetation', a concept of 'corn-spirits' and a 'spirit of the tree'. Mannhardt claimed

---

45. Charles H. Long, 'Primitive Religion', *A Reader's Guide to the Great Religions*, p. 5.

46. Eliade, *Patterns*, p. 17. Of course, at this stage we have no assurance that a position incorporating such terms as 'sacred-profane', 'dialectic of hierophanies', and 'ontological' will be more adequate in analyzing religious phenomena than were such animistic or pre-animistic theories.

47. Sir James Frazer, *The Golden Bough: A Study in Magic and Religion*. Other significant works on 'magic and religion' include Malinowski's *Magic, Science, and Religion* and studies by H. Hubert, M. Mauss, and Evans-Pritchard.

that the 'lower mythology' still 'surviving' in the culture of various peasants disclosed an earlier stage than even Müller's naturalistic mythologies. Frazer adopted, developed, and popularized these points.

In the first two volumes of *The Golden Bough*, entitled *The Magic Art,* Frazer discusses the nature of magic and his pre-animistic theory of the origin of religion. As is well known, he discusses magic in terms of his 'Law of Sympathy' and distinguishes two types of 'Sympathetic Magic': 'Homeopathic' or 'Imitative Magic' and 'Contagious Magic'. Magic is older than and inferior to religion. (It is 'psychologically simpler', 'more uniform', etc.) It may evolve into religion, although this doesn't always occur. In fact, much data which have usually been considered part of 'primitive religion' are classified under the prior stage of magic by Frazer.

Although Frazer probably had had more general popularity than any of the other early scholars, Historians of Religions have tended to consider him neither an original nor a careful thinker and have been especially critical of his methodological disregard of historical details. His vital contribution to the field lies in the unbelievable amount of factual material he compiled.[48]

Anti-evolutionary pre-animism

Finally, we may dicuss Andrew Lang's pre-animistic theory of a 'High God' (supreme being, 'All-Father'), a view which seems completely at odds with the cultural context of the nineteenth and early twentieth centuries.

In *Custom and Myth, Modern Mythology*, and especially in *Myth, Ritual and Religion*, Lang decisively criticized Müller's theories and strongly undermined the field of comparative mythology. Strangely enough, he did this from the position of an evolutionary anthropologist, who believed that myths arose not from a 'disease of language' but from the stage of animism. 'His system began with the premise that the history of mankind followed a uniform development from savagery to civilization, and that relics of primitive belief and

48. See Robert H. Lowie's *Primitive Religion*, pp. 137–147, for a criticism of Frazer's theories.

custom survived still among the rural peasantry, and among contemporary savages.'[49]

However, in *The Making of Religion*, Andrew Lang completely broke away from Tylor's position: a 'progressive evolutionary' view was unjustified and animism was not the first stage of religion. Among such 'low savages' as the Andamanese, Fuegians, and Australians, European scholars often spoke of the divine beings of these 'primitives' as 'spirits'; but Lang claimed that the natives themselves did not appear to advance 'the metaphysical idea of spirit': 'Are these beings spiritual or material?' Rather these 'moral and creative deities' are simply envisaged as 'beings', and there is no justification in assuming that they everywhere evolved out of the theory of spirits or ghosts.[50]

Among some very primitive tribes, Lang found the presence of a belief in High Gods: 'the belief in a primal being, a Maker, undying, usually moral. . . . However the ancestors of Australians, or Andamanese, or Hurons arrived at their highest religious conception (of a "Father" or "Master of Life"), they decidedly possess it.'[51] But Lang's data disclosed that

> there coexist the mythical and the religious elements in belief. The rational factor . . . is visible in religion; the irrational is prominent in myth. The Australian, the Bushman, the Solomon Islander, in hours of danger and necessity 'yearns after the gods,' and has present in his heart the idea of a father and friend. This is the religious element. . . . Religion, in its moral aspect, always traces back to the belief in a power that is benign and works for righteousness.[52]

This belief in High Gods did not evolve from a belief in nature-spirits. On the contrary, this pre-animistic belief in High Gods was the original religious form which later 'deteriorated' into such forms as worship of the ghosts of tribal heroes, theriomorphic ancestors, or nature-spirits. Although Lang's anti-evolutionary approach had little

49. Dorson, 'The Eclipse of Solar Mythology', pp. 22–23.
50. Andrew Lang, *The Making of Religion*, pp. 201–209.
51. Andrew Lang, *Myth, Ritual and Religion*, vol. 1, pp. 3, 5.
52. *Ibid.*, pp. 306–307.

immediate influence, we have seen that pre-animistic theories soon came to dominate research in the History of Religions.

To understand the nature of the History of Religions at this time, we may observe the positions taken in the heated controversy over the so-called High Gods, especially over the All-Fathers or Sky Beings of the southeastern tribes of Australia.[53] Eliade points out that this controversy over the nature of the Australian High Gods 'was entangled in a series of prejudices' on both sides.

For the 'evolutionists' (Tylor, Baldwin Spencer, Frazer, E. S. Hartland), it was simply inconceivable that the Australian aborigines could have such a 'lofty' religious conception of a 'Creator, an omniscient and ethical All-Father'. These 'savages' still exemplified first stages of religion; hence, they could not possibly entertain such a religious conception, one which would be found only at the apex of religious evolution.

If these 'stone-age' people claimed to believe in a High God, there was undoubtedly some further explanation. Tylor tried to explain the belief as the result of the influence of Christian missionaries. Baldwin Spencer wrote to Frazer that he was convinced that 'a high ethical religion amongst the lowest savages' does not exist, and 'it is the easiest thing possible to be misled by what a native tells you in regard to such a point as this'.[54]

Yet the supporters of the 'anti-evolutionary' interpretation shared many of these ideological prejudices, mainly stemming from an equally 'rationalistic' approach. The evolutionists refused to attribute anything 'rational' to primitive religion; Lang found it impossible to accept anything 'irrational' about this original form.

Therefore, he also had to 'explain away' much of his data. He accepted the general interpretation of myth as 'irrational and debas-

53. Mircea Eliade, 'Australian Religions, Part I: An Introduction', *History of Religions* 6, no. 2 (1966): 108–134. Eliade carefully presents the research of A. W. Howitt in the nineteenth century and 'the story of a controversy', involving Lang's debates with Hartland and others. The two positions we are about to present are summarized on pages 116–117. This article is reproduced as chapter 1 in Eliade's *Australian Religions: An Introduction*.

54. E. B. Tylor, 'Limits of Savage Religion', *Journal of the Anthropological Institute* 21 (1891): 283–301; J. G. Frazer, *Totemism and Exogamy*, vol. 1, p. 148. See E. S. Hartland, 'The "High Gods" of Australia', *Folk-lore* 9, no. 4 (1898): 328.

ing', whereas for him religious belief was 'rational and even elevated'. Rather than go to the usual extreme of completely identifying primitive religion with this irrational and aberrant state, Lang embraced the extreme opposite position: he denied that the mythical was essential to primitive religion.[55] Indeed, he even tried to account for the deterioration of the High Gods in terms of the later influences of the mythological imagination.

In analyzing certain 'ideological presuppositions' with which investigators approached the 'primitive world', Eliade compares the above 'two antagonistic orientations' in broader terms and refers to them as 'evolutionist' and 'romantic-decadentist'. He submits that the following question more or less tacitly guided the inquiries of both: 'do the contemporary "Primitives" represent, religiously speaking, a stage very near the "absolute beginning" or, on the contrary, do the Primitives (or most of them) display a more or less catastrophic "degeneration", a fall from a primordial perfect situation?'

As was the case with the animists and evolutionary pre-animists, Eliade seems much more impressed by the methodological similarities in these 'antagonistic orientations' than in their obvious differences.

> Notwithstanding their radical differences, these ideologies have two things in common: 1) their obsession with the *origin* and the *beginnings* of religions; 2) their taking for granted that the beginning was something 'simple and pure'. Of course, the evolutionists and the romantic-decadentists understood quite differently this primordial simplicity. . . . Both of these ideologies postulated the unfolding of archaic religions as a linear movement from the simple to the complex, though in opposite directions; up (the evolutionists) or down (the romantic-decadentists). Both such interpretations implied a *naturalistic* or a *theological* approach, not a *historical* one.[56]

55. Lang, *Myth, Ritual and Religion*, p. 4: 'Now, the whole crux and puzzle of mythology is, "Why, having attained (in whatever way) to a belief in an underlying guardian, 'Master of Life', did mankind set to work to evolve a chronique scandaleuse about Him? And why is that chronique the elaborately absurd set of legends which we find in all mythologies?" '

56. 'On Understanding Primitive Religions', *Glaube, Geist, Geschichte*, p. 500. This article is reproduced as the Preface in Eliade's *Australian Religions: An Introduction*.

Eliade's phenomenology will be seen as a reaction against each of the methodological tendencies described above.

SUMMARY AND CONCLUSIONS

What can one say about the essential characteristics of the History of Religions during this first period?

1. As we have seen, there are two major 'schools': philologists and ethnologists. One must guard against an explication of a rather unilinear series of developments in which each position arises out of and completely refutes the previously prevailing viewpoint. The complex interrelationships, the subtle influences, and the lasting contributions of earlier positions will become evident as we elucidate more recent tendencies in the field.

2. These Historians of Religions felt that they had established an 'autonomous' discipline, a 'scientific' study of religion. This 'new science', with its extraordinary enthusiasm and its unlimited confidence in the prodigious discoveries about to be made, was largely shaped by the values of the Enlightenment and the scientific progress of the nineteenth century.

By accumulating 'religious facts' and looking for common elements or 'parallels', by locating and translating the 'original sources', and by assuming a critically 'rationalistic' attitude marked by personal detachment, these scholars felt that they could attain a 'scientific objectivity' in understanding the nature of religion.[57]

Thus we have seen how Müller in his analysis of myth as a 'disease of language', Tylor's treatment of animism as a 'mistaken logical inference', and the theories of the pre-animists rested upon a very narrowly-conceived, rationalistic approach. Religious documents were approached with a detachment not unlike that of the nineteenth century naturalist classifying some biological species.

---

57. Wilfred Cantwell Smith, 'Comparative Religion: Whither — and Why?', *The History of Religions: Essays in Methodology*, p. 31, sees the thirteen-volume *Encyclopaedia of Religion and Ethics*, ed. by James Hastings (Edinburgh: 1908–21), as 'typifying a culmination of the first great stage of scholarship in this field: the accumulation, organization, and analysis of facts'.

3. This 'positivistic' approach to the facts was combined with a view of historical and cultural evolutionism. For a few, this evolutionary approach still took the apologetical form of defending one's own religion as the culmination of religious evolution. However, most Historians of Relgions took from the Enlightenment a confidence in reason and scientific progress and from nineteenth century organic evolutionism the possibility of approaching human history in a similar fashion. Religion was usually identified with the earliest stages of cultures. Even if scholars interpreted Christianity as exemplifying the culmination of the laws of evolution in religion, their historical evolutionism usually included stages beyond all forms of religion.

4. We have seen that this evolutionary approach naturally was concerned with the question of origins and 'primordial forms'. Since religion was usually identified with the first stages of culture, ethnologists had reason to believe that by studying primitive peoples they would understand the origin and nature of religion. Lang's theory of a belief in High Gods and Marett's theory of the universal experience of mana did not deviate from the nineteenth century obsession with 'the primordial': they claimed to have found an earlier stage than Tylor's animism; indeed, they had discovered the very origin of religion.

5. Similar here to the approach of the Darwinian naturalist seems to have been an assumption as to the uniform reaction of the human mind to the phenomena of Nature. Without such a belief, it is difficult to understand how a Tylor or a Frazer, after accumulating so much empirical data, could then speak of primitive myth or ritual or belief with so little regard for the particular time or place of a specific datum. In understanding a religious manifestation in Australia, for example, one could then speak of the 'same' form manifested throughout the world, because there was a uniformity in the human reaction before natural phenomena.

6. Despite their concern with objective, impersonal descriptions of the religious data, these Historians of Religions have usually been criticized for their highly normative and speculative judgments. 'The early historians of religions [Historians of Religions] notwithstanding their conscious "emancipation" from philosophy, had definite

philosophical assumptions, be they rationalistic or romantic, and they dealt with religio-scientific data "philosophically." '58

> The image that our nineteenth century created of 'inferior societies' was largely derived from the positivistic, antireligous, and ametaphysical attitude entertained by a number of worthy explorers and ethnologists who had approached the 'savages' with the ideology of a contemporary of Comte, Darwin, or Spencer. Among the 'primitives' they everywhere discovered 'fetishism' and 'religious infantalism' — simply because they could *see* nothing else.[59]

In short, it seems that these scholars approached their studies with many 'prior' beliefs about the evolution of cultures. These often served as the interpretive schema by which religious manifestations were described and evaluated. There was little patience with trying to understand what a religion meant for its believer. Built into the very act of description were the evaluative principles provided by the triumph of the modern scientific spirit.

These normative principles rendered possible the great syntheses and generalizations: animism, High Gods, mana, magic, astral mythologies, pan-Babylonianism, etc. Only because one already possessed universal norms for culture, history, and language could he or she then find, in countless numbers of myths, everywhere a 'disease of language'; or, in voluminous collections of 'primitive' data, everywhere a 'belief in Spiritual beings' based on a 'mistaken logical inference'.

TRANSITION

If we rather arbitrarily stop here and classify the above as the 'first period' of the History of Religions, our justification for this imperfect division is the following: new disciplines and new discoveries during the first few decades of the twentieth century seem to have gradually created a new hermeneutical situation in the History of Religions. In

58. Kitagawa, 'The History of Religions in America', p. 18.
59. Mircea Eliade, *Yoga: Immortality and Freedom*, pp. xii–xiv. Cited hereafter as *Yoga*.

light of the discoveries in such areas as archaeology, ethnology, Oriental studies, and depth psycholgy, and especially with the increased
historical consciousness and the rise of phenomenology, the various
assumptions and conclusions of a Tylor or a Müller were rendered
somewhat obsolete.

We may conclude this chapter with what seems to be a rather
remarkable observation on the relationship between Mircea Eliade's
phenomenological method and the early methodological aproaches to
religious phenomena. On the one hand, Eliade sees his approach as a
definite rejection of the above mentioned methodological characteristics. On the other hand, we shall see that most critics of Eliade's
approach claim that his method incorporates the very same characteristics of early approaches, that Eliade is simply a new Tylor or a new
Frazer.[60] Thus, he will be attacked for not paying attention to the
specific historical conditionings of his data; for making hasty uncritical generalizations; for 'reading into' his data all kinds of universal
meanings, based upon his own 'prior' assumptions and normative
principles.

It seems to us that Eliade's phenomenological method is usually
directed against these characteristics of early approaches: a narrowly-
rationalistic, impersonal, detached, positivistic approach distorts the
basic intentionality of the religious phenomena; religious data, as far as
we know, have always been very complex and do not reveal a
unilinear evolutionary process. At the same time, we shall submit that
Mircea Eliade does assume a certain 'uniformity' regarding the human
mode of being in the world; and he does go 'beyond' the descriptions
of most twentieth century 'specialists' and attempts to compare and to
evaluate his data.

If Mircea Eliade is not to be criticized on the same grounds as the
early methodological approaches, then we must show that his

60. It is true that Eliade wishes to dissociate himself from the 'confusionist' position
of a Tylor or a Frazer, who felt free to compare data which had 'no geographical or
historical contiguity', because they assumed the existence of the same 'uniform
reaction of the human mind before the phenomena of Nature'. According to Eliade,
the later historico–cultural and other historicist approaches represent an 'undeniable
progress'. *Images and Symbols*, pp. 175–176. Nevertheless, in chapters 6 and 7, we shall
analyze Eliade's attempt to describe 'the human condition, as such', and 'primordial'
existential situations.

phenomenological approach reveals a very different hermeneutical situation. More specifically, we must determine whether Eliade provides us with some 'objective', underlying hermeneutical framework, some phenomenological foundation, in terms of which he can go beyond the limitations of the specialist, compare and descriptively evaluate his data, and gain insight into the universal structures of religious experience.

2

Twentieth Century Methodological Approaches

INTRODUCTION

During the twentieth century, many scholars have identified themselves with the History of Religions and have sought to define the
specific nature of their discipline. Among the studies of religions, it has
thus often become possible to distinguish the approach of an
anthropologist, sociologist, or psychologist from that of a Historian
of Religions.

This 'second period' is characterized by a new hermeneutical situation, which arose from the founding of previously unknown disciplines and the increased specialization within older fields. The study of
religions was radically changed by the accumulation of new data and
the development of new techniques and methodological principles.

To give but one example, we can discern the emphasis now placed
upon history.

> Almost without noticing it, the historian of religions [Historian of
> Religions] found himself in a cultural milieu quite different from
> that of Max Müller and Tylor, or even that of Frazer and Marett. It
> was a new environment nourished by Nietzsche and Marx, Dilthey,
> Croce, and Ortega; an environment in which the fashionable cliché
> was not *Nature* but *History*.[1]

Without here discussing the emergence of various fields (such as
prehistory and archaeology) or the development of historical methods
(such as cultural stratification), we may simply note the 'discovery' of
the irreducibility of history: the human being is always a historical
being, and one must respect the historical nature of all religious data.

Now it is true that scholars of 'the first period' expounded a theory
of progress, an evolutionary history. But, as we observed, these

1. Eliade, 'The Quest for the "Origins" of Religion', p. 166.

evolutionary histories actually reflected a general disregard for the historical dimension of the religious data. Because of numerous assumptions and theories accepted by the investigators, they were able to superimpose their evolutionary schemes upon history, were able to 'reconstruct' history largely independent of the actual historical process, and were able to analyze their religious data without sufficiently considering their specific and irreducible, historical conditionings.

What gradually developed were difficult conceptions as to the nature and significance of history, and these in turn demanded new methodological approaches. Religious data were historical data, to understand religion one had to do justice to the concrete and unique conditionings of any historical manifestation. We shall see that this constitutes the basis for one of the major criticisms of Eliade's approach.

By dividing the study of religions into various 'schools' or approaches, we shall elucidate the multifarious factors which have contributed to the present nature of the History of Religions. Of course, one realizes that there are no clear-cut divisions.

For example, what is one to subsume under 'anthropological approaches'?[2] Much of the recent anthropological research on religions has been undertaken by 'social anthropologists'. What is the meaning and scope of this increasingly used classification of 'social anthropology'? Radcliffe-Brown and his followers in British anthropology clearly distinguish their comparative sociological approach of social anthropology both from ethnology, which is concerned with the historical study of cultural processes, and from sociology.[3] However, G. P. Murdock and most American anthropologists seem to object to this classification. They prefer the category 'cultural anthropology' and relegate social anthropology to the status of one of

2. In some countries, anthropology is simply limited to physical anthropology. In the United States and many other countries, anthropology also includes archaeology, ethnology, linguistics, folklore, and numerous other fields. See Sol Tax et al., *An Appraisal of Anthropology Today*, pp. 221–222.

3. A. R. Radcliffe-Brown, 'Historical Note on British Social Anthropology', *American Anthropologist* 54, no. 2, pt. 1 (1952): 275–277; and A. R. Radcliffe-Brown, *Method in Social Anthropology*, pp. 133 ff. and *passim*. Maurice Merleau-Ponty attempts to distinguish earlier sociologists, such as Durkheim, from social anthropologists: 'From Mauss to Claude Lévi-Strauss', *Signs*, p. 114 and *passim*.

many branches of cultural anthropology. Lévi-Strauss submits that there is no great difference between the approaches of cultural anthropology and social anthropology: 'the difference is only one of standpoint, not of the subject matter investigated.'[4]

Such difficulties in clearly delineating and differentiating positions will be apparent throughout this chapter. Nevertheless, it should become evident that the study of religion during 'the second period' became highly specialized. We should gain some insight into the nature of the specialized approaches and their significance for the History of Religions.

The following presentation will seem greatly fragmented, with isolated treatments of numerous positions and without a pronounced sense of development. To a considerable extent, this fragmented presentation mirrors the actual nature of the highly specialized approaches to religion in the twentieth century. It seems unwise to impose some artificial unity. Nevertheless, if we remain cognizant of our purpose in this historical sketch, some sense of direction will emerge, especially as our presentation is related to later chapters.

Our general purpose is to lay the foundation for an adequate understanding of contemporary History of Religions — a foundation largely constructed from the fragmented treatments of earlier periods. By examining previous approaches, we shall have some grasp of the issues and problems confronting the Historian of Religions today. In Chapter 3, we shall attempt to formulate 'the hermeneutical situation today'.

In addition, we shall distinguish the phenomenological perspective from other approaches and shall define the present nature of the History of Religions in terms of a certain 'tension' between historical and phenomenological approaches. It remains to be seen whether Mircea Eliade can harmoniously relate and do justice to both the historical and the phenomenological.

More specifically, we wish to see how Mircea Eliade confronts the central issues and problems that follow, what he rejects from past approaches, and how he incorporates many of the previous contributions in his phenomenology of religion. What may initially seem to be

4. 'Cultural/Social Anthropology', *An Appraisal of Anthropology Today*, p. 224; Claude Lévi-Strauss, 'The Place of Anthropology in the Social Sciences and Problems Raised in Teaching It', *Structural Anthropology*, pp. 353–357.

a mere hodgepodge (a little Durkheim, some Freud, then to Schmidt) of unrelated approaches will begin to assume some order. We shall observe Eliade's endeavor to develop a methodological framework which can do justice to the sociological, the psychological, the historical, etc. — that is, to all dimensions of religious data.

SOCIOLOGICAL APPROACHES

It seems possible to distinguish two major trends in the sociological approaches to the study of religions. First, there is Émile Durkheim and the 'French school of sociology', which often has associated with it such scholars as Henri Hubert, Robert Hertz, Marcel Granet, Louis Gernet, Marcel Mauss, Lucien Lévy-Bruhl, Roger Caillois, and Georges Dumézil.[5] The second major sociological approach to religion can be seen in the works of Max Weber. This tradition includes studies by such scholars as Ernst Troeltsch, H. R. Niebuhr, Howard Becker, Talcott Parsons, J. Milton Yinger, and Joachim Wach.

Because of our limited time for analysis, we shall only concentrate on the sociological approach of Émile Durkheim. More of the 'second tradition' will be discussed in the following chapters, especially through the contributions of Joachim Wach.

Émile Durkheim and the 'first tradition'

In 1912, Durkheim published *Les formes élémentaires de la vie religieuse*, in which he attempted to account for the origin and nature of religion. The first characteristic of religion is its division of things into sacred or profane. In opposition to many previous scholars, Durkheim contended that 'naturism' does not explain this division; nature as such cannot inspire the religious attitude. Religion does not rest upon an 'illusion', as the positivists had thought, but rather upon a 'basic fact of experience'. Durkheim defines religion as 'a unified system of beliefs

5. Depending upon one's classification, many of these scholars are often said to have been influenced by the 'French sociological school', although they are distinguished from it.

and practices relative to sacred things, that is to say, things set apart and forbidden—beliefs and practices which unite into one single moral community called a Church, all those who adhere to them'.[6]

By analyzing Australian religions, Durkheim arrived at the most primitive religious form: totemism.[7] In the totem, one can decipher the religious attitude, since the 'totemic principle' is a symbol of the clan. Unable to exist alone, humans become totally dependent upon society which they then consider sacred; because of the complexity of society, humans represent their clan in terms of a symbol, and thus direct their religious attitude toward the totem. The 'reality' '. . . which is the universal and eternal objective cause of these sensations *sui generis* out of which religious experience is made, is society'. 'If religion has given birth to all that is essential in society, it is because the idea of society is the soul of religion.'[8]

Therefore, that which human beings have meant by God and that which has served as the object of their religious emotions and practices is *society*. Society has deified itself; religion is the means of *symbolically expressing* the total collective life.

We must distinguish between Durkheim's theory of the origin of religion, which has been generally dismissed, and his view of the *function* or role of religion, which many sociologists accept. Sociologists and ethnologists have rejected Durkheim's theory of totemism as the primordial form of religion.[9] Durkheim limited himself to the Arunta and Central Australia, whereas the Southeastern Australians, forming the oldest stratum, do not have totemism.

By emphasizing only the sociological dimension of religious experiences, Durkheim failed to realize that the manifestation of the sacred as social 'does not exhaust the manifestations of sacrality'. Charles H. Long has enumerated several ways in which the 'ontologi-

6. Émile Durkheim, *The Elementary Forms of the Religious Life*, p. 47.

7. 'In regard to the word totem, we may say that it is the one employed by the Ojibway, an Algonquin tribe, to designate the sort of thing whose name the clan bears.' *Ibid.*, p. 103

8. *Ibid.*, pp. 418–419 and *passim*. See Lessa and Vogt, pp. 2, 66–67.

9. See Alexander Goldenweiser, 'Religion and Society: A Critique of Émile Durkheim's Theory of the Origin and Nature of Religion', *Journal of Philosophy, Psychology, and Scientific Methods* 14 (1917): 113–124; Robert H. Lowie, *The History of Ethnological Theory*, pp. 205–212.

cal dimension as the modality of the sacred may show itself', and these include various nonsocial and nonritual expressions.[10]

On many methodological issues, it seems to us that contemporary Historians of Religions might view Durkheim as a transitional figure. Like the nineteenth century evolutionists, Durkheim is obsessed with the quest for the origin of religion, and, like those earlier scholars, explains the nature of religion by means of an oversimplified reductionism of his religious data.[11]

But even in Durkheim's reductionistic approach, we can discern potential *'openings'* for more fruitful interpretations. There is not a negative prepossession toward the religious data; this renders possible more objective analyses. The positivists had reduced religion to a state of ignorance and superstition, an anachronism in a modern, scientific world. Durkheim challenged many of the 'negative' assumptions and theories of 'the first period'. His data revealed that 'the roots of religious belief and practice lie in the very fabric of society itself and in the nature of human interrelations'. Religious institutions are 'an integral and necessary element in any stable social system'.[12]

Durkheim went too far in identifying the religious with the sociological, but it is also true that he opened up the sociological dimension of the religious. No contemporary Historian of Religions can overlook the sociological nature of his or her data.

Finally, by emphasizing the importance of religious symbolism, Durkheim opened up new possibilities of interpretation. Earlier scholars had been too 'narrow' in their interpretative approaches; many hidden layers of religious meaning remained to be deciphered. Mircea Eliade will submit that it is of the essence of religious sym-

---

10. Charles H. Long, 'Prolegomenon to a Religious Hermeneutic', *History of Religions* 6, no. 3 (1967): 260–262. See Long, *Alpha*, p. 14. In *Yoga: Immortality and Freedom*, p. 95 and *passim*, Mircea Eliade has shown that the different techniques of (Patañjali's) Yoga all have one common characteristic: 'They are antisocial, or, indeed, antihuman. The worldly man lives in society, marries, establishes a family; Yoga prescribes absolute solitude. . . .'

11. 'Things are above all sacred or profane, pure or impure, friends or enemies, favourable or unfavourable, i.e. their most fundamental characteristics are only expressions of the way in which they affect social sensibility.' Émile Durkheim and Marcel Mauss, *Primitive Classification*, pp. 85–86.

12. Lenski, pp. 3–4.

bolism, as an autonomous mode of cognition, that it brings into a structural whole the diverse levels of religious meaning.

Let us say a few words about Lucien Lévy-Bruhl, especially since we still find philosophers and other scholars who seem to adopt many of the distinctions and categories first propounded by Lévy-Bruhl. Like Durkheim, Lucien Lévy-Bruhl is concerned with 'group ideas' (*représentations collectives*) and submits that these can be described in terms of a *participation mystique* to which all 'primitive mentality' conforms.[13] Primitive mentality, which pays no attention to the law of contradiction, is completely different from modern logical thought. By 'a law of mystical participation', Lévy-Bruhl seems to mean that the primitive feels that a 'mutual participation' holds between him or her and some object, locality, etc. In other words, if the primitive declares that he or she is a parrot, this person means precisely that: there is an inexplicable mystical identity of him or herself and the parrot.

These hypotheses were rejected by ethnologists and sociologists. Under his 'primitive mentality', Lévy-Bruhl even included the sophisticated thought of China and India; he neglected individual variability; there is no absolute dichotomy between modern and primitive thought, which is often quite logical.[14] Nevertheless, Lévy-Bruhl had a great influence on scholars in other fields and directed attention to the behavior of 'premoderns' and the importance of analyzing myths and symbols.

The 'second tradition'

We shall emphasize only one crucial methodological feature of this 'second' major sociological approach to religious phenomena: a certain *antireductionist* tendency. In Chapter 3, we shall see that a general antireductionist approach is one of the distinguishing characteristics of contemporary History of Religions. In Chapter 4, we shall discuss

13. Lucien Lévy-Bruhl, *Primitive Mentality*. Before his death, Lévy-Bruhl, seems to have abandoned his hypothesis of this prelogical primitive mentality. Cf. Lévy-Bruhl's *Les Carnets*, published posthumously by Maurice Leenhardt (Paris: Presses Universitaires de France, 1949).

14. Lowie, *The History of Ethnological Theory*, p. 220. See Paul Radin, *Primitive Man as Philosopher* and Bronisław Malinowski, *Magic, Science and Religion*.

Mircea Eliade's assumption of 'the irreducibility of the sacred'. Thus, from the modern perspective of the History of Religions, one might say that this 'second tradition' is the sociology of religion *sensu stricto*.

Wach submits that Max Weber was the first to conceive of a systematic sociology of religion. What Wach intends to stress here is that Weber, unlike a Marx or a Comte or a Durkheim, is not guilty of a reductionism of the religious: Weber rejects the interpretation that 'the characteristic feature of a religious attitude can be simply the function of the social condition of the social stratum appearing as its representation; that this attitude would be only its "ideological" expression or a reflex of it material or ideal interests'.[15]

Undoubtedly the most famous illustration of Weber's antireductionism appears in *The Protestant Ethic and the Spirit of Capitalism*. Far from maintaining that religion was simply a reflection of, or was determined by, the prevailing economic conditions, Weber contended that the very source of the spirit of modern Western capitalism was to be found in the values of the Protestant Reformation. Throughout his writings, Weber assumes that the specific religious features are at least partially independent of the relevant social and economic conditions, and he tries to show how religion influences economic, educational, scientific, artistic, governmental, and other societal institutions.[16]

Although we shall refer to Joachim Wach when we consider the nature and methodology of the History of Religions today, a few words on his sociology of religion would be appropriate here. As we noted at the beginning of Chapter 1, Wach divided the 'general science of religion' into four branches: history, phenomenology, psychology,

15. Max Weber, *Gesammelte Aufsätze zur Religionssoziologie*, vol. 1, p. 240. See W. E. H. Stanner, *On Aboriginal Religion*, pp. vi, 27: Australian religion must be studied '*as* religion and not as a mirror of something else'; it is a fallacious presupposition 'that the social order is primary and in some sense causal, and the religious order secondary and in some sense consequential'. Cf. Mircea Eliade, 'Australian Religions, Part V: Death, Eschatology, and Some Conclusions', *History of Religions* 7, no. 3 (1968): 265–266. This article is reproduced as chapter 5 in Eliade's *Australian Religions: An Introduction*.

16. Max Weber, *The Protestant Ethic and the Spirit of Capitalism*; Weber, *From Max Weber: Essays in Sociology*, pt. 3, especially pp. 267–270; Lenski, pp. 3–8. We shall not discuss Weber's 'interpretive' approach in attempting to understand an 'ethos' in its distinctive character, his method of *Verstehen*, and other important features of his methodology. One may detect his influences in much of our later analysis.

and sociology of religion. Comparative studies reveal that there are three major forms of religious expression: theoretical forms (myth, doctrine, dogma), practical forms (in cultus and forms of worship), sociological forms (religious grouping and fellowship).[17]

The question arises as to whether the sociology of religion is to be regarded as a branch of the History of Religions or of sociology. Wach admonishes the sociologist not to be 'deceived' by the 'apparent identity of religious and social behavior' and thus commit the 'fallacy of regarding religion as a function of natural social grouping'. In religion, 'communion with the numen is primary and is basic in achieving religious integration'. The gap between the study of religion and the social sciences can be bridged from the perspective of *Religionswissenschaft*: 'We like to believe that, though there is a Catholic and Marxian philosophy of society, there can be only one sociology of religion which we may approach from different angles and realize to a different degree but which would use but one set of criteria.'[18]

Nevertheless, Joseph Kitagawa seems justified in distinguishing two kinds of sociology of religion, one as a subdivision of sociology and the other as a branch of the History of Religions. Despite Wach's admonition, the sociologist in studying religion starts with the basic assumption that 'the conduct of the person— his way of thinking and ways of acting — and the nature of the social order — its structure, function and values — are to be understood as a product of group life'.[19] Thus it would seem that the same 'religious expressions' taking 'sociological forms' could be viewed either by a sociology of religion from the perspective of sociology or by a sociology of religion from the perspective of the History of Religions.

Here we have the basis for one of Eliade's primary antireductionist principles: the methodological 'scale' we employ 'makes the difference'; the various approaches, using different 'scales', will interpret the

17. Joachim Wach, *Sociology of Religion*, pp. 1–2; Wach, *Types of Religious Experience*, p. 34.

18. Wach, *Sociology of Religion*, pp. 107–108; Wach, 'Sociology of Religion', *Twentieth Century Sociology*, p. 418.

19. Kitagawa, 'The Nature and Program of the History of Religions Field', *Divinity School News* (November, 1957), p. 19; Philip M. Houser, 'Sociology', *Encyclopaedia Britannica* (1957).

same religious data in different ways. We shall be able to relate this principle to the phenomenological claim as to the 'perspectival' nature of all knowledge, and we shall question whether Mircea Eliade violates his own antireductionist principle.

PSYCHOLOGICAL APPROACHES

We shall concentrate on the influence of Freud and Jung, but should at least acknowledge the contributions to the understanding of religion made by other scholars utilizing psychological approaches. We should mention the contributions of Wilhelm Wundt and 'Völkerpsychologie', of people in the Freudian tradition (Géza Róheim, Bruno Bettelheim) and of scholars strongly influenced by Jung (Heinrich Zimmer, Joseph Campbell, Karl Kerényi, Henry Corbin). In citing William James, Starbuck, Leuba, and Pratt, Erwin R. Goodenough submits that the psychology of religion was America's special contribution to the field of *Religionswissenschaft*.[20]

Sigmund Freud

In 1913, Sigmund Freud published *Totem and Taboo*, in which he theorized 'that the beginnings of religion, ethics, society, and art meet in the Oedipus complex': religion originated with the 'first parricide', a 'primordial murder' which is ritually repeated in the 'totemic sacrifices'.[21] Accepting two hypotheses — Atkinson's 'primordial horde' and Robertson Smith's 'totemic sacrifice-communion' — Freud believed that he had explained the origin and nature of religion in terms of the Oedipus complex.

20. Erwin R. Goodenough, 'Religionswissenschaft', *Numen* 6, fasc. 2 (1959): p. 80. Under a section entitled 'Two American Psychologists', Jan de Vries discusses the psychology of religion of William James and J. H. Leuba in *The Study of Religion*, pp. 149–153. See Ira Progoff, *The Death and Rebirth of Psychology*, for its analysis of Freud, Adler, Jung, and Rank; Goodwin Watson, 'A Psychologist's View of Religious Symbols', *Religious Symbolism*, with its emphasis upon Fromm; and the works of Ernst Neumann.
21. Sigmund Freud, *Totem and Taboo*, p. 258. Cf. Alfred L. Kroeber, 'Totem and Taboo: An Ethnologic Psychoanalysis', *American Anthropologist* 22 (1920): 48–55.

In the 'primal horde' the father kept all the women for himself, and, when his sons became old enough to evoke his jealousy, he drove them off. Finally, the expelled sons banded together, slew their father, ate him, and appropriated his females. At this point the ambivalence of feelings toward the father emerged: having assuaged their 'hate impulse', the brothers now felt remorse and guilt. Consequently they created the two oldest and most significant taboos: 'not to kill the totem animal [the totem being "the father substitute"] and to avoid sexual intercourse with totem companions of the other sex'.

The totemic banquet both reenacts the original parricide and establishes 'a kind of reconciliation' with the 'father-totem'. Culture began with this primordial sacrificial ritual, and 'all later religions have been reactions aiming at the same great event'.[22] As Wilhelm Schmidt has noted, for Freud, God is nothing other than the sublimated physical father; in the totemic sacrifice it is God himself who is killed and sacrificed. 'This slaying of the father-god is mankind's original sin. The blood-guilt is atoned for by the bloody death of Christ.'[23]

We shall not carefully elucidate the widely known Freudian theory, expressed in *The Future of an Illusion* and elsewhere, as to the psychological basis of why human beings developed the 'illusion' of religion. Let us simply recall that human beings were unable to cope with the more threatening forces of nature. They then regressed to a childhood, wish-fulfillment experience, in which they had felt protected by their fathers whom they depended upon, admired, and feared. Thus religion provides the individual with an imaginary fulfillment of his or her repressed infantile desires and needs. Comparing religion with the obsessional neurosis he found in children, Freud contends that 'Religion would thus be the universal obsessional neurosis of humanity.'[24]

Freud's interpretation of religion, as based upon an 'objective historical event'— the primordial 'totemic banquet'— has been decisively refuted by such ethnologists as Rivers, Boas, Kroeber, Malinowski, and Schmidt.[25] To cite just a few objections: totemism is

22. Freud, pp. 53, 238–239.
23. Wilhelm Schmidt, *The Origin and Growth of Religion*, p. 112.
24. Sigmund Freud, *The Future of an Illusion*, chap. 8 and *passim*.
25. Schmidt, pp. 112–115; Kroeber, pp. 48–55.

not found at the beginnings of religion; it is not universal, nor have all peoples passed through a 'totemic stage'; Frazer had shown that out of hundreds of totemic tribes, only four knew of the 'totemic sacrifice-communions'.

Neo-Freudians have tended to interpret Freud's hypotheses as 'psychological' and not necessarily 'historical' descriptions. Thus, in terms of the Oedipus complex, one might envisage sacrificial rites as symbolic expressions of our unconscious desire for parricide.

We may detect naturistic and positivistic influences from 'the first period' in Freud's analysis of religion in terms of wish-fulfillment and illusion: religion originating in our confrontation with the forces of nature; a strongly 'rationalistic' interpretation; an evolutionary theory, in terms of which religion is seen as a pre-rational, pre-scientific stage.

Undoubtedly Freud revealed the psychological roots of much of religion. However, in his preoccupation with pathological phenomena, he was not justified in identifying all religious phenomena with 'the irrational nature found in the neurotic compulsion'. Erich Fromm has shown that there are religious rituals which are 'rational', meaningful, symbolic expressions and which are 'without any obsessional or irrational component'.[26]

Because of the many inadequacies in his theories on the origin and nature of religion, one must not underestimate Freud's monumental contributions to the History of Religions: his 'discovery' of the unconscious and of the method of psychoanalysis. The significant methodological implications of these discoveries for the History of Religions will be elucidated at the end of this section.

C. G. Jung

We shall not discuss C. G. Jung's theory of 'the collective unconscious' and its 'archetypes' or 'the process of individuation', but shall simply elucidate several Jungian features of special significance for the History of Religions. We shall observe that Mircea Eliade is often criticized for having a Jungian approach and for adopting Jung's notions of

26. Erich Fromm, *Psychoanalysis and Religion*, pp. 108–109.

'the collective unconscious' and its 'archetypes'. In Chapter 5 and especially in Chapter 7, we shall contend that such an interpretation is inadequate; that several of Eliade's works do reveal Jungian influences, but that Eliade's phenomenological approach can be distinguished from Jung's approach to religious phenomena.[27]

If we contrast Freud's discussion of religion with that of Carl Jung, we can see that whereas it seems to be implied by Freud's theory that a perfectly healthy individual (no repressed fears, hostilities, needs, or desires) would have no inclination to be religious, Jung considers religion to be a normal and necessary psychic function. It is clear that the one theory is antithetical to religious belief in a way in which the other is not.[28]

Jung opposes Freud's attempt to 'explain away' religious phenomena. He asserts that his psychological approach is 'scientific', is from 'a purely empirical point of view', and refrains from 'any application of metaphysical or philosophical considerations'. Thus, for example, psychology may use its comparative research to determine whether an 'imprint found in the psyche can or cannot reasonably be termed a "God-image" '. But this psychological approach says nothing about 'the actual existence of God'. From the standpoint of psychology, it is a 'fact' that the patient has an idea of a religious phenomenon: 'it [the idea] is psychologically true in as much as it exists.' Jung goes on to assert that the religious experiences are not only meaningful, but the religious symbols often are of the greatest therapeutic aid. Therefore, on the level of psychology, he rejects the characterization of religion as an 'illusion'. 'The thing that cures a neurosis must be as convincing as the neurosis; and since the latter is only too real, the helpful experience must be of equal reality.'[29]

We may view Jung's approach as 'broadening' Freud's analysis of

27. The best treatment of this topic is Mac Linscott Ricketts's 'The Nature and Extent of Eliade's "Jungianism" ', *Union Seminary Quarterly Review* 25, no. 2 (1970): 211–234.

28. William P. Alston, *Religious Belief and Philosophical Thought*, p. 228.

29. C. G. Jung, *Psychology and Religion*, pp. 2–3, 114. C. G. Jung, *Psychological Reflections*, p. 299. William James arrives at a similar conclusion in *The Varieties of Religious Experience*, p. 389. Fromm (pp. 15–17) strongly criticizes the Jungian approach presented above.

the unconscious by declaring that there are universal structures of the unconscious that keep reappearing in the dreams, hallucinations, art, myths, etc., of insane and 'so-called normal' minds throughout the world. With therapeutic intentions, Jung, in his effort to understand more adequately the processes of the mind, was gradually led to the study of archaic and Oriental religions and alchemy. He was struck by the similarity between the symbolic structures and images manifested by some of his patients and the symbolism in these other areas.[30]

Jung claims that these universal symbols 'arise from levels within us deeper than our conscious self and deeper than the personal unconscious which contains, as Freud has shown, memories repressed during the course of our early years'.[31] These psychic structures were not constituted by our individual, historical experiences. Hence, we can analyze symbolic expressions and the human 'situation' they express in terms not entirely limited to an individual's historical conditioning.

Several methodological contributions

We may conclude this section on psychological approaches by formulating several significant contributions by psychologists to the hermeneutics of the History of Religions.

Mircea Eliade compares the discovery of the unconscious to the maritime discoveries of the Renaissance and the astronomical discoveries that followed the invention of the telescope: 'for each of these discoveries revealed worlds whose very existence had been previously unsuspected. Each of them effected a sort of "breakthrough in plane", in the sense that it shattered the traditional image of the Cosmos and revealed the structures of a Universe previously unimaginable.'[32] Through the discovery of the unconscious and through the techniques developed by depth psychologists, the Historian of Religions was forced to challenge many of the uncritical assumptions and theories of earlier investigators, was presented with a new world of religious

30. See Mircea Eliade, *The Forge and the Crucible*, pp. 199–204.
31. Goodwin Watson, 'A Psychologist's View of Religious Symbols', p. 125. See Long, *Alpha*, pp. 22–23.
32. Eliade, 'Encounters at Ascona', *Spiritual Disciplines* (Papers from the *Eranos-Jahrbach*; Bollington Series 30, vol. 4), p. xviii.

manifestations, and was given the opportunity for a more adequate understanding of religious phenomena.

Much of the interest in symbols and myths and in archaic and Oriental religions can be traced back to the impact of Freud's discoveries. More specifically, the psychologists of religion exposed a 'misunderstanding' so frequent during 'the first period' interpretations: 'The misunderstanding consists mainly in taking the contents of symbolic language for real events in the realm of things instead of for symbolic expression of the soul's experience.'[33] Eliade's methodology will be seen as directed toward an understanding of the symbolic structures and meanings revealed through the religious data.

It seems unnecessary to stress the paramount significance of the opening up of the psychological dimension of the religious. But we may emphasize the methodological danger of completely reducing the religious to its psychological analysis. In this regard Eliade concludes that 'there can be no question of confusing their [the Historian of Religions and the depth psychologist] frames of reference, nor their scales of value nor, above all, their methods'.[34] That the religious must be approached *on its own 'plane of reference'*, that religious phenomena reveal an *irreducibly religious dimension* which can only be understood by the Historian of Religions — these will be seen as central methodological concerns in the History of Religions today.

Finally, we may observe that

> The historian of religions [Historian of Religions] is especially grateful to Freud for proving that images and symbols communicate their 'messages' even if the consciousness remains unaware of this fact. The historian [Historian] is now free to conduct his hermeneutical work upon a symbol without having to ask himself how many individuals in a certain society and at a given historical moment understood all the meanings and implications of that symbol.[35]

33. Fromm, p. 112.

34. *Myths, Dreams and Mysteries*, p. 20. For Eliade's attempt to establish this conclusion, see pp. 13–20.

35. Mircea Eliade, 'The History of Religions in Retrospect: 1912–1962', *Journal of Bible and Religion* 31, no. 2 (1963): 102. This article is presented in revised and expanded form as chapter 2 in *The Quest: History and Meaning in Religion*.

Obviously, this discovery opens up many new possibilities for interpretation by the Historian of Religions. However, we may recall the highly subjective interpretations of the 'first period', evolutionary anthropologists when they attempted to go 'beyond' what *homo religiosus* was actually saying and to understand what 'primitive' religion 'really' meant. Consequently, if Historians of Religions are to go 'beyond' the conscious awareness of *homo religiosus*, they must provide the *methodological framework* in terms of which their interpretation will be seen to evidence some sense of objective understanding.

ANTHROPOLOGICAL APPROACHES

During the twentieth century, anthropological approaches have become highly specialized. Within cultural anthropology alone, we can distinguish functional, diffusionist, *Kulturkreis*,[36] and evolutionary approaches. Because of the diversification and specialization of anthropological approaches, it will not be possible to formulate a somewhat unified perspective as we attempted to do in Chapter 1. Our presentation will be greatly fragmented. Some sense of unity may emerge in the following chapters, as we analyze Mircea Eliade's endeavor to incorporate the contributions of the diverse anthropological approaches (diffusionist, functionalist, etc.) in his phenomenological method, and as we analyze how Eliade deals with the challenges (such as Boas's criticism of almost all generalizations as highly subjective) raised by these anthropologists.[37]

36. 'The area that is characterized by, and radiates outward, a specific culture circle. The theory . . . postulates a diffusion of successive culture aggregates.' Charles Winick, *Dictionary of Anthropology* (Patterson, N. J.: Littlefield, Adams), p. 305. See 'The Theory of Culture Circles', pp. 175–180, in *The Study of Religion* by Jan de Vries.

37. Among the works which outline the diversification and specialization of anthropological approaches are the following: Michael Banton, ed., *Anthropological Approaches to the Study of Religion*, which includes Clifford Geertz's 'Religion as a Cultural System' and Melford E. Spiro's 'Religion: Problems of Definition and Explanation'; Allan W. Eister, ed., *Changing Perspectives in the Scientific Study of Religion*; Lessa and Vogt, eds., *Reader in Comparative Religion*; Sol Tax, ed., *Horizons of Anthropology*, which includes Edward Norbeck's 'The Study of Religion'; and Anthony F. C. Wallace, *Religion: An Anthropological View*.

Several specialist approaches

The foremost proponent of the *Kulturkreistheorie*, Wilhelm Schmidt, illustrates the culture historical approach[38] in his monumental *Ursprung der Gottesidee* (twelve volumes; 1912–55). His major significance for the History of Religions lies in his rejection of ahistorical and naturalistic approaches to religious phenomena.

Deeply impressed by Andrew Lang's pre-animistic theory and by Fritz Graebner's method for identifying various cultural and religious strata, Schmidt now used his culture historical approach to prove that the oldest strata revealed the belief in an eternal creator, an omniscient and beneficent High God (a sort of *Urmonotheismus*).[39] Starting from the 'survivals' in such 'living fossils' as Southeastern Australian tribes, one could reconstruct the *Urreligion*. From this 'original monotheism' in the *Urkultur*, Schmidt traced the gradual corruption, confusion, and degeneration of this belief in a High God.[40]

Unfortunately, Schmidt's contributions have been neglected because of certain obvious inadequacies. Even more than Lang he utilizes an excessively rationalistic approach and identifies Western conceptions of God among archaic cultures. Schmidt not only claims the existence of this belief in a High God but also submits that this notion is 'the product of logicocausal thought'; it 'arises out of man's supposed intellectualistic need of becoming aware of the origin and wherefore of things'.[41]

38. 'Culture Historical (method): follows the principles of general history but makes use of the culture itself and its productions as methodological media to reconstruct the history of man in those times for which we have no written documents.' Wilhelm Schmidt, *The Culture Historical Method of Ethnology*, p. 346.

39. Schmidt, *The Origin and Growth of Religion*, pp. 177 ff. (Lang's theory); pp. 262 ff. ('The Primitive Religion of a High God a True Monotheism'); pp. 269 ff. ('Attributes of the Supreme Being'); and *passim*.

40. This should indicate the subtle interaction between different approaches and the artificially in clear-cut distinctions. See Franz Boas, 'Evolution or Diffusion?', *American Anthropologist* 26 (1924): 340–344. Yet the highly diffusionist opponent of evolutionism, Father Schmidt, when he detects 'survivals' and reconstructs 'the stages of the whole development', certainly expounds a type of evolution, albeit not a unilinear evolution. See Lowie, *The History of Ethnological Theory*, p. 190. Another traditional opposition — 'diffusionism' or 'functionalism' — also does not necessarily occur. (See Claude Lévi-Strauss, 'Social Structure', *Anthropology Today*, pp. 532–533.)

41. Raffaele Pettazzoni, 'The Supreme Being: Phenomenological Structure and

Schmidt was inclined to think that all the irrational elements represent a 'degeneration' of genuine religion. The truth is that we do not have any means to investigate this 'primordial religion.' Our oldest documents are relatively recent. . . . It is true that the belief in High Gods seems to characterize the oldest cultures, but we also find there other religious elements. As far as we can reconstruct the most remote past, it is safer to assume that religious life was from the very beginning rather complex, and that 'elevated' ideas coexisted with 'lower' forms of worship and belief.[42]

In America the major tendencies can be observed in Franz Boas and his followers.[43] Reacting against the monistic interpretations of the evolutionists, and their penchant for broad generalizations, these American anthropologists emphasized the study of particular cultures and the importance of cultural pluralism and cultural relativity. The 'ethnic phenomena which we compare are seldom really alike'. The 'selection of the material assembled for the purpose of comparison is wholly determined by the subjective point of view according to which we arrange diverse mental phenomena'.[44]

This has been determinative for the formation of anthropological research in the United States: a stress upon the absolute inviolability of the individual phenomenon and a consequent unwillingness to subordinate it to any more general system of interpretation. In

Historical Development', *The History of Religions: Essays in Methodology*, p. 60. Cf. Eliade, 'Australian Religions, Part I', p. 119.

42. Eliade, 'The History of Religions in Retrospect: 1912–1962', p. 103. There have been a number of other Continental anthropologists who have contributed to the History of Religions. We may cite the followers of Schmidt and the present Vienna School; German and Austrian ethnologists, such as L. Frobenius, H. Baumann, and W. Müller; Marcel Griaule and the French School of ethnology; the French social anthropologists. See the above Eliade article ('The History of Religions in Retrospect: 1912–1962') and Lessa and Vogt for a more complete listing of anthropologists interested in the study of religions.

43. Exceptions should be noted. At times such anthropologists as Clyde Kluckhohn and Ruth Benedict have attempted to overcome the highly diffusionistic and relativistic position of a Boas. We have cited the important works of Lowie, have referred to Paul Radin, and could have analyzed the contributions of Clifford Geertz and several other contemporary American anthropologists.

44. Franz Boas, 'The Origin of Totemism', *American Anthropologist* 18, no. 3 (1916): 320. Cf. the similar positions of Stith Thompson and Melville Herskovitz.

practice, this has made for, on the one hand, an amassing of immense amounts of data upon any given subject, but, on the other hand, a denial that any common structures could be perceived to inform these data, that any comparisons could therefore legitimately be made between them, and, finally, that scarcely any generalizations of any kind could be genuinely applied to them.[45]

Cultural uniformities are usually only 'apparent similarities', and, in the case of 'genuine parallels', we can explain them in terms of diffusion due to the contacts between various cultures.

In England, although anthropological research has also reacted against the evolutionistic approaches, there have been attempts to account for uniformities: 'underlying this diversity (in the actual cultural content) there may be impressive similarities in basic functions, involving the culturally prescribed solutions of human social and psychological problems and the ways of expressing and reaffirming the central values of a society.' As Radcliffe-Brown wrote in *Taboo*, 'I would suggest that what Sir James Frazer seems to regard as the accidental results of magical and religious beliefs really constitute their essential function and the ultimate reason for their existence.'[46] 'Since we cannot define cult and creed by their objects, perhaps it will be possible to perceive their function'; the unity in religion can be seen 'in the function which it fulfills'.[47] This *functionalist school* can best be seen in the works of Malinowski, Radcliffe-Brown, Evans-Pritchard, and Raymond Firth.[48]

In recent years the *'structural anthropology'* of Claude Lévi-Strauss has received considerable attention. Using his structural linguistic

45. Robert Luyster, 'The Study of Myth: Two Approaches', *Journal of Bible and Religion* 34, no. 3 (1966): 238.

46. Lessa and Vogt, p. 85.

47. Bronisław Malinowski, *Magic, Science and Religion*, pp. 20 and 68.

48. For their fundamental differences, especially the comparative sociological emphasis of the latter three, see David Bidney, 'The Concept of Value in Modern Anthropology', pp. 694–696 and Lessa and Vogt, chapter 2. Cf. Carl G. Hempel, 'The Logic of Functional Analysis', *Symposium on Sociological Theory*, ed. Llewellyn Gross (Reprinted in *Readings in the Philosophy of the Social Sciences*, ed. May Brodbeck); Kingsley Davis, 'The Myth of Functional Analysis as a Special Method in Sociology and Anthropology', *American Sociological Review* 24 (1959): 757–772; Hans H. Penner, 'The Poverty of Functionalism', *History of Religions* 11 (1971): 91–97.

approach, Lévi-Strauss asserts that 'In every one of its practical under-takings, anthropology thus does no more than assert a homology of structure between human thought in action and the human object to which it is applied.'[49] By regarding 'religious systems as co-ordinate wholes', by trying to understand their system of classification and decode the messages they communicate, Lévi-Strauss's structuralistic approach has yielded highly controversial and often enlightening results. Thus, although 'the properties to which the savage mind has access are not the same as those which have commanded the attention of scientists', he submits that 'the savage mind is logical in the same sense and the same fashion as ours. . . . Its thought proceeds through the understanding, not affectivity, with the aid of distinctions and oppositions, not by confusion and participation.'[50] Although the forms of primitive expressions may not seem rational, careful analysis reveals a logical structure in their symbolic expressions.

Here we observe that the earlier evolutionary views concerning the nature of religion and of primitive culture, and the oversimplified distinctions and distortions of a scholar such as Lévy-Bruhl, are being challenged. 'Recent anthropologists and historians of religion [Historians of Religion] have agreed courageously that we can no longer believe in a gulf between primitive man and ourselves.'[51]

That clear-cut 'gulf' between the primitive and ourselves, between the premodern and the modern, which we observed in the evolutionary theorists of 'the first period' and in such later scholars as Lévy-Bruhl, has been rendered dubious by the brilliant findings of Alexander Marshak and other investigators. Using a technique of 'microscopic

49. Claude Lévi-Strauss, *Totemism*, p. 91. Note Lévi-Strauss's discussion of previous theories on totemism and his own position, especially in 'Totemism from Within', pp. 92–104. See Mircea Eliade's 'Cultural Fashions and the History of Religions', *The History of Religions: Essays on the Problem of Understanding*, pp. 21–38, for an analysis, from the perspective of History of Religions, of the popularity of Lévi-Strauss. This article appears as chapter 1 in Eliade's *Occultism, Witchcraft, and Cultural Fashions*.
50. Claude Lévi-Strauss, *The Savage Mind*, pp. 268–269.
51. Kees W. Bolle, Introduction to Jan de Vries's *The Study of Religion*, p. xvi. By looking at Jensen, Lanternari, and Lévi-Strauss, Kees Bolle shows that each anthropologist has a different conception as to why this 'gulf' between primitive and modern should be opposed. This diversity Bolle traces to 'the philosophical presuppositions of each scholar', his 'underlying or presupposed idea of man'.

analysis', Marshak was able to interpret the 'almost invisible signs engraved on stones and bones from Upper Paleolithic levels in Europe' as revealing a 'system' of 'time notations based on lunar periodicities'.

> The evidence for a ubiquitous tradition of Upper Paleolithic notation would seem to verify a modern level of cognitive capacity and symbolic usage in early, prewriting, prearithmetic phases of *sapiens* culture. The complexity of the tradition in the typical Aurignacian [ca. 32,000 years ago] implies an earlier origin. The latter complexities of the tradition in the terminal Magdalenian [ca. 10,000 years ago] may indicate that formal writing, arithmetic, and the true calendar, which appear in the first agricultural civilizations, may have had reference to this earlier symbolizing tradition, one that was at least 25,000 years old.

As Eliade has written: 'Such conclusions brilliantly vindicate those scholars — from Wilhelm Schmidt and Oliver Leroy to Karl Narr and Claude Lévi-Straus — who were convinced neither by the "prelogical" structure of the *mentalité primitive* nor by the supposed *Urdummheit* of archaic man.'[52]

Because of limited space, we have refrained from entering into a discussion of the contributions of Malinowski, Leenhard, Lévi-Strauss and others toward understanding such phenomena as myths and rituals. We should note the heated controversy over the relationship of myths and rituals. Are rituals 'prior' and only later myths develop to justify them (Hyman)? Or are myths prior and then rituals develop to enact them (Bascom)? Or, in their usual interrelation, is there no necessary primacy of one over the other (Kluckhohn)?[53]

Most 'ethnologists have tended to interpret myth literally as an

52. Alexander Marshak, 'Cognitive Aspects of Upper Paleolithic Engraving', *Current Anthropology* 13, nos. 3–4 (1972): 461; Marshak, *The Roots of Civilization: The Cognitive Beginnings of Man's First Art, Symbol, and Notation*; Eliade, 'On Prehistoric Religions', *History of Religions* 14, no. 2 (1974): 141.

53. Stanley Edgar Hyman, 'The Ritual View of Myth and the Mythic', *Myth: A Symposium*, pp. 84–94; William Bascom, 'The Myth-Ritual Theory', *Journal of American Folklore* 70 (1957): 103–114; Clyde Kluckhohn, 'Myths and Rituals: A General Theory', *Harvard Theological Review* 35 (1942): 45–79. See Lessa and Vogt, chap. 2, 'Myth and Ritual', pp. 134–202; Joseph M. Kitagawa, 'Primitive, Classical, and

expression of primitive thought but have differed in their evaluation of myth'.[54] But certain anthropologists (such as Griaule, Berndt, and Lévi-Strauss), in attempting to understand what myths or rituals mean for those who believe and practice them and in allowing religious phenomena 'to speak for themselves', have arrived at some startling results.

To give one illustration, the Berndts have found that a seemingly simple ritual (during a ceremony in northeastern Arnhem Land, an emblem signifying a goanna's tail and vertebrae is ritually displayed) hides a complex symbolism and rich mythology. Down the trunk of the emblem, totemic designs are painted and feathered penchants are attached. 'Slowly the actor removes it from its shade, posturing as he does so; he writhes along the ground, holding the sacred stick close to his breast.' Rather than tracing the diffusion of this ritual, or classifying it as a prescientific stage of 'literal confusion', or determining its function in maintaining the cohesiveness of the society, and then concluding that one had exhausted its significance as a religious phenomenon, the Berndts continue:

What does this mean? Here is an emblem which is a symbol of a goanna's tail and vertebrae, withdrawn from its shade. But to the neophyte it is much more than this. The shade or hut symbolizes a special conically-shaped mat, brought by the Dyanggawul Fertility Mothers from a spirit land away in the sunrise, beyond the Morning Star. This mat is really a womb. When the goanna tail emblem is removed from it on the sacred ground, this signifies that the first people, ancestors of the present-day eastern Arnhem Landers, are being born from their Mother; and they, in turn, are associated with a combination of fertility symbols. Actually, there is symbol within symbol, meaning within meaning, much of it connected with fundamental drives.[55]

Modern Religions: A Perspective on Understanding the History of Religions', *The History of Religions: Essays on the Problem of Understanding*, pp. 45–49. Note also the methodological debates over the 'Myth and Ritual School' or 'patternism', especially the volumes edited by S. H. Hooke and the criticisms of H. Frankfort.

54. Bidney, 'Myth, Symbolism, and Truth', pp. 12–13.

55. R. M. and C. H. Berndt, *The First Australians*, pp. 78–79. See Mircea Eliade, 'Australian Religions, Part II: An Introduction', *History of Religions* 6, no. 3 (1967): 222–225. This article appears as chapter 2 in *Australian Religions: An Introduction*.

Of course, we have not indicated how one would arrive at and check this sort of interpretation. Our purpose at this point is to show the *new hermeneutical situation* in which Historians of Religions find themselves, a situation with many potential 'openings' for new understandings of religious phenomena.

Several significant influences

We are now in a position to enumerate several of the significant influences of anthropologists on the History of Religions, with emphasis upon the methodological issues and problems arising from these anthropological approaches.

1. The anthropologists have amassed a vast quanity of religious data, and this has greatly assisted Historians of Religions in their interpretations. For example, through the meticulous research of historically oriented anthropologists, documentation on premodern religions has been pushed back further into Paleolithic times (decisively proving the earlier theories about religious origins and growth were inadequate), and our information about every historical period has been greatly increased. A. E. Jensen's interpretation of a 'Dema-type', V. G. Childe's views on prehistoric cultures, and numerous positions on 'megalithic religion' have been invaluable in identifying religious forms and deciphering their meanings.

2. The Historian of Religions must be congnizant of all of the specific anthropological approaches. Each approach reveals *different aspects* of the religious phenomena. The cultural historical approaches remind the Historian of Religions to avoid the earlier mistakes of the ahistorical and naturalistic approaches. The significance and meaning of an isolated religious datum often seem unintelligible until one begins to unravel its pattern of diffusion. A phenomenon, such as shamanism, may appear to be nothing less than sheer madness until the interpreter begins to comprehend its religious function. What is required of the History of Religions is an approach which can incorporate *all* of the different anthropological perspectives into its methodological framework.

At the same time, the Historian of Relgions recognizes that many anthropologists have *reduced* the religious to their specific perspective.

After tracing the diffusion or determining the function of a religious phenomenon, the Historian of Religions has not completed his or her investigation. Each anthropological perspective sheds light upon but does not exhaust the total significance of the religious.

3. The general insistence of most anthropologists upon *specialization*, with a respect for cultural relativism and pluralism, is reflected in the studies of most contemporary Historians of Religions. 'The situation that one finds today is as follows: a considerable improvement in information, paid for by excessive specialization and even by sacrificing our own vocation (for the majority of historians of religions [Historians of Religions] have become orientalists, classicists, ethnologists, etc.), and a dependence upon the methods elaborated by modern historiography or sociology. . . .'[56]

Following the admonishments of Boas and others, most Historians of Religions greatly limit the scope of their work. They may specialize in one culture, attempting to trace the diffusion of myths or to determine the function of rituals in that specific culture.

This emphasis upon highly specialized research in the History of Religions has severely restricted efforts at comparative analysis. Oscar Lewis[57] has distinguished two general types of comparative studies in anthropology: very modest comparisons between societies that are historically related, broad comparisons between historically unrelated societies. As a reaction against the latter, usually associated with the 'failure' of those universal typologies and evolutionary sequences of a Tylor or a Freud or a Durkheim, the Historian of Religions often refrains from comparative analysis.

Mircea Eliade not only attempts the very modest comparisons between historically related societies, but he often makes the most general comparisons between societies which are not historically or geographically related. Indeed, Eliade will claim that there are certain 'primordial' religious phenomena, such as 'ecstasy', which 'reappear

56. Mircea Eliade, *Images and Symbols*, p. 29. Note the section entitled 'The Inhibitions of the Specialist', in Eliade's *Mephistopheles and the Androgyne*, pp. 193–195.

57. Oscar Lewis, 'Comparisons in Cultural Anthropology', *Yearbook of Anthropology — 1955*, pp. 259–292. The attempt to reach fairly general conclusions through 'small-scale comparative studies' and 'controlled comparisons' has been attempted by such scholars as Dumézil, Nadel, Evans-Pritchard, and Eggan. See Lévi-Strauss, 'Social Structure', pp. 548–549; Lessa and Vogt, p. 5.

spontaneously' in all kinds of heterogeneous and historically unrelated societies. We can compare such phenomena and decipher universal structures of religious experience. Obviously such a position leaves Eliade open to the severe criticisms of contemporary historicists and other 'specialists', especially to the charge that he is just as uncritical as the earlier 'generalist' approaches.

In addition to specialization in one culture or tribe, Eliade locates another reason for documentation that is insufficiently broad to permit valid comparisons and generalizations: by limiting our research to primitive religions, we have no measure of the role of that religious phenomenon (such as myth) in highly developed religions. A few comparativists, such as Jensen and Baumann, attempt to 'deal with all categories of mythological creativity, those of the "primitives" as well as of the peoples of high cultures'.[58]

While recognizing the need for specialization, we must also stress that there are many dangers in overspecialization on the part of Historians of Religions. In the ensuing chapters, we shall observe that there are many hermeneutical advantages in having at least some Historians of Relgions taking a more 'generalist' approach.

The anthropological specialists have been justified in stressing that one must do justice to the individuality of the specific religious phenomenon. The methodological problem confronting the Historian of Religions seems to be one of formulating a systematic framework, in terms of which he or she can both interpret the particular religious manifestation and make adequate comparisons and generalizations.

4. There has been a definite reaction against the 'prior' assumptions and theories of earlier anthropologists. From the perspective of contemporary anthropology, the research of 'the first period' was often more normative than descriptive. More attention has been devoted to

58. Mircea Eliade, 'Cosmogonic Myth and "Sacred History" ', *Religious Studies* 2, (1967): 172. Some Historians of Religions, realizing this neglect of 'highly developed religions', have gone to the opposite extreme of entirely eliminating the study of primitive religions. For example, R. C. Zaehner, in contrasting his view with that of E. O. James, understands Comparative Religion to be the comparison of ' "the great religions and ethical systems . . . of the East" . . . with each other and with the religions and ethics of the West'. *The Comparison of Religions*, pp. 11–12.

describing what *homo religiosus* says and what religious phenomena mean for him or her.

This same emphasis is reflected in the interpretations of the History of Religions. We shall see that with some scholars, such as the phenomenologist W. Brede Kristensen, there is almost a complete unwillingness to go beyond the descriptions of the believer. However, without minimizing the necessity for describing what *homo religiosus* says, most Historians of Religions also agree with Freud that there are dimensions of religious phenomena of which the believer may remain consciously unaware and that these must be interpreted.

5. Merleau-Ponty claims that with Marcel Mauss we find the attempt to regard a 'social fact' (e.g. the phenomenon of magic) as 'an efficacious system of symbols or a network of symbolic values'. 'Concomitant variations and external correlations leave a residue', and this can only be understood by thinking 'our way into the phenomenon'.[59] Such an approach, which can be seen in the investigations of Lévi-Strauss and many other anthropologists, plays a large part in the History of Religions: the attempt to understand a religious phenomenon *from within*, to penetrate it and communicate with it, especially by deciphering its meaning through its *symbolic structures*.

Now, if the History of Religions really wants to understand what religious phenomena mean for *homo religiosus* and if it really wants to understand the religious data 'from within', then the possibility for such interpretations must be reflected in its methodological approach. To supply only one illustration to which we shall return, the History of Religions will emphasize such methodological requirements as the need on the part of the scholar for a 'sympathetic understanding' and 'participation' in the religious phenomena of 'the other'.

6. A major difficulty in determining the influence of anthropology on the History of Religions arises from the fact that it is not at all clear the extent to which modern anthropology is even interested in religion. Although anthropologists still devote most of their attention to primitive cultures, the study of religion seems to have fallen into the background.

In his 'Introduction' to *Anthropology Today* — a collection of fifty

59. Merleau-Ponty, 'From Mauss to Claude Lévi-Strauss', *Signs*, p. 115.

'inventory papers' from 'The International Symposium on Anthropology'— A. L. Kroeber writes that 'in short, this volume is a summary of what we know in and around anthropology in 1952'. In his paper, 'Social Structure', Lévi-Strauss notes 'that the word "religion" does not even appear in the program of this symposium' (p. 548). Indeed, in almost 1000 pages — most of them dealing with primitive cultures — references to religion appear only a few times.

In an earlier study, 'The Structural Study of Myth', Lévi-Strauss submits that 'during the past twenty years anthropology has been increasingly turned from studies in the field of religion' and that the field of mythology has been invaded by all sorts of 'amateurs'.[60] Hans H. Penner claims that

> It is only since the appearance of Lévi-Strauss's article ['The Structural Study of Myth'], in fact, that anthropology has returned to religion by means of a study of myth and ritual. I am not saying that he alone is responsible for the return. Since 1960, however, we have had a number of books, anthologies, and articles on anthropological approaches to 'religion' — which means myth and ritual. Whether this new interest has resulted in a new understanding of myth and ritual remains a debatable point.[61]

At a conference in 1963, eight years after the publication of Lévi-Strauss's article, Clifford Geertz began his 'Religion as a Cultural System' by submitting that anthropological work on religion since the second world war 'has made no theoretical advances of major importance'. He goes on to maintain that those significant concepts which anthropological studies of religion do use are almost always drawn from the contributions of only four men: Durkheim, Weber, Freud, and Malinowski.[62]

60. 'The Structural Study of Myth', *Structural Anthropology*, pp. 202–203. This article first appeared in *Journal of American Folklore* 78 (1955): 428–444.

61. Hans H. Penner, 'Myth and Ritual: A Wasteland or a Forest of Symbols?', *On Method in the History of Religions*, ed. James S. Helfer, pp. 46–47. Penner contends that 'the new interest in anthropology concerning myth and ritual, though revised after the gap between, let us say, Tylor and the studies of Leach, Turner, Wallace, Evans-Pritchard, Douglas, and Spiro (that is, from the late 1950's onward), has not involved an essential change in methodological assumptions'.

62. Clifford Geertz, 'Religion as a Cultural System', *Anthropological Approaches to the Study of Religion*, ed. Michael Banton, pp. 1–2. John Henry Morgan, 'Religious Myth

In recent years, there certainly have been numerous publications by anthropologists[63] on myth and ritual and other religious phenomena, on attempts to formulate new scientific approaches, and on such topics as 'civil' and 'secular' religious expressions, drug experiences and contemporary youth cults. To what extent these studies will produce significant *openings*, radically changing the hermeneutical situation of the Historian of Religions, remains to be seen.

PHENOMENOLOGICAL APPROACHES

Of all the twentieth century approaches in the History of Religions, the phenomenology of religion has been the most revolutionary: it has rendered possible a more systematic study of religions and has shaped much of the nature of the History of Religions today. Charles J. Adams asserts that 'the phenomenological approach, or some variation on it, whatever it may be called, has gained more adherents — until today almost every historian of religions [Historian of Religions] is a phenomenologist. . . .'[64] Adams does overstate his point: there is significant research being done in the History of Religions by scholars who are not phenomenologists; and, as we shall observe in our discussion of the historical-phenomenological 'tension' and elsewhere, many 'specialists' vehemently oppose any phenomenological interpretation, and some 'generalists' do not consider themselves phenomenologists. Nevertheless, it does seem to be the case that many scholars identified as Historians of Religions do take some sort of phenomenological approach, and many of the major methodological concerns in the History of Religions today are issues raised by the phenomenology of religion.

---

and Symbol: A Convergence of Philosophy and Anthropology', *Philosophy Today* 18 (1974): 68–84, submits that it is in fact the philosophical anthropology of such anthropologists as Victor Turner, Clifford Geertz, and Claude Lévi-Strauss that presents us with 'advances of major importance'.

63. For a partial listing of publications, see n. 27 in chap. 1 (p. 12) and n. 37 in chap. 2 (p. 45), as well as the references listed by Penner, 'Myth and Ritual', and Morgan, 'Religious Myth and Symbol'.

64. Charles J. Adams, 'The History of Religions and the Study of Islām', *The History of Religions: Essays on the Problem of Understanding*, p. 178.

At this point, it is not possible to explicate what is meant by a phenomenological approach in the History of Religions. Our major objective will be to determine the nature of such a phenomenological method and to assess the value of Eliade's phenomenology of religion. For now, let us begin with a general, introductory formulation offered by C. Jouco Bleeker.

According to Professor Bleeker, there is no agreement as to the nature and the task of the phenomenology of religion. He claims that at present we can distinguish three types of phenomenology of religion: '1) the descriptive school which is content with a systematisation of the religious phenomena, 2) the typological school, which aims at the research of different types of religion, 3) the phenomenological school in the specific sense of the word, which makes inquiries into the essence, the sense and the structure of the religious phenomena'.[65]

In focusing on the third, more specific type, Bleeker submits that 'the word phenomenology gets a double meaning'. The phenomenology of religion is 'an independent science' which creates monographs and handbooks, but it is also 'a scholarly method' which utilizes such principles as the phenomenological *epoché* and eidetic vision. Although these concepts 'are borrowed from the philosophical phenomenology of Husserl and his school', they are used by the phenomenology of religion only in a 'figurative sense'. Indeed, Bleeker asserts that 'the phenomenology of religion would be greatly served if its scope of activities was clearly distinguished at the one side from that of the philosophical phenomenology and at the other hand from that of anthropology'. He warns that the Historian of Religions is a 'layman' in matters relating to philosophical phenomenology and 'should refrain from meddling in these difficult affairs'. 'In my mind phenomenology of religion is not a philosophical discipline, but a systematization of historical facts with the intent to understand their religious meaning.'[66]

It is our position that the above not only illustrates the orientation of many who consider themselves phenomenologists of religion, but it also reveals the limitations and methodological inadequacy of their approaches. It is our position that many of the fundamental issues

65. Bleeker, 'The Contribution of the Phenomenology of Religion', p. 39.
66. *Ibid.*, pp. 39–41, 51.

raised by philosophical phenomenology *must* be taken seriously by the phenomenology of religion or it will remain methodologically naive and uncritical.

For now, it will suffice simply to say that we are using 'phenomenology of religion' in its 'broadest sense, including under "phenomenology" those scholars who pursue the study of structures and meanings' of religious phenomena.[67] More than any other approach, phenomenologists have emphasized the experiential basis of religion and have attempted to describe and to systematize the basic *structures of religious experience*. In describing such structures, phenomenologists of religion have attempted to approach their data in a specific *antireductionist* manner, and, unlike the other approaches to religious phenomena, have insisted upon the irreducibility and uniqueness of the religious dimension of experience.[68]

We shall now consider the approaches of three phenomenologists: Rudolf Otto, G. van der Leeuw, and W. Brede Kristensen. Since Chapters 4–7 will be devoted almost entirely to the phenomenology of religion, there will be no effort to be comprehensive in the following analyses.

Rudolf Otto

Rudolf Otto's interpretation of religion, especially as formulated in *Das Heilige* (1917), is well-known and has profoundly influenced later phenomenology of religion. Otto was familiar with the anthropologi-

67. Mircea Eliade, 'History of Religions and a New Humanism', *History of Religions* 1, no. 1 (1961): 7. This article appears in revised and expanded form as chapter 1 in *The Quest: History and Meaning in Religion*.

68. An exception to this general pattern of reductionist approaches was seen in Max Weber's sociology of religion. It seems to us that this is the primary reason why various phenomenologists interested in the social sciences, such as Alfred Schutz and Maurice Natanson, trace so much of their methodology back to Max Weber. For example, Natanson uses Weber's analysis, especially his method of *Verstehen*, to distinguish and compare the 'naturalistic approach' (which is 'reductionistic') and the 'phenomenological approach' to the methodology of the social sciences. See Maurice Natanson, 'A Study in Philosophy and the Social Sciences', *Literature, Philosophy, and the Social Sciences*, pp. 160–165. It will become clear that much of Eliade's opposition is directed against the very characteristics Natanson identifies with the 'naturalistic approach'.

cal theories of religion. With special emphasis on the aspect of 'prodigious power', he attempted to relate all of the religious phenomena (magic, totemism, mana, animism, etc.) 'by a common — and that a *numinous* — element'.[69] Concentrating on the nonrational aspect of religious experience, Otto spoke of the *sui generis* numinous experience, which presented itself as 'wholly other' (*ganz andere*) and could be characterized as *mysterium tremendum et fascinosum*.

We shall focus on two significant methodological contributions which Rudolf Otto made to the phenomenology of religion: his experiential approach, involving the description of the essential structures of religious experience; his antireductionist approach, involving the unique numinous quality of all religious experience. These interdependent methodological contributions helped to transform the hermeneutical situation of the Historian of Religions.

Rather than emphasizing various religious 'ideas' or conceptions, as had Tylor, Lang and others in their highly 'rational' explanations, Otto directed his attention to the different modalities of the numinous. He emphasized the religious encounter, the experiential basis of religion. Instead of formulating various 'negative' normative judgments regarding such issues as whether religion was 'illusory' or was based upon some sort of 'mistake', instead of speculating regarding such issues as whether religion did in fact reveal the 'primordial' forms or the 'origin' of the evolutionary process, Rudolf Otto examined certain data which disclosed specific structures of the numinous experience. He attempted to describe and analyze the structures of the experiences expressed in his data.[70]

Otto attempted to formulate a universal phenomenological struc-

69. Rudolf Otto, *The Idea of the Holy*, p. 117 and *passim*.

70. Cf. the similar emphasis by William James, who could easily be included under 'phenomenological' (as well as 'psychological') approaches to religions. For example, James finds 'a certain uniform deliverance in which religions all appear to meet'. Every religion has the following pattern or structure: there is a vision of perfection or of an ideal; secondly, there is an uneasiness: as compared to the ideal, 'there is something wrong about us as we naturally stand'; finally, there is a solution of this 'flaw': 'we are saved from the wrongness by making proper connection with the higher powers'. Cf. also his analysis of the structure of mysticism in terms of four essential 'marks'. James, by elucidating these structures, affords us the opportunity of organizing and comparing the multifarious religious manifestations. *The Varieties of Religious Experience*, pp. 383–384, 292–294, and *passim*.

ture of religious experience in terms of which the phenomenologist could organize and analyze the specific religious manifestations. Not only will this be Eliade's purpose in formulating a phenomenological foundation of universal symbolic structures, but Eliade will adopt much of Otto's structural analysis: the transcendent ('wholly other') structure of the sacred; the 'ambivalent' structure of the sacred (*mysterium tremendum* and *mysterium fascinosum*).

We must not overlook serious weaknesses in Otto's analysis of religious experience, primarily stemming from a too-narrowly-conceived phenomenological approach. In reacting against previous 'rational' interpretations, Otto stressed the nonrational dimension of religious experience to such an extent that he tended to define religious experience too narrowly; his analysis is often quite illuminating, especially with regard to certain mystical experiences, but it does not do justice to the total realm of religious phenomena in all its complexity.[71]

In his antireductionist approach, Otto insisted upon the unique a priori quality of the numinous. He thus protested against the 'one-sidedly intellectualistic and rationalistic' bias of most interpretations and against the reduction of religious phenomena to the interpretive schema of linguistic analysis, anthropology, sociology, psychology, etc.[72] In emphasizing the a priori quality of the religious and the universal structure of religious experience, Otto was also attacking the reductionisms of the historicistic approaches to religious phenomena.[73]

In his emphasis upon the irreducibility of the religious, Rudolf Otto

---

71. Eliade, *The Sacred*, p. 10. Cf. Th. P. van Baaren, 'Science of Religion as a Systematic Discipline', *Religion, Culture and Methodology*, p. 40: 'Rudolf Otto, while theorizing about the Holy as the *ganz Andere*, has made the rare exceptions the general norm and has thus greatly impeded our understanding of religion as it actually is.' See Charles H. Long, 'The Meaning of Religion in the Contemporary Study of the History of Religions', *Criterion* 2, no. 2 (1963): 25–26, for a discussion of why this 'narrowness' necessitates an extensive schematization and the problems involved therein.

72. Otto, pp. 3–4 and *passim*.

73. *Ibid.*, p. 175; 'the holy' is 'an a priori category of mind' and is 'not to be derived from "experience" or "history" '. See Charles H. Long, 'Archaism and Hermeneutics', *The History of Religions: Essays on the Problem of Understanding*, pp. 69–70; Charles H. Long, 'Where is the History of Religions Leading Us?', *Criterion* 6, no. 3 (1967): 19.

was correct in realizing that most earlier investigators, not to mention many contemporary scholars, were incapable of empathizing with the numinous experience, and this led to analyses which distorted the nature of religious phenomena. But Otto's appeal to the 'unique religious element' in the reader's 'deeply-felt religious experience'[74] also will not do, since experience is necessary but not sufficient in understanding religious phenomena. There is no 'pure' encounter; experience is not wholly self-interpreting. We always need *criteria* of what counts.

Otto insisted upon the irreducibility of the numinous, but he did not succeed in providing an adequate hermeneutical framework for perceiving and interpreting these irreducible manifestations. What Otto lacks and what the contemporary phenomenologist must provide is a comprehensive structural analysis, in terms of which the reader can empathize with the numinous experience, distinguish authentic religious phenomena, and interpret the religious meanings of such manifestations.

Unfortunately, Otto's antireductionistic concerns, focusing on the rationalistic and historicistic reductions of previous interpretations, led him too far in the opposite direction: he was not justified in identifying religion with the nonrational, and he was not sufficiently concerned either with the forms of the world through which the numinous manifests itself or with the specific meaning of each historical manifestation of religion. As Charles Long has written, Otto's 'theory of the religious a priori operated as one of Kant's regulative ideas'. Otto seems to provide us 'with an explanatory *law* of religious experience and expression — a law not derivative from historical experience'.[75]

---

74. Otto, p. 8. Those who cannot identify this unique numinous element in their experience — as would seem to be the case with most readers in our modern desacralized age — are 'requested to read no farther'.

75. Long, 'Archaism and Hermeneutics', p. 69. We have emphasized Otto's antireductionist *claim*, especially as a reaction against the reductions evident in previous approaches. But the above should make clear that Otto himself was a reductionist. Not only is his phenomenology founded on certain Kantian assumptions and categories and on a preference for certain ('nonhistorical', 'mystical') types of experience, but even more obvious are his underlying, personal, Christian, theological beliefs. This is evident in the many passages in *Mysticism East and West*, *The Idea of the*

This is why contemporary Historians of Religions, who recognize the need to do justice to the historical and particular dimension of religious experience, claim to be using an empirical approach which is devoid of any a priori judgments. Here lies a crucial methodological problem for Eliade's phenomenology. As we shall see in Chapters 4 and 5, Eliade will claim to employ an empirical method, which is free from any a priori judgments and describes only what the data reveal; and at the same time, he will proceed to uncover various universal structures, which seem incapable of being falsified by future data. In Chapter 6, we shall suggest how the phenomenologist might arrive at such contingent, yet necessary structures.

G. van der Leeuw

Many of the methodological contributions made by Gerardus van der Leeuw have already been suggested in our analysis of Rudolf Otto. For example, we need not analyze van der Leeuw's insistence on the irreducibility of the religious and his opposition to various reductionist approaches. Van der Leeuw, unlike Otto, attempted to analyze and *systematize* a tremendous number of historical expressions of religious experiences. His *Religion in Essence and Manifestation* is a classic in the systematic research of the phenomenology of religion.

Probably more than any other Historian of Religions, van der Leeuw was impressed by the religious aspect of '*power*', as evidenced in the findings of such investigators as Codrington and Hewitt. But unlike Marett, in his pre-animistic theory of mana or dynamism, he realized that the object of religion was not an 'impersonal force': 'the idea of Power . . . empirically, and within some form of experience, becomes authenticated in things and persons. . . .'[76]

The key to van der Leeuw's phenomenology lies in this notion of power, which is at the basis of every religious form and which defines that which is religious. Beginning by simply characterizing the object

---

Holy, and other works in which Otto 'describes' the 'superiority' of Christianity — a Christianity whose truth is for the most part known in a nonhistorical and introspective manner.

76. G. van der Leeuw, *Religion in Essence and Manifestation*, vol. 1, p. 28 and chaps. 1–3.

of religious experience as a vague 'Somewhat', his phenomenological analysis leads to the following typical assertions: 'Phenomenology describes how man conducts himself in his relation to Power'; 'Taken all together ["holy", *sanctus, tabu,* etc.], they provide the description of what occurs in all religious experience: *a strange, "Wholly Other", Power obtrudes into life.'*[77]

In his 'epilegomena' van der Leeuw shows some knowledge of phenomenological analysis,[78] but it is difficult to discern how this approach is utilized in his study of religious phenomena. Although he maintains that one must respect the specific intentionality of religious phenomena and simply describe 'what appears into view', so convinced is he of the primacy of the notion of 'power', that he forces all of his data into this interpretive scheme. Consequently, he is often insensitive to the rich complexity and individuality of the religious expressions.

Van der Leeuw realized that phenomenology must constantly appeal to history, that it must be open to 'perpetual correction by the most conscientious philological and archaeological research', and that 'it becomes pure art or empty fancy' when it withdraws itself from such historical control.[79] Yet here lies the greatest weakness in his phenomenology of religion: he is not concerned with the historical conditioning and specific existential character of all religious expressions and structures.

This raises what is probably the foremost challenge for the phenomenologist of religion. His or her methodological approach to religious phenomena must do justice to the interdependence of the historical and the phenomenological, fact and essence, the particular and the universal.

W. Brede Kristensen

The methodological point we wish to focus upon in the descriptive phenomenology of W. Brede Kristensen is his extreme antireduc-

77. Van der Leeuw, vol. 1, pp. 23, 191; vol. 2, p. 681.
78. Van der Leeuw, vol. 2, pp. 671–695. Especially note chap. 107 ('Phenomenon and Phenomenology') and chap. 109 ('Phenomenology of Religion').
79. *Ibid.*, p. 677.

tionistic tendencies, in terms of which he would criticize Eliade's phenomenological approach as being highly subjective and normative.

Professor Kristensen proposed that the usual systematic classifications, which were formulated as objective and essential categories of religion, were to be placed outside the domain of descriptive phenomenology: all investigations into the essence and evaluation of religious phenomena are undertaken from the viewpoint of the interpreter, are necessarily normative, and belong to such fields as philosophy and theology.

The phenomenology of religion is the systematic and comparative approach which attempts to describe what various religious phenomena have in common.[80] This common basis is their 'inner meaning' which can only be understood by combining a knowledge of the historical facts with an 'indefinable sympathy', 'empathy', 'feeling' for the religious data.[81]

What the phenomenologist of religion attempts to understand and describe is the sole 'religious reality': the faith of the believers. 'For the historian [Historian of Religions] only one evaluation is possible: "the believers were completely right." Only after we have grasped this can we understand these people and their religion.' One finds that the believers themselves always ascribe an absolute value to their faith, and phenomenologists must respect this absoluteness in their descriptions. We are interested in determining the value of religious manifestations, 'but this is the value that they had for the believers themselves, and this has never been relative, but is always absolute'.[82]

After attempting to understand and describe how the believers understand their faith (this knowledge is always 'approximate'), the

---

80. This may appear to contradict Kristensen's earlier point that all investigations into the essence of religious phenomena are beyond the domain of phenomenology, since most phenomenologists intend by 'essence' precisely what various 'phenomena have in common'. The history of philosophy reveals many conceptions of 'essence' which are clearly normative, and we would guess that Kristensen is referring to those metaphysical and theological formulations, in terms of which the scholar goes 'beyond' the affirmations of *homo religiosus*, evaluates his or her data, and establishes what is ultimately true or 'really real' in religion.

81. W. Brede Kristensen, *The Meaning of Religion*, pp. 3, 7, 10.

82. *Ibid.*, pp. 14, 418, 2.

scholar may try to classify the phenomena according to essential types and to make comparative evaluations. But this takes us beyond the limits of a descriptive phenomenology.[83]

In Eliade's methodology we shall discern numerous points of agreement with Kristensen's descriptive phenomenology. Yet we shall observe an effort to surmount the severe restrictions that Kristensen has placed upon a phenomenological approach. Eliade will attempt to include such vital questions as typological classifications and comparative evaluations within the domain of phenomenology of religion.

TRANSITION: RAFFAELE PETTAZZONI AND THE HISTORICAL-PHENOMENOLOGICAL 'TENSION'

Raffaele Pettazzoni attempted to define the nature of the History of Religions in terms of its 'two complementary aspects': the historical and the phenomenological. This point can serve as a 'transition' not only to Chapter 3, where we investigate the present nature of the History of Religions, but also to the following chapters, because Eliade is well aware of the need to provide a method which can do justice to both the historical and the phenomenological. First, we shall direct our attention to several other features of Pettazzoni's approach.

Raffaele Pettazzoni was primarily concerned with the historical factor in all religious expressions and referred to his approach as 'a historical–religious way'. Eliade distinguishes Pettazzoni from most historians of religions:

> He wanted to be a historian of religions, and not a specialist in a single field. This is an important distinction. Many excellent scholars likewise consider themselves 'historians of religions,' because they accept exclusively historical methods and presupposi-

83. *Ibid.*, p. 271: 'Grouping religions according to a particular characteristic is not a task for historical or phenomenological inquiry, but rather for philosophical inquiry concerning the essence of religions. For philosophical inquiry does not aim to determine the autonomous value and significance of the divergent types, but attempts to give normative generalizations. It is impossible for the phenomenologist to make such normative distinctions.'

tions. They are in fact, however, experts in just one religion, and sometimes in only one period or one aspect of that religion. . . . Pettazzoni aimed always at a historico-religious interpretation, i.e., he articulated the results of the different investigations within a general perspective.[84]

Pettazzoni tended to consider religious manifestations as purely historical phenomena. The notion of a Supreme Being is a product of the mythical imagination, arising from the existential needs of the particular historical-cultural reality. For example, in pastoral patriarchal civilizations, the notion of the Heavenly Father arose from the existential anxieties of these peoples. But in the historical-cultural context of agricultural matriarchal civilizations, the new existential anxieties necessitated the emergence of a different notion of a Supreme Being, the Mother Earth, which more adequately satisfied the existential needs of that period. 'This historicism is of value for religious phenomenology. Existential anxiety is the common root in the structure of the Supreme Being, but this structure is historically expressed in different forms: the Lord of animals, the Mother Earth, the Heavenly Father. All these structures have profound cultural realities which have conditioned them and of which the various Supreme Beings are expressions.'[85]

We may conclude our analysis of approaches during 'the second period' in the History of Religions by citing Pettazzoni's historical-

84. Eliade, 'The History of Religions in Retrospect: 1912–1962', p. 105. Among specialists who are also competent in other areas, Eliade cites M. P. Nilsson, Jan de Vries, Franz Altheim, Georges Dumézil, and Theodor H. Gaster; among contemporaries of Pettazzoni who also attempted to cover the entire field of *allgemeine Religionsgeschichte*, he cites Carl Clemen, E. O. James, and G. van der Leeuw.

85. Pettazzoni, 'The Supreme Being: Phenomenological Structure and Historical Development', pp. 65–66. Charles Long ('Archaism and Hermeneutics', p.73) presents several criticisms of Pettazzoni's position. Granted that certain symbols are discovered and predominate in different cultural-historical periods, one cannot 'limit the meaning of the symbolism simply to a reflection of the world-view of the period'. Granted that existential anxiety is a general characteristic of all periods, 'the modalities through which man expresses this anxiety take on different forms. What more than existential anxiety is expressed in religious symbolism?' Pettazzoni's interpretation cannot explain 'the wide variety of religious symbolism' and 'the persistence of the same symbolism in different cultural historical periods'.

phenomenological formulation, which broadly identifies the directions in *Religionswissenschaft* today.

'The peculiar nature, the very character, of religious facts as such give them the right to form the subject of a special science.' This is the 'science of religion' [History of Religions]: 'the essential character of religious facts is the necessary and sufficient reason for its existence.' Within the science of religion, one can distinguish 'a historical science, the history of religion'. But we are not satisfied with knowing 'precisely what happened and how the facts came to be; what we want above all to know is the meaning of what happened'. The history of religion does not yield this 'deeper understanding'; 'it springs from another religious science, phenomenology'.[86]

Yet the historical approaches have reacted against the phenomenological attempt to grasp the 'essence' and 'structures' of religious phenomena. It is this *tension*, with the attempt to find a *broader perspective* which can incorporate both of these approaches, which defines much of the direction of the History of Religions today.

Phenomenology and history complement each other. Phenomenology cannot do without ethnology, philology, and other historical disciplines. Phenomenology, on the other hand, gives the historical disciplines that sense of the religious which they are not able to capture. . . . Religious phenomenology and history are not two sciences but are two complementary aspects of the integral science of religion, and the science of religion as such has a well-defined character given to it by its unique and proper subject matter.[87]

86. Raffaele Pettazzoni, 'History and Phenomenology in the Science of Religion', *Essays on the History of Religions*, pp. 215, 216, 217. Three articles in U. Bianchi, C. J. Bleeker, and A. Bausani, eds., *Problems and Methods of the History of Religions* discuss the crucial methodological issue of the relationship between history and phenomenology within the History of Religions: G. Widengren, 'La méthode comparative: entre philologie et phénoménologie', pp. 5–14; Ugo Bianchi, 'The Definition of Religion. On the Methodology of Historical-Comparative Research', pp. 15–34; Jouco Bleeker, 'The Contribution of the Phenomenology of Religion to the Study of the History of Religions', pp. 35–54.

87. Pettazzoni, 'The Supreme Being: Phenomenological Structure and Historical Development', p. 66. See Pettazzoni, 'History and Phenomenology in the Science of Religion', pp. 217–219.

3

The Hermeneutical Situation Today

Our purpose in this chapter is to arrive at a general view of the central methodological issues and problems confronting the Historian of Religions today. To a considerable extent, such a perspective emerges from the contributions and errors of previous approaches. Our major purpose in formulating this hermeneutical situation is to lay the foundation for an analysis of Eliade's phenomenological approach and to see how he deals with these central methodological concerns. We shall begin by focusing upon Pettazzoni's crucial historical-phenomenological 'tension'. Then we shall consider two contemporary 'generalist' approaches, which will be seen as alternatives to Eliade's 'generalist' approach and as criticisms of much of his methodology. Finally, we shall formulate various problems, issues, and concerns, and this will lay the foundation for an understanding of the present hermeneutical situation in which Mircea Eliade investigates religious phenomena.

'SPECIALISTS' AND 'GENERALISTS'

We concluded our sketch of the History of Religions by defining its present nature in terms of a tension between the historical and the phenomenological approaches. As Kitagawa has stressed, 'the problem of "understanding," which is the central task of *Religionswissenschaft*, requires a hermeneutical principle which would enable us to harmonize the insights and contributions of both historical and structural inquiries, without at the same time doing injustice to the methodological integrity of either approach'.[1]

Unfortunately, no one appears to have formulated such a hermeneutical principle, and the complete harmonization of these two

1. Kitagawa, 'Primitive, Classical, and Modern Religions', p. 42.

approaches may be a methodological impossibility. Not that this broader perspective cannot serve as a regulative ideal, but, as Eliade has written, these two approaches reflect to some degree different philosophical temperaments.[2] He goes on to maintain that such an inevitable tension is creative; the two approaches complement each other by guarding against the dogmatic extremes inherent in each, and together they yield a more complete knowledge of *homo religiosus*.[3]

It should be noted that those Historians of Religions who are not concerned with phenomenology do not usually express this hermeneutical difference in terms of the historical-phenomenological tension we have formulated. Considering the entire discipline, it is probably most adequate to conceive of this methodological *tension* as between approaches tending toward *either specialization or generality and synthesis*. As we shall see, specialist approaches tend to emphasize the unique, particular, historical conditions of the religious phenomenon. Phenomenology of religion, with its search for universal structures and its comparative and systematic research, will be considered one kind of generalist approach. Mircea Eliade will be seen as a generalist who uses a phenomenological approach.

During 'the first period', we observed ambitious syntheses and sweeping generalizations. Historians of Religions found parallels and uniformities everywhere: the quest for the universal primordial stage of religion, the delineation of a universal evolutionary scheme for religion, the formulation of a simple yet universal definition of religion, etc. To what extent Eliade can overcome the methodological errors of earlier 'generalists' will greatly determine the success of his phenomenological approach.

During 'the second period', we observed a pronounced reaction against the sweeping comparisons and assumed uniformities of earlier ethnologists and philologists. With the emergence of new disciplines and the differentiation of numerous 'schools', the investigation of religion became highly specialized. Eliade, in both describing and

2. In conversation, Eliade has suggested that this methodological tension may be viewed as a fundamental atomistic-holistic difference in approach.

3. Eliade, 'History of Religions and a New Humanism', pp. 7–8. We shall observe that Eliade attempts to formulate such a hermeneutics which does justice both to the historical and the phenomenological. However, it will be seen that he stresses the latter, often at the expense of the historical.

criticizing this tendency, claims that 'from Max Müller and Andrew Lang to Frazer and Marett, from Marett to Lévy-Bruhl, and from Lévy-Bruhl to historians of religions [Historians of Religions] of our day one notices a progressive loss of creativity and an accompanying loss of interpretive cultural synthesis in favor of fragmented, analytical research'.[4] Those Historians of Religions, whom we have subsumed under the category of historical approaches, have continued this emphasis upon more intensive investigations, usually limiting their research to a particular culture, or to a specific period, or to one aspect of religious phenomena.

In quoting Pettazzoni, we described this more specialized approach in terms of 'the history of religions', especially emphasizing the endeavor to know 'precisely what happened and how the facts came to be'. Joachim Wach describes the 'historical approach' as attempting 'to trace the origin and growth of religious ideas and institutions through definite periods of historical development and to assess the role of the forces with which religion contended during these periods'.[5]

By 'history', we shall often mean not only history 'proper' but also all of the highly specialized disciplines which provide data for the phenomenologist: ethnological studies, archaeological discoveries, etc. In a similar fashion, Eliade sometimes substitutes for 'history' such terms as 'philology'— 'understanding by this term knowledge of the language, history, and culture of the societies whose religion he [the scholar] studies'.[6]

Today we can observe an increasing number of 'generalists', who, while cognizant of the methodological inadequacies of earlier research, have reacted against what they consider the overspecialization of recent decades. This is evidenced in the efforts to formulate a general systematic framework, in terms of which one can then interpret the particular religious manifestation and make adequate comparisons and generalizations. It is in this light that one must see efforts such as Charles Long's attempt to articulate 'some logical framework

---

4. Mircea Eliade, 'Crisis and Renewal in History of Religions', *History of Religions* 5, no. 1 (1965): 5. This article is reproduced as chapter 4 in *The Quest: History and Meaning in Religion*.

5. Joachim Wach, *The Comparative Study of Religions*, p. 21.

6. Eliade, 'Crisis and Renewal in History of Religions', p. 6.

which does justice to all of these ingredients': not only the phenomenological and morphological, 'but equally the existential, social and practical dimensions of religion'.[7]

Although all phenomenologists of religion seem to adopt a broad systematic approach, it must be emphasized that many use the term 'phenomenology' in such a manner that it bears little if any resemblance to contemporary philosophical phenomenology.[8] 'We use the term not in the sense of Husserl and Scheler but to indicate the systematic, not the historical, study of phenomena like prayer, priesthood, sect, etc.' 'Are types . . . the last word which the historian of religions [Historian of Religions] has to contribute? Very possibly, yes; *qua* historian [Historian of Religions] he cannot go further.'[9] Here one means by phenomenology what is meant by the term in many fields such as Phenomenological Quantum Mechanics: the systematic study of the various types of phenomena within one's discipline.

However, in Pettazzoni, Eliade, and others we have cited, 'phenomenology' is given a more specific meaning — one that will be seen to be not greatly at odds with its present philosophical usage. Mircea Eliade will be taken as the outstanding phenomenologist of religion. First we shall indicate several essential points of disagreement among contemporary generalists.

Two 'Generalist' Approaches

Most systematic approaches consist of a series of classifications, illustrated by several references and claiming to be objective and universally applicable. But why are these 'the essential categories', 'the relevant data', 'the appropriate evaluations'?

7. Charles H. Long, 'Prolegomenon to a Religious Hermeneutic', p. 254. This need for a 'framework' is the predominant goal in Wach's works. See *The Comparative Study of Religions*, p. x and *passim*.

8. Note Bleeker's formulation of different 'types' of 'phenomenology of religion', which we presented in chapter 2 under 'Phenomenological Approaches'.

9. Wach, *Sociology of Religion*, p. 1; *Types of Religious Experience*, p. 229; *The Comparative Study of Religions*, pp. 25–26. In his hermeneutics, Wach is definitely influenced by philosophical phenomenology. He acknowledges that his methodology greatly depends on the perspective of Scheler, and he is deeply concerned with a descriptive analysis of the intentionality of religious experience. See *Types of Religious Experience*, p. 30.

Consider the classification of mysticism. Bouquet finds two categories of mystical religion: 'specifically Christian and specifically non-Christian'.[10] Similarly, in describing 'the four characteristics of true mysticism', Underhill asserts that 'the business and method of Mysticism is Love'. One can imagine the reaction of a Buddhist to the description of this essential characteristic of all mysticism: the intense, passionate love of God, the 'attraction, desire, and union as the fulfillment of desire'.[11]

In short, it seems that most systematic approaches have been methodologically uncritical and have rested upon a highly normative foundation. Interpreters' classifications are plausible only if we make their assumptions, restrict our investigation to their evidence, and ask their questions. Several systematic approaches have attempted to deal with such methodological difficulties.

Our rationale for selecting these generalist approaches may be expressed in the following manner. These approaches are easily differentiated from one another as well as from Eliade's phenomenology. The positions exemplify divergent tendencies in *Religionswissenschaft* today and raise different methodological problems and issues. Each can be seen as a contemporary alternative to Eliade's methodological approach.

A brief consideration of each of these approaches will enable a greater comprehension of the hermeneutical situation of the History of Religions today. The major points of agreement among contemporary scholars and the central methodological issues and problems confronting the Historian of Religions will become evident. We shall then be in a better position to understand what Eliade's methodology

10. A. C. Bouquet, *Comparative Religion*, pp. 288–289. Incidentally, according to this classification, mystics such as Eckhart are 'non-Christian'.

11. Evelyn Underhill, *Mysticism*, pp. 85–90. It is true, as A. L. Basham notes (*The Wonder That Was India* [New York: Grove Press, 1959], pp. 284–285), that *mettā* (loving kindness) is occasionally described with great passion. Nevertheless, an overall view of Buddhism clearly discloses that such an intense passionate love, so admired in Christianity, is a manifestation of *tanhā* (desire, craving) which is the 'cause' of *dukkha* (sorrow, etc.). Buddhists generally emphasize a 'spirit of benevolent harmlessness', 'the detached radiation of *mettā*' — not 'love aflame with all desire, but love at peace'. Winston L. King, *In Hope of Nibbana* (La Salle, Illinois: Open Court Publishing Co., 1964), pp. 150–158; and Christmas Humphreys, *Buddhism* (London: Penguin Books, 1962), pp. 125–126.

is attempting to do and to what extent he succeeds in interpreting the religious phenomena.

Dependence on a normative (theological) basis

If Kristensen is correct and the History of Religions is a descriptive discipline which stops short of comparative classifications and evaluations, most scholars have conceived of it as preparatory to those normative fields which consider such questions. Probably most Western Historians of Religions who have granted their descriptive research this preliminary role have been Christian theologians. Usually they understood their research to be descriptive in its initial stages; it served an indispensable preparatory role for their overriding comparative and evaluative concerns.

Unfortunately, it would seem that their methodology and conclusions as Historians of Religions were considerably influenced by, and were often completely dependent upon, their theological beliefs. For nineteen hundred years, the Christian theological understanding of non-Christian religions has usually taken some variation of the basic apologetic approach which early Christian theologians took toward the pagan religions.[12] The aim was to demonstrate the insufficiency of other religions when compared to Christianity. At best, these other religions had some limited value, especially in preparing one to receive the true Christian revelation. At worst, they were completely false and even demonic.

We should notice that the relationship between one's theology and his or her History of Religions is far from simple. Both the nature and scope of one's History of Religions are greatly influenced by his or her specific theology. Liberal theologians have tended to be more interested in and 'sympathetic' toward other religious phenomena; many orthodox theologians have been unwilling to grant other religions even the slightest positive value.

Philip H. Ashby traces the change in American theological attitudes toward non-Christian religions.[13] A liberal attitude produced considerable interest in the History of Religions in the late nineteenth and

12. Philip H. Ashby, 'The History of Religions', *Religion*, p. 19.
13. *Ibid.*, pp. 18–24.

early twentieth centuries. In the 1930s, under the influence of such European theologians as Karl Barth and Emil Brunner, the theological understanding of non-Christian religions greatly changed and interest in the History of Religions sharply declined.

In a similar manner, Erwin R. Goodenough maintains that the change in theological attitude and decline in the scientific study of religion are related to the 'collapses which followed upon the catastrophe of 1914'. The conditions in defeated Germany of 1918, the great financial depression, the horrors of the Hitlerian war, etc., led many to emphasize 'the inherent sinfulness of man and the mockery of his analytical and scientific efforts'. 'Men's only hope is in a divine act of revelation'; the scientific study of religion is futile and even impious.[14]

It would seem that those contemporary theologians who are concerned with the History of Religions often bear a marked resemblance to the generalists of 'the first period': they approach their descriptive studies with prior beliefs, and inherent in their very act of description are evaluative principles provided by these accepted beliefs. In short, as Historians of Religions their descriptions do not do justice to 'the other'.

No one would deny the value of the History of Religions for theology or the value of a theology of the History of Religions. But the position we wish to question insists that the History of Religions is *not possible* unless aided by or based upon a normative discipline such as theology. To illustrate such a position, let us briefly consider the view of Hendrik Kraemer, Kristensen's pupil and successor as Professor of the History and Phenomenology of Religions at the University of Leiden.

While recognizing the preliminary value of Kristensen's descriptive phenomenology, Kraemer defends the 'ultimate rightness of a theological approach'. Only a theological approach can deal with 'the majestic problem of Truth' and with such a 'problem as that of the perennial ambiguity of Religion'.[15]

It seems to us that Kraemer, as well as most theologians in the History of Religions, is not simply contending that theology should

14. Erwin R. Goodenough, *'Religionswissenschaft'*, *Numen* 6, fasc. 2 (1959): 81–82.
15. Hendrik Kraemer, Introduction to W. Brede Kristensen's *The Meaning of Religion*, pp. xxiv–xxv.

continue where the descriptive History of Religions limits itself. He is not endorsing Kristensen's view of phenomenology and then asserting that this preliminary discipline should be supplemented by normative investigations. Rather his point seems to be the following: A descriptive History of Religions which is not grounded in theology cannot hope to understand the very religious phenomena it attempts to describe.

By examining the forms of expression of a religion (myth, cultus, dogma, etc.), the phenomenologist attempts to understand the religious phenomena and to claim an objectivity for her or his descriptions. But any such analysis and claim to objectivity is always 'from the "scientific" standpoint, a psychological and sociological reality which may have great significance but is quite different from what is suggested by *objektiver Geist*, which points to the realm of metaphysics. . . . [Historians of Religions overlook] the fact that the category of faith is essentially a different category from psychological understanding or experience, however penetrating the latter may be.'[16]

To understand religious phenomena one must view them '*from within*'. It is for this reason that *only theology* 'is able to produce that attitude of freedom of the spirit and of impartial understanding, combined with a criticism and evaluation transcending all imprisonment in preconceived ideas and principles as ultimate standards of reference'.[17]

Unfortunately, Kraemer's Neo-Calvinist approach is conspicuous both by its excessive 'criticism and evaluation' and its lack of 'impartial understanding'. His normative position is that no one can 'know' God except through the absolute revelation of 'Biblical realism'.[18] Kraemer, 'whose books are valuable precisely because he makes no attempt to be impartial, but takes Biblical Christianity as the absolute standard against which he judges all religions including historical Christianity, does not seem to be worried by the fact that Muslims have a precisely similar absolute standard against which the religions,

16. Hendrik Kraemer, *Religion and the Christian Faith*, pp. 50–51.
17. *Ibid.*, p. 53.
18. Hendrik Kraemer, *The Christian Message in a Non-Christian World*, pp. 61 ff.

including Dr. Kraemer's own Biblical realism, must be judged'.[19] Invariably such a normative standard renders one's History of Religions unsatisfactory to all save the minority who adopt this particular theological viewpoint.

What concerns us is not Kraemer's specific approach, which we believe distorts any understanding of 'the other'. But the Historian of Religions must recognize serious objections raised by any view which submits that the History of Religions is not an autonomous discipline; it is both aided by and dependent upon a normative discipline such as theology.

If one proceeds beyond the 'descriptive limitations' of a Kristensen, can such normative questions as those of comparison and evaluation only be understood through an approach which has a normative basis? Is any approach which is free from such a normative grounding only capable of yielding an apparent 'objectivity', which is lacking in depth and produces a distorted understanding of the religious phenomena?

The *dilemma* facing Historians of Religions may be summarized as follows: When we ground our approach on some normative basis, our conclusions seem acceptable only to those who share our normative position; when we refuse any such normative foundation, the scope of our inquiry is severely restricted and our conclusions may indicate a lack of depth and a distortion in understanding the religious phenomena. Eliade's methodology will attempt to preserve the autonomy of a descriptive phenomenology and at the same time to deal adequately with the comparative and evaluative religious questions.

The study of religious persons

There is a contemporary 'generalist' approach which attempts to disassociate itself from all positions we have examined. In many respects it will appear as antithetical to the theological approach of a Kraemer. Comparative religion, according to Wilfred Cantwell Smith and several others, is *'the study of persons'*. 'All religions are new religions, every morning. For religions do not exist up in the sky

19. R. C. Zaehner, *The Comparison of Religions*, p. 195. See pp. 172–173.

somewhere, elaborated, finished, and static; they exist in men's hearts.'[20] Smith delineates several steps leading to the understanding of 'religious persons':

> The traditional form of Western scholarship in the study of other men's religion was that of an impersonal presentation of an 'it.' The first great innovation in recent times has been the personalization of the faiths observed, so that one finds a discussion of a 'they.' Presently the observer becomes personally involved, so that the situation is one of a 'we' talking about a 'they.' The next step is a dialogue, where 'we' talk to 'you.' If there is listening and mutuality, this may become that 'we' talk with 'you.' The culmination of this progress is when 'we all' are talking with each other about 'us.'[21]

In light of this view of what it is to study religion, Smith offers several revolutionary methodological recommendations. We should desist from using the terms and concepts 'religion, the religions, and the specific named religions'. The concept 'religion' is 'confusing, unnecessary, and distorting'. The 'vitality of personal faith' and the attempt to understand 'the traditions of other people throughout history and throughout the world, are both seriously blocked by our attempt to conceptualize what is involved in each case in terms of (a) religion'. In short, the Historian of Religions should not be concerned with 'religion' or 'the religions' but with 'man's religiousness', with persons who have lived and are 'living religiously'.[22]

If 'religion' is 'the faith in men's hearts', and if we recall how Historians of Religions from early ethnologists to contemporary theologians have attributed to 'the other' what they themselves believed, we may better appreciate Smith's second recommendation: 'that no statement about a religion is valid unless it can be acknowledged by that religion's believers'.[23]

Although this standard of 'validity' should be used as a 'pedagogic

20. Wilfred Cantwell Smith, 'The Comparative Study of Religion: Reflections on the Possibility and Purpose of a Religious Science', *McGill University, Faculty of Divinity, Inaugural Lectures*, p. 51.

21. Wilfred Cantwell Smith, 'Comparative Religion: Whither — and Why?', p. 34.

22. Wilfred Cantwell Smith, *The Meaning and End of Religion*, pp. 50, 119–153, and 194–195; 'Comparative Religion: Whither — and Why?', p. 55.

23. Smith, 'Comparative Religion: Whither — and Why?', p. 42.

principle',[24] we would submit that it not only has practical difficulties (Which adherents? How many adherents?), but it often is a false standard of validity. Central importance must be given to what the other believes; but this is only preliminary to the understanding of religious phenomena.

Here Kraemer was justified in distinguishing 'psychological reality' from a deeper understanding of the religious phenomena. Kristensen was wrong: the faith of the believer is not 'final'. Believers often have a strong apologetic tendency when discussing their beliefs. Often they may not understand certain things about their religion or themselves which another person can. Sometimes their faith takes the form of 'superstition' and other 'aberrations'; usually they are unaware of the subconscious and unconscious dimensions of their faith; frequently they are unaware of the richness and complexity implicit in their beliefs.[25]

In short, we must be able to *interpret and evaluate* what the other believes. But can we avoid the pitfalls of the highly subjective, evaluative approaches of the past? Can we have a hermeneutical approach which does justice to the other's faith and at the same time is able to evaluate his or her descriptions in terms of some larger methodological framework?

Smith has correctly elucidated difficulties in traditional approaches. When we eliminate 'the personal', we are no longer investigating 'the religious'. Our methodological approach must always preserve the central importance of 'the religious person'. Analyses based upon the concepts of 'religion' and 'the religious' have proven confusing and highly polemical (as in 'Christian versus non-Christian' religious phenomena). Historians of Religions have been oblivious to the paramount importance of listening to what the believer has to say about her or his own religion.

What Smith seems to be lacking is a *methodological structure* to his approach. Yes, he is correct in stressing that we must learn to communicate with each other, we must approach other religious beliefs

24. Isma'il Ragi A. al Faruqi, 'History of Religions: Its Nature and Significance for Christian Education and the Muslim-Christian Dialogue', *Numen* 12, fasc. 1 (1965): 45.

25. For example, see Eliade, *Patterns*, pp. 6–7; and *The Forge and the Crucible*, p. 108.

with love, humility, tolerance, and respect.[26] But there is a difference between believing and understanding. It is not apparent that Smith has ever really raised such questions as those of hermeneutics and objectivity. Any Historian of Religions must be mindful of Smith's insights. But without raising these questions of hermeneutics and objectivity, no methodology is adequate for understanding the scope and profundity of religious phenomena.

COMMON METHODOLOGICAL ISSUES AND PROBLEMS

In gaining some insight into the hermeneutical situation of the History of Religions today, we described the historical–phenomenological tension, which was seen to be a particular formulation of the specialist–generalist tension. We then analyzed two contemporary generalist approaches, which revealed different methodological tendencies today and will be seen as challenges to Eliade's phenomenology.

It is now time to formulate several common methodological issues, problems, and concerns, largely arising from past approaches and defining the hermeneutical situation in which Eliade interprets the meaning of religious phenomena. Our enumeration of general points of agreement, problems, and issues is in little more than skeleton form. It is imperative that we realize that the following is not intended as a satisfactory analysis of any of these methodological points. We are simply delineating several of the issues with which Eliade's phenomenology will be concerned. Thus, under our first point, we simply and bluntly assert that most contemporary Historians of Religions seem to assume that religion presupposes religious experience.

26. Smith urges the following 'general principle' in arguing against Kraemer's position: 'that an outsider cannot understand a civilization or a great religion unless he approaches it with humility and love' ('Comparative Religion: Whither — and Why?', p. 50, n. 39). Previously we presented Smith's position as antithetical to the theological approach of a Kraemer. However, it seems to us that his approach may also depend upon a religious foundation. Unlike Kraemer, his religious basis stresses love, tolerance, and mutual respect. With Kraemer, we have a narrow methodological approach which is unsatisfactory; with Smith, we cannot discern a self-critically formulated, methodological structure to his approach.

We in no way attempt to analyze the nature of that religious experience, how one can distinguish religious from nonreligious experience, etc. Our intention is to present and to evaluate Eliade's response to these and similar methodological questions in the ensuing chapters.

Religious experience and the irreducibility of the religious

The general starting point for most Historians of Religions seems to be the assumption that 'religion presupposes "religious experience," however this term may be interpreted, on the part of *homo religiosus*. Call it the experience of the Holy, the Sacred, or the Power, it is that something which underlies all religious phenomena.'[27]

While starting with this assumption, Historians of Religions readily concede that they do not possess direct knowledge of the religious experiences of others. What they begin with are the religious *expressions* of *homo religiosus*. Whether we consider the religious experiences of antiquity or of our contemporaries, we must still interpret what others express. By carefully examining the religious data, Historians of Religions attempt to understand the nature of the religious experiences expressed in their data.

To give but one illustration, we have seen that Joachim Wach subsumes religious expressions under three major classifications: theoretical, practical, and sociological forms of expression. Wach attempts to determine 'if anything like a structure can be discovered in all these forms of expression' and 'to what kind of experience this variegated expression can be traced'.[28]

Probably the primary methodological task facing Historians of Religions is the need for an adequate methodological framework or

27. Kitagawa, 'Primitive, Classical, and Modern Religions', p. 40. When we write 'most Historians of Religions', we are referring to scholars who publish in such journals as *Numen* and *History of Religions* and in such anthologies as *History of Religions: Essays in Methodology* and *History of Religions: Essays on the Problem of Understanding*.

28. Wach, *Types of Religious Experience*, p. 30. Kitagawa observes that Wach assumed 'that subjective religiousness is objectified in various expressions, and that these expressions appropriate definite structures which can be comprehended'. Joseph M. Kitagawa, 'The Life and Thought of Joachim Wach', *The Comparative Study of Religions* by Joachim Wach, pp. xxiii–xxiv.

structure in terms of which they can interpret their data. The sheer quantity of accumulated religious data is impressive. What is now demanded is a hermeneutics which does justice to the complexity and specificity of the religious expressions, and, at the same time, provides a rigorous methodological structure in terms of which we can interpret our data and understand the nature of religious experience.

Concerning the nature of this religious experience, most Historians of Religions would concur with the following:

> The notion that religious experience underlies all religious phenomena has a serious methodological implication in the study of religions. In this respect, Mircea Eliade rightly reminds us that 'to try to grasp the essence of such a [religious] phenomenon by means of physiology, psychology, sociology, economics, linguistics, art or any other study is false; it misses the one unique and irreducible element in it — the element of the Sacred.'[29]

Here we have the point made by Otto, van der Leeuw, Wach, and many others: the Historian of Religions must respect the fundamentally *irreducible* character of the religious experience. Although someone like Wilfred Cantwell Smith would be unhappy with such talk of 'the religious' or 'the sacred', he would also insist upon the irreducible character of the experience of religious persons.

One recalls that Max Müller proclaimed the autonomous nature of *Religionswissenschaft*. However, we have seen that Historians of Religions were invariably reductionists: religious phenomena were interpreted in terms of notions borrowed from other fields (philology, ethnology, etc.).

In defining the *autonomous* nature of their discipline, contemporary Historians of Religions contend that religious phenomena must be grasped as irreducibly religious, that one must 'make an effort to understand them on their own plane of reference'.[30] In contrast to most of the previous investigators (sociologists, psychologists, etc.), Historians of Religions attempt to define their own unique perspective

---

29. Kitagawa, 'Primitive, Classical, and Modern Religions', p. 40; Eliade, *Patterns*, p. xiii.

30. Eliade, 'History of Religions and a New Humanism', p. 4; and *Myths, Dreams and Mysteries*, p. 13.

qua Historians of Religions. If there are certain irreducible modes by which religious experiences and their expressions are given, then our 'method of understanding must be commensurate with the givenness of the mode'.[31]

Although Historians of Religions, in opposing the psychological, sociological, and other reductionisms, maintain that their data reveal 'an irreducible reality, the experience of the sacred', they 'do not agree among themselves even apropos of the nature of this experience'.

> For some of them, the 'sacred' as such is a historical phenomenon, i.e., it is the result of specific human experiences in specific historical situations. [Recall Pettazzoni's interpretation.] Others, on the contrary, leave open the question of 'origins'; for them the experience of the sacred is *irreducible*, in the sense that, through such an experience, man becomes aware of his specific mode of being in the world and consequently assumes responsibilities which cannot be explained in psychological or socio-economic terms.[32]

This last statement illustrates the type of assertion — about the human mode of being in the world, the human condition, etc. — which is the source of much of the criticism of Eliade's phenomenology. In Chapters 6 and 7, when we analyze Eliade's 'more-than-historical-explanation' claim and especially the different 'levels of meaning' in his methodology, we shall determine whether such assertions entail ontological moves on his part.

Of course, these general features will require considerable development and refinement. We may simply note that by 'autonomous' Historians of Religions do not mean that *Religionswissenschaft* is a 'self-sufficient' discipline. It depends heavily upon such fields as linguistics, anthropology, and sociology. In addition, by 'irreducible' we do not mean that there are 'purely religious' phenomena. The religious phenomena can also be approached from the perspectives of sociology, anthropology, and other disciplines.

All that is claimed is that certain experiences or phenomena exhibit a

31. Long, 'The Meaning of Religion in the Contemporary Study of the History of Religions', p. 25. See Wach, *The Comparative Study of Religions*, p. 15.

32. Mircea Eliade, 'Historical Events and Structural Meaning in Tension', *Criterion* 6, no. 1 (1967): 30.

fundamental religious character and that our method must be commensurate with the nature of our subject matter. From the perspective of the History of Religions, the sociological, economic, or anthropological dimensions of the phenomena are 'secondary'. At the same time one acknowledges that from the perspectives of economics, sociology, or anthropology the 'religious' dimensions of the phenomena are 'secondary'. What is insisted upon is that the sociological, economic, linguistic, and other studies of certain phenomena do not exhaust the nature or meaning of those phenomena. What 'remains' to be studied is the fundamentally irreducible religious character of those phenomena, and this can only be understood from the perspective of the History of Religions.

The personal dimension of religious phenomena

What is the nature of this approach which attempts to understand the fundamentally irreducible religious phenomena? In answering this question most Historians of Religions now emphasize several characteristics which sharply contrast with many earlier positions.

Perhaps foremost in this regard is the point so stressed by Wilfred Cantwell Smith: our approach must do justice to the *personal* dimension of religious phenomena. One recalls earlier attempts at creating an 'autonomous', 'scientific' discipline. A 'positivistic' approach to the 'religious facts', marked by an impersonal detachment and a narrowly 'rationalistic' attitude, was the ideal.

Contemporary Historians of Religions contend that such an approach leads to the reduction of 'living' data to 'dead' data, of the personal to the impersonal; in short, of the religious to the nonreligious. If our method be adequate for our subject matter, our hermeneutics must lead to an understanding of the highly personal dimension of the irreducibly religious data.

In this regard Smith may be placed at the opposite end of the spectrum from the nineteenth century scholar. It seems to us that this sheds some light on the difficulties each encounters. It was not by chance that earlier Historians of Religions adopted an impersonal, detached attitude and a highly rationalistic and positivistic approach to their data; in endeavoring to rid their discipline of all personal and 'subjective' elements, they aimed for a rigorous 'scientific objectivity'. They did attain a sense of 'scientific objectivity': we can observe what data they accumulated and how they reached their conclusions. Unfortunately, this was a false sense of objectivity, because these Historians of Religions were strong reductionists who were not sensitive to the specific demands of their subject matter. The approach which the naturalist might use in classifying types of insects produced less success for a scholar attempting to understand religious phenomena.

In emphasizing the irreducibly personal dimension of religious experience, Smith is more aware of the demands of his subject matter. 'The externals of religion— symbols, institutions, doctrines, practices . . . are not in themselves religion, which lies rather in the area of what these mean to those that are involved. The student is making effective progress when he recognizes that he has to do not with religious systems basically but with religious persons; or at least, with something interior to persons.'[33]

But in moving so far from the impersonal approach of the earlier Historians of Religions, scholars like Smith seem to encounter the very difficulties these previous investigators wanted to avoid. One's approach appears highly 'subjective' and seems to be lacking any methodological structure or framework in terms of which we can determine whether the scholar has understood the religious phenomena, i.e., whether her or his conclusions have some degree of 'objectivity'.

Smith, in overstressing the personal, does not provide the criteria for objective understanding; earlier Historians of Religions, in trying to eliminate the personal, provided criteria— but not criteria sufficient for objective understanding of religious phenomena, since any approach must do justice to the essentially personal dimension of all religious experience.

How we understand 'the personal' and what part it plays in our History of Religions will vary from one scholar to the next. The 'externals' of religion ('symbols, institutions, doctrines, practices') are highly personal and not nearly as 'external' as had been thought. But if

33. 'Comparative Religion: Whither — and Why?', p. 35.

we go too far in undermining their religious significance— as Smith and several others seem to do — then we encounter the aforementioned difficulties. Indeed, we would submit that it is these very symbols, institutions, doctrines, and practices, when approached in a manner which does justice to the personal nature of all religious phenomena, that provide the hermeneutical framework in terms of which our interpretations assume some sense of objectivity.

Participation and sympathetic understanding

We have seen that this emphasis upon the personal nature of the subject matter has focused attention on the highly personal role of the investigator. If Historians of Religions are to understand religious phenomena 'on their own plane of reference', they must attempt to place themselves within the perspective of *homo religiosus*. What is needed is a capacity for participation in the religious phenomena of the other. 'What is required is not indifference, as positivism in its heyday believed — "Grey cold eyes do not know the value of things," objected Nietzsche— but an engagement of feeling, interest, *metexis*, or participation.'[34] One must approach the religious phenomena with a sympathetic attitude. 'The inquirer must feel an affinity to his subject, and he must be trained to interpret his material with sympathetic understanding.'[35]

Concentrating on the task of understanding Hinduism, Ashby examines many of the difficulties involved in endeavoring 'to participate in Hinduism'.[36] The Historian of Religions must attempt to 'become as fully as possible at one' with the Hindu; it is only as the investigator 'participates by reenactment within himself of the long continuous unfolding of Hinduism . . . that he can begin to understand the voice of Hindu religiosity'. What renders this task of participation even more complex and difficult is the fact that there seems to be no uniform nature of *homo religiosus*. As Ashby points out, the participation necessary for understanding 'the less intellectual Hindu,

---

34. Wach, *The Comparative Study of Religions*, p. 12.
35. Wach, *Sociology of Religion*, p. 10.
36. Philip H. Ashby, 'The History of Religions and the Study of Hinduism', *The History of Religions: Essays on the Problem of Understanding*, pp. 143–159.

the *homo religiosus* of the countryside, the village, and the large city slums of today' requires a religious and emotional capacity which few scholars possess.[37]

Almost all Historians of Religions stress the need for personal participation, sympathetic understanding, an 'adequate emotional condition', 'empathy', a 'feeling' for the religious data. But these terms tend to be vague, and it is not clear how such a participation is to be achieved. Insufficient attention has been devoted to developing a rigorous methodology in terms of which one might check whether he or she has reenacted within him or herself the experience of the other and whether one has understood the religious phenomenon under investigation.

Historians of Religions admit that there are inevitable limitations to the personal participation of the investigator. We attempt to participate in religious experiences of the other; and by becoming as fully as possible at one with the other, we can partially surmount the barriers standing in our way of understanding the religious phenomena of the other. But, as Kristensen stated, the knowledge of the religion of others is always 'approximate'. The other is always to some extent other. Recognizing this limitation to our participation, Historians of Religions strive to decrease the distance separating them from the other and thus to understand the religious experience of the other as fully as possible.

The commitment of the historian of religions

Who can best participate in and sympathetically understand the religious phenomena of others? Is only the nonbeliever capable of investigating the religious data impartially? Is only the person who identifies him or herself with a religion or has some other specific religious commitment capable of understanding the religious phenomena 'from within'?

Most Historians of Religions now reject the view that 'only agnostics can be expected to achieve complete objectivity because they alone

37. *Ibid.*, pp. 155–157.

might be expected to be free from religious prejudice'.[38] Indeed, it is contended that the atheist or agnostic often lacks 'the adequate emotional condition', the sympathetic attitude, and the capacity for personal participation in the religious phenomena.

Some maintain that the scholar who is a committed member of a religion can best participate in the phenomena of religion. Yet when we recall the highly apologetic approach of Kraemer and of most theologians or missionaries who have taken part in the History of Religions, we realize why scholars tend to view such religious commitment with suspicion. Various criteria have been suggested to ensure that investigators suspend their particular religious viewpoints when interpreting the other. Kitagawa even goes so far as to list as one of the 'three essential qualities underlying the discipline . . . an attitude of self-criticism, or even scepticism, about one's own religious background'.[39]

Far more subtle than the 'narrow' normative interpretations of a 'committed' theologian such as Kraemer are the investigations of several Western and numerous Eastern scholars who do not seem motivated by a specific religious commitment. On the contrary, these Historians of Religions most emphasize such qualities as tolerance and sympathetic understanding. But careful examination reveals that they do so from a specific religious commitment.

Friedrich Heiler condemns 'the falsity of numerous polemical judgments of past times' and delineates 'seven principal areas of unity which the high religions of the earth manifest'.[40] With such 'sympathetic understanding', he finds 'one and the same reality' everywhere. But Heiler's analysis, albeit in reaction to an 'exclusivist' Christian tradition, is nonetheless from a Western, and more specifically Christian, viewpoint.[41] Here the History of Religions assumes a most 'liberal' Christian orientation: Christian love and brotherhood are so all-embracing that one humbly subsumes the religious phenomena of

38. Zaehner, *The Comparison of Religions*, p. 12.
39. 'The History of Religions in America', p. 15.
40. Friedrich Heiler, 'The History of Religions as a Preparation for the Co-operation of Religions', *The History of Religions: Essays in Methodology*, pp. 132–160.
41. *Ibid.*, pp. 142–152. 'The reality of the Divine is ultimate love. . . .'; 'The way of man to God is universally the way of sacrifice'; 'Love is the most superior way to God'; etc. Cf. Isma'il R. A. al Faruqi, pp. 53–54.

others under Christian categories and then proclaims the religious unity of humankind.

Especially appealing in the History of Religions is the non-exclusivism and tolerance of Easterners such as Radhakrishnan. 'The Hindu thinker readily admits other points of view than his own and considers them to be just as worthy of attention.' The Hindu maintains 'that every human being, every group and every nation has an individuality worthy of reverence'; 'the more religious we grow the more tolerant of diversity shall we become'.[42]

Yet thinkers as different from one another as Kraemer, Zaehner, and Wach[43] have correctly criticized Radhakrishnan's 'sympathetic attitude' and 'tolerance' toward all religious phenomena as grounded in a specifically Hindu interpretation of 'religious tolerance'. This gives rise to highly apologetic treatments and to misrepresentations of Christianity.

To give but one illustration, Hindu nonexclusiveness and religious tolerance are manifested in the views of *avatāras*: God may have many human incarnations, such as Rāma, Krishna, or Buddha. Thus, 'Jesus is an *avatar*' and 'the resources of God which were available to him are open to us, and if we struggle and strive even as he did, we will develop the God in us'. In general, Radhakrishnan minimizes or neglects the unique and absolute Christian claims and indicates that Jesus 'should be brought in line with the other great saints of God'.[44]

But if one is attempting to participate in and understand the religious experience of Christians, it may not be so 'tolerant' to regard the notion of Christ as 'the Son of God' in the same manner as Indians view their *avatars*. Because one finds such Christian views 'dogmatic' (making for 'narrowness and intolerance'),[45] the Historian of Religions *qua* Historian of Religions does not show a sympathetic under-

---

42. Sarvepalli Radhakrishnan, *The Hindu View of Life*, pp. 16, 34–44. See chapter 2 ('Conflict of Religions: The Hindu Attitude'), pp. 26–44.

43. Kraemer, *Religion and the Christian Faith*, pp. 119–136; Zaehner, *The Comparison of Religions*, pp. 13–15; Joachim Wach, 'Radhakrishnan and the Comparative Study of Religion', *The Philosophy of Sarvepalli Radhakrishnan*, pp. 445–458.

44. Sarvepalli Radhakrishnan, *The Heart of Hindusthan*, pp. 101–102, 165; Wach, 'Radhakrishnan and The Comparative Study of Religion', p. 453.

45. Sarvepalli Radhakrishnan, *Eastern Religions and Western Thought*, p. 59. (See pp. 160 ff.); Kraemer, *Religion and the Christian Faith*, pp. 129–130.

standing in 'converting' the other's religious experience into something the scholar considers more religiously tolerant.

At this point, we can appreciate the question of the nonbeliever as to whether one can have a particular religious commitment and at the same time some sense of impartiality and objectivity. Most Historians of Religions would agree that their discipline is uncommitted in the sense that 'not by believing, but by imaginative participation is understanding achieved'.[46] This is not meant to exclude the committed members of a religion from the History of Religions, but only to affirm that such specific religious commitment is not a necessary prerequisite for Historians of Religions. If they do identify themselves with specific normative religious positions, investigators must not allow their religious beliefs to color their investigation of other religious phenomena.

However, in a sense different from the commitment of the 'believer', it is necessary for the investigator to be *committed*. 'It is of course true, as van der Leeuw notes, that the phenomena cannot be grasped by one who is unconcerned, and a person who had no awareness of the religious could not really engage in this discourse.'[47] The commitment of the Historian of Religions manifests a sympathetic attitude and interest in the religious experiences of humankind, a sensitive awareness of what is religiously expressed in her or his data, a respect for the irreducibly religious nature of the phenomena. Only from such a commitment, grounded in a sympathetic attitude, interest, sensitivity, and respect for the phenomena of religion, can the investigator participate in and understand the religious experiences of others.

---

46. William A. Beardslee, 'Truth in the Study of Religion', *Truth, Myth, and Symbol*, p. 65.
47. *Ibid*. Beardslee's reference to van der Leeuw is from *Religion in Essence and Manifestation*, vol. 2, p. 675. Winston L. King, in his *Introduction to Religion: A Phenomenological Approach*, pp. 6–8, describes such an approach as a 'detached withinness'. By 'detached', King does not mean the impersonal, positivistic sense of detachment we observed in earlier approaches. His combining a sense of 'withinness' with 'detached' makes this clear. What he wants to exphasize is that the Historian of Religions is detached from any particular religious viewpoint and does not pass value judgments on one religion on the basis of another religion.

The complexity of religious phenomena and the 'total person'

In reaction to past Historians of Religions, we have observed a pronounced antireductionist tendency in contemporary History of Religions: the irreducibly religious nature of religious experience, the irreducibly autonomous nature of the History of Religions, and the irreducibly personal dimension of religious phenomena.

This antireductionism is evidenced in the insistence of Historians of Religions on the complexity of religious phenomena. Most scholars of 'the first period' accepted a view of historical and cultural evolutionism. There was a unilinear evolution from the simple to the complex. Religion was usually identified with the earliest (and hence, most 'primitive' and simplest) stages of cultures. Recent investigations have disclosed the surprising complexity of religious phenomena.

> The religious life appears complex even at the most archaic stages of culture. Among the peoples still in the stage of food-gathering and hunting small animals (Australians, Pygmies, Fuegians, etc.), the belief in a Supreme Being or 'Lord of the Animals' is intermingled with beliefs in culture-heroes and mythical ancestors; prayers and offerings to the gods coexist with totemic practices, the cult of the dead, and hunting and fertility magic.[48]

We have noted that even those Historians of Religions of 'the second period' who repudiated a unilinear evolutionary interpretation and did not subsume the religious under some homogeneous category such as totemism or 'primitive mentality' invariably oversimplified the nature of religious phenomena. Usually they identified the religious with only one of its perspectives: the psychological, the sociological, the anthropological, etc.

This antireductionist insistence on the complexity of religious phenomena is often expressed by claiming that religion is the concern of the 'total person'. Charles Long describes the person's religious experience as 'the experience of his totality in relationship to that which he experiences as ultimately real'.[49] Joachim Wach maintains

48. Mircea Eliade, 'Structure and Changes in the History of Religion', *City Invincible*, p. 351. See *Patterns*, pp. xiv, 7.
49. Long, *Alpha*, p. 10.

that 'the statement that experience must be conceived of as a total response of the total being to Ultimate Reality means that it is the integral person which is involved, not just the mind, the emotion, or the will'. Wach contends that many previous theologians and philosophers have failed to realize that religion was concerned with the total or integral person and have argued about the 'seat' of religion: 'From Schleiermacher to James, Whitehead, and Otto it was sought in feeling; from Hegel and Martineau to Brightman, in the intellect; and from Fichte to Reinhold Niebuhr, in the will.'[50]

If *homo religiosus* represents the 'total person', then several methodological consequences seem to follow for the History of Religions. Since the approach must be commensurate with the subject matter, the History of Religions 'must become a total discipline, in the sense that it must use, integrate, and articulate the results obtained by the various methods of approaching a religious phenomenon'.[51] This is not to deny the unique perspective of *Religionswissenschaft*. What is maintained is that unless the History of Religions can integrate the results of other approaches within its own unique approach, it will commit the same kind of reductionism of past approaches which did not realize that the religious 'totality' included, but was not exhausted by, the psychological, sociological, or some other perspective.

Furthermore, if religion concerns the total person and if the investigator must participate in the religious experience of the other, then Historians of Religions must themselves participate in the religious phenomena as total persons. We have seen that early investigators were highly 'rationalistic' and lacked the 'emotional condition' necessary to understand the religious phenomena. The evolutionists relegated the religious to the status of the irrational, unsophisticated, and 'primitive'; Lang 'exalted' the religious to the status of the rational, ethical, and sophisticated. But both did so on highly rationalistic grounds and thus failed to appreciated the complexity of religious phenomena. Someone like Otto strongly undermined this past intel-

50. Wach, *The Comparative Study of Religions*, pp. 32, 33. This stress upon the 'total person', the 'integral person' is undoubtedly a major factor in the Jungian evaluation of religion as a therapeutic system which contributes to the equilibrium and unity of the individual personality.

51. Eliade, 'History of Religions and a New Humanism', p. 7.

lectualistic bias, but he also reduced the complexity of the religious by overemphasizing its nonrational and nonhistorical aspects.

The History of Religions must employ a hermeneutics which does justice to the rational and the irrational; to the intellectual and the emotional and the volitional; to the anthropological and the sociological and the psychological. In short, its methodology must do justice to the complexity and totality of religious phenomena.

Religion as 'practical' and 'soteriological'

Recalling past characterizations of religious phenomena in terms of animism, mana, magic, totemism, taboo, *mysterium tremendum*, etc., we may understand why Historians of Religions agree that religion is 'practical', soteriological, aiming at a complete transformation of the human being. 'Religion is more than a system of beliefs, doctrines and ethics. It is a total orientation and way of life that aims at enlightenment, deliverance, or salvation. In other words, the central concern of religion is nothing less than soteriology; what religion provides is not information about life and the world but the practical path of transformation of man according to its understanding of what existence ought to be.'[52]

It is interesting to note that many Historians of Religions assert that the discipline has 'practical' effects upon the investigators themselves. The History of Religions is not merely an intellectual exercise. Kristensen felt that 'the student of religion "grows himself religiously" with and by his work'.[53] Wach says that the 'practical significance' of *Religionswissenschaft* is that 'it broadens and deepens the *sensus numinus*, the religious feeling and understanding; it prepares one for a deeper conception of one's own faith; it allows a new and comprehensive experience of what religion is and means'.[54]

When we remember that the investigator must attempt to participate personally in the transforming, soteriological experience of the

---

52. Kitagawa, 'Primitive, Classical, and Modern Religions', p. 41.
53. Kraemer, Introduction to Kristensen's *The Meaning of Religion*, p. xxii.
54. Joachim Wach, 'Introduction: The Meaning and Task of the History of Religions', *The History of Religions: Essays on the Problem of Understanding*, p. 4. This article first appeared in *Zeitschrift für Missionskunde und Religionswissenschaft* 50, no. 5 (1935).

other, we may realize why the religious understanding of the Historian of Religions often has these 'practical' effects. Nevertheless, one must not identify the study of religious experience with the experience itself. What is agreed upon is that religious experience is practical, producing a profound transformation of *homo religiosus*.

Beyond 'mere' description

At the very beginning of our sketch, we observed that Max Müller used the term *Religionswissenschaft* to distinguish this new discipline from normative fields such as the philosophy of religion and theology. By becoming 'purely descriptive', the History of Relgions might attain the autonomy and objectivity of the descriptive sciences.

Kristensen conceived of the phenomenology of religion as 'purely descriptive', and we noted the severe restrictions this placed upon the task of the phenomenologist. Wach repeatedly employs a similarly sharp descriptive-normative distinction. Thus, he asserts that theology is 'a normative discipline'; the 'general science of religion' is 'essentially descriptive'. The method of the former is normative; that of the latter is descriptive.[55]

P. L. Pemberton correctly criticizes Wach as remaining 'too Kantian, where descriptive and normative functions must be sharply divided'.[56] Wach does seem to realize this when he speaks of the History of Religions in terms of 'relative-normativeness' and 'relative objectivity'. *Religionswissenschaft* must have 'the right and the courage to evaluate'; it must make use of 'scales and standards'.[57]

Contemporary Historians of Religions reject the ideal of a 'purely descriptive' discipline, which avoids comparative evaluations and other seemingly normative questions. C. J. Bleeker, discussing the phenomenology of religion, states that 'nowadays nobody confines

55. *Sociology of Religion*, p. 1; *Types of Religious Experience*, p. 229.

56. Prentiss L. Pemberton, 'Universalism and Particularity: A Review-Article', *Journal of Bible and Religion* 20, no. 2 (1952): 98.

57. Wach, 'Introduction: The Meaning and Task of the History of Religions', p. 16; Wach, *Types of Religious Experience*, p. 57; Kitagawa, 'The Nature and Program of the History of Religions Field', (The University of Chicago) *Divinity School News* (November, 1957): 20–21.

himself to a mere description of the religious phenomena, which is like the stock-taking in an antiquated museum, but the general trend is for an inquiry into the meaning and structure of these facts'.[58]

However, it is not clear how an autonomous History of Religions is to go beyond the descriptive and deal adequately with normative questions. These scholars, such as Kraemer, who ground their discipline in a normative basis, seem to compromise the irreducibility and complexity of religious phenomena and fail to provide the means for an objective understanding of 'the other'.

Kitagawa analyzes the History of Religions as being 'neither a normative discipline nor solely a descriptive discipline, even though it is related to both'. He submits that 'the discipline of *Religionswissenschaft* lies between the normative disciplines on the one hand and the descriptive disciplines on the other'. What Kitagawa intends by this status of the discipline becomes evident later in his analysis: the History of Religions starts with the historically given religions, and, while it 'has to be faithful to descriptive principles, its inquiry must nevertheless be directed to the meaning of the religious phenomena'.[59] Thus, it would seem that any approach, such as phenomenology, which is concerned with 'meaning' takes one beyond the descriptive.

Now it seems to us that this reflects the sharp descriptive-normative bifurcation — even if Kitagawa tries to place the History of Religions 'in between' — which philosophical phenomenologists have never accepted. In fact, if there is no possibility of *describing meanings*, then philosophical phenomenology rests upon a totally misconceived foundation. It seems to us that this traditional descriptive-normative dichotomy must be challenged. Indeed, we shall attempt to show that Mircea Eliade's phenomenological approach attempts not only to *describe meanings* but even to *evaluate descriptively*.

It will be our position that the History of Religions is essentially a descriptive discipline, but one that must go beyond the 'mere' description of religious phenomena. In Eliade, we shall attempt to elucidate a hermeneutics in terms of which one can compare and evaluate descriptively. What is needed is a methodological framework in terms of

58. C. Jouco Bleeker, 'The Phenomenological Method', *Numen* 6, fasc. 2 (1959): 104.

59. Kitagawa, 'The History of Religions in America', pp. 19, 21.

which one can deal with such interpretative questions as the structure and meaning of religious facts, and, at the same time, provide the basis for an objective understanding which does not distort the nature of the phenomena under investigation.

THE ISSUE OF REDUCTIONISM

What follows is little more than a very incomplete listing of a number of antireductionist claims as found in the works of such scholars as Mircea Eliade, G. van der Leeuw, Wilfred Smith, and Paul Ricoeur. Although this brief delineation could be extended for many pages, it should provide some indication of the complexity and richness of the various antireductionist methodological assumptions.

1. In most general terms, our approach must do justice to the irreducibly religious nature of *religious experience*. Some scholars have insisted on a unique, irreducibly religious structure of consciousness which comes into play only in religious experience. Many have argued that we must avoid 'naturalistic reductions': those methodological approaches which attempt to find the religious structures in the 'natural' secular facts negate the basic intentionality of the religious phenomena.

2. Our approach must do justice to the autonomous nature of the *History of Religions*. The scholar attempts to provide an irreducibly religious interpretation of religious phenomena, to investigate religious phenomena 'on their own plane of reference'.

3. Our approach must do justice to the irreducibly *personal dimension* of religious phenomena. Earlier 'positivistic' approaches to the 'religious facts', characterized by an impersonal detachment and a narrowly 'rationalistic' attitude, led to the reduction of 'living' data to 'dead' data, of the personal to the impersonal.

4. Our approach must do justice to the nature of *religious symbolism*. To cite but two formulations of this contention which we shall examine in Chapter 5, it is argued that we must not provide a simple 'unilateral' interpretation by reducing the 'multivalence' of a religious symbolism to one symbolic frame of reference. In addition, we must not reduce the nature and meaning of religious symbolism by some

very narrow, 'rational' interpretation, as seen in attempts to analyze religious symbolism by some method of 'logical analysis'.

5. Our approach must do justice to the *complexity and totality* of religious phenomena. We must avoid reducing this complexity of the religious either by interpreting our data in terms of some oversimplified scheme or by identifying the religious with only one of its perspectives.

In an excellent article, 'Reductionism in the Study of Relgions', John Y. Fenton has severely criticized such antireductionist approaches. By 'theologism', Fenton means 'a concept properly and primarily developed and used in a theological context that has been transferred with some residue as a non-theological concept to another domain such as that of the secular scholarly study of religions'. Fenton then attacks one of these central theologisms:

> The conception of religion as *sui generis*, i.e., as a primary datum which can be understood only in its own terms, has generally been accompanied in theological circles by its natural corollary: reductionistic explanations of religion are entirely incorrect. . . . [The secular study of religions] should no longer be restricted by the need to defend the faith, or to defend its theologistic residue, the anti-reductionistic *sui generis* character of the so-called 'discipline of religion.'[60]

Fenton correctly argues that 'every systematic attempt to understand phenomena reduces the phenomena'. In the study of religious or any other phenomena, 'systematic interpretation necessarily translates the phenomena into disciplinary terms, simplifies, and narrows the perspective'. Fenton contends that there is 'nothing wrong with reductionism in the study of religions, unless the investigator does not self-consciously realize that he is reductionistic, unless the reductionistic scholar thinks that his discipline alone allows him to isolate the essence of religious phenomena from their accidents, unless he overextends his method beyond its legitimate scope'.[61]

60. John Y. Fenton, 'Reductionism in the Study of Religions', *Soundings* 53, no. 1 (1970): 62.

61. *Ibid.*, pp. 63, 64. Fenton goes on to argue for the value of various reductive studies of religions (pp. 64–67) and to challenge the view that religions must be studied as something religious (pp. 67–71).

Now it is not our aim to defend all of those scholars who insist on the irreducibility of the religious. In many cases, Fenton's criticisms seem justified. But the insistence on the irreducibility of the religious, on studying religious phenomena within a religious perspective, need not be 'theologistic'. In this regard, we shall formulate two, very general methodological observations.

First, in a very fundamental way, all methodological approaches are necessarily reductionistic. This is why we shall refer to Eliade's *assumption* of the irreducibility of the religious. We recognize that starting with the assumption of the irreducibility of the religious is itself reductionistic. Our methodological assumptions necessarily limit what we shall see: what phenomena will be included within our field of inquiry, how we shall describe and analyze those phenomena, etc.

Very few philosophers would endorse some Cartesian model of a completely presuppositionless philosophy. Indeed, very few phenomenologists since the 'early Husserl' have attempted to formulate a completely presuppositionless phenomenological approach. In describing the phenomenological *Lebenswelt*, even in formulating the phenomenological *epoché*, phenomenologists attempt to render explicit our presuppositions and not to deny their existence.

In the methodological assumption of the irreducibility of the religious and in our interpretation of the religious phenomena as religious, we recognize the *perspectival* nature of all knowledge and acknowledge the fact that we are utilizing one perspective and that there is value to other perspectives. In analyzing such issues as the economic and social basis of many contemporary religious institutions, various Marxist perspectives seem much more insightful than most perspectives within the History of Religions.

Indeed, if Historians of Religions, in their insistence on the irreducibility of the religious, ignored these other perspectives, their research would be exceedingly limited and shallow. For example, in their interpretations of shamanism, Historians of Religions must be aware of the studies by ethnologists, psychologists, sociologists, philologists, and others. What they attempt to do is to integrate the contributions of other approaches within their own unique religious perspective.

Our second observation involves the attempt to grant a certain *methodological primacy* to this perspective in which we assume the irreducibility of the religious. It is possible to distinguish different kinds of reductionisms, not all of which are methodologically necessary and not all of which are on the same level of analysis. More specifically, while granting that all methodological approaches are necessarily reductionistic in the above mentioned sense and that there is value to other perspectives, one may argue for the methodological primacy of approaches which do not reduce the religious to the nonreligious.

We submit that the antireductionist claim that we ought to interpret the religious on a religious plane of reference and not reduce the religious to some nonreligious scale need not be a 'theologism'. Our justification for the assumption of the irreducibility of the religious need not involve some normative theological justification. Our justification is *phenomenological* and involves an insistence on the phenomenological *epoché*. In fact, such a phenomenological orientation could not involve some theological 'defending the faith', since the phenomenologist must 'suspend' all such normative concerns, such as whether or not the religious life-world is 'illusory', whether or not *homo religiosus* really experiences ultimate reality, etc.

One may attempt to justify the primacy of the assumption of the irreducibility of the religious by criticizing past reductionist approaches which reduced the religious to some nonreligious perspective. Yes, all approaches make assumptions, but it is possible for us to uncover and examine such assumptions.

Thus, we were able to uncover and examine various methodological assumptions and beliefs at the foundation of E. B. Tylor's ethnological approach to religious phenomena: certain 'rationalistic' and 'positivistic' assumptions; unilinear evolutionary assumptions; etc. We were able to criticize Tylor's assumptions and his interpretation of religious phenomena. From the perspective of the phenomenology of religion, Tylor's reductionist approach destroyed the basic intentionality of the religious data.

Our phenomenological justification for this assumption of the irreducibility of the religious involves an insistence on the phenomenological *epoché*. By suspending all of our interpretations of what is 'real', the phenomenologist attempts sympathetically to reenact the experiences of *homo religiosus* and to describe the meaning of the religious phenomena. The phenomenologist of religion attempts to describe and interpret the meaning of the religious experience as it is for the religious person who has had such an experience. The phenomenologist wants to deal faithfully with phenomena as phenomena, to see just what such religious phenomena reveal.

What is claimed by Otto and other phenomenologists of religion is that certain people have experienced phenomena which they have considered religious. *Homo religiosus* experiences the numinous as something *sui generis*. If we want to describe and interpret the meaning of such a religious *Lebenswelt*, we must approach such religious phenomena as something religious.

The justification for the methodological primacy of some descriptive phenomenological level of analysis, in which we sympathetically reenact the religious *Lebenswelt* of *homo religiosus*, in which we interpret the meaning of religious phenomena within a religious perspective, in no way negates the value of psychological, sociological, and other perspectives. Indeed, it does not negate the value of normative theological or metaphysical perspectives, so long as the theologian or metaphysician self-consciously realizes the nature of his or her particular assumptions and normative reductionism. For example, there are numerous creative possibilities for theological projects, such as that envisioned by Paul Tillich, when he attempted to construct a theology based upon a phenomenological foundation.

We may conclude this discussion of reductionism by emphasizing that although all approaches are necessarily reductionistic, there are different kinds and degrees of reductionism. In this regard, we may note James S. Helfer's excellent analysis of how Historians of Religions have been guilty of 'methodological solipsism': the position that insists that all interpretations and descriptions are necessarily based on ' "our own" observational experiences'.[62]

In the earlier investigations, which usually reduced the religious to some nonreligious perspective, we attempted to formulate the cultural

62. James J. Helfer, 'Introduction', *On Method in the History of Religions*, pp. 1–7. Helfer takes the term 'methodological solipsism' from Karl Popper's *Conjectures and Refutations*; Popper, in turn, took the term from Rudolf Carnap.

context within which the investigator was situated and to suggest how that context shaped his or her particular interpretation. Even with those Historians of Religions who insisted on the irreducibility of the religious, we observed this 'methodological solipsism'. Theologians, such as Kraemer, were transparent in reducing religious data to their own, personal, theological perspective. But even phenomenologists, such as van der Leeuw and Otto, interpreted religious phenomena from their own particular standpoint, thus reducing the complexity and specificity of the religious manifestations and distorting the intentionality expressed in much of their data.

It does seem that our methodological approach and interpretation are situated, are at least partially determined or influenced by the economic, social, and historical context. But this does not end the issue of reductionism.

We must examine each particular reductionism and determine whether this reductionism was 'necessary', in the sense that all approaches are situated, perspectival, and limiting; and we must determine whether this reductionism was helpful or not in shedding light on various dimensions of religious phenomena. True, phenomenologists cannot claim that their approach is presupposition-less; but past phenomenologists, such as van der Leeuw and Otto, could have done better in rendering explicit their assumptions and in 'neutralizing' as much as possible the subjective nature of their interpretations.

In Chapter 4, we shall acknowledge Mircea Eliade's 'assumption' of the irreducibility of the sacred; in Chapter 7, we shall submit that his entire approach rests on the assumption of a privileged status for certain religious phenomena. At the same time, we shall be concerned with determining whether such reductions can be justified in terms of formulating some basis for an objective hermeneutical framework, of providing some sense of methodological rigor and verification, and of offering us a satisfactory treatment of many of the fundamental issues and problems raised in Part 1 of this study.

PART TWO

Eliade's Phenomenology:
Key Methodological Notions

4

Distinguishing Religious Phenomena

INTRODUCTION

It seems possible to make the distinction between providing the criteria for separating religious from nonreligious phenomena and providing the criteria for interpreting the meaning of a religious phenomenon. This is analogous to the distinction between formulating the criteria for distinguishing a work of art and supplying the criteria for understanding the meaning of the work of art.

In terms of this distinction, it is our thesis that there are two key notions in Mircea Eliade's methodology: the dialectic of the sacred and the profane[1] and the central position of symbolism or symbolic structures. Eliade's interpretation of the dialectic of the sacred allows him to distinguish religious phenomena; his interpretation of symbolism provides the theoretical framework in terms of which he is able to understand the meaning of most of these sacred manifestations. Eliade's general view of symbolism establishes the phenomenological grounds for his structural hermeneutics; the dialectic of the sacred, when combined with Eliade's analysis of symbolism, conveys the irreducibly religious 'sense' evidenced throughout his approach.

In this chapter, we shall focus on the first of these key notions: Eliade's attempt to provide criteria for distinguishing religious phenomena. For the sake of analysis, we shall abstract several principles from his methodology. Such an approach might suggest a temporal order in Eliade's hermeneutics: first Eliade insists on the irreducibility of the sacred, which involves the phenomenological *epoché* and the sympathetic effort to participate in the experience of *homo religiosus*; next he attempts to recreate imaginatively the conditions of the sacred manifestation and captures the intentionality of the sacred manifestation in terms of the dialectic of the sacred; then he

1. We shall use 'the dialectic of the sacred', 'the dialectic of the sacred and the profane', and 'the dialectic of hierophanies' interchangeably.

attempts to understand the meaning of the sacred manifestation in terms of a structural hermeneutics grounded in his interpretation of religious symbolism.

It is imperative that we clearly recognize that such an interpretation, suggesting this temporal sequence in Mircea Eliade's methodology, will not do. For example, we shall describe Eliade's methodological insistence on suspending one's own interpretation and seeing just what one's data reveal. But surely even the most conscientious phenomenologist cannot simply 'perform' or 'invoke' the *epoché*. The phenomenological *epoché* must involve some explicit method of self-criticism, intersubjective check, factual (as well as 'free') variations. Consequently, we could not possibly understand the nature of Eliade's phenomenological *epoché* until we had elucidated the additional methodological principles and hermeneutical framework in terms of which one can suspend his or her own normative judgments, grasp the meaning of the experiences of *homo religiosus*, etc.

In short, we cannot overemphasize that the following hermeneutical principles, along with the structuralistic principles not elucidated in this chapter, must be viewed as functioning together in Mircea Eliade's methodology. Any illusion of temporal order is an unfortunate consequence of the need for an analytic exposition.

Before proceeding with our systematic treatment of Mircea Eliade's phenomenological approach, we may acknowledge that our analysis is in contrast with most of Eliade's interpreters, who seem to feel that Eliade has never developed a systematic methodology. For example, Thomas J. J. Altizer repeatedly describes Eliade's phenomenological method as 'mystical' and 'romantic'; such a method is completely divorced from any approach which is 'rational' and 'scientific'.[2] Indeed, the proponent of this mystically grounded approach is identified with such roles as 'prophet, seer, and shaman'.[3]

We must acknowledge that Mircea Eliade himself lends considerable credence to the view that he has never really dealt with the crucial

2. Thomas J. J. Altizer, *Mircea Eliade and the Dialectic of the Sacred*, pp. 30, 36, 41, 84, and *passim*; and Altizer, 'The Religious Meaning of Myth and Symbol', *Truth, Myth, and Symbol*, p. 97 and *passim*.

3. Altizer, *Mircea Eliade and the Dialectic of the Sacred*, p. 17. See 'Myths for Moderns', *The Times Literary Supplement*, no. 3, 337 (February 10, 1966): 102.

phenomenological issues and consequently lacks a critical systematic methodology. When asked how he arrived at his frequently unexpected and bewildering interpretations, this scholar is apt to reply that he simply looked at his religious documents and this was what they revealed.[4] It is little wonder that such a seemingly uncritical approach is often viewed as either incredibly naive or charlatanical or at best the brilliant intuitions of a true mystic. In any case, this approach would have little value for the methodological concerns of the rigorous phenomenologist.

Now it is our thesis that Mircea Eliade does in fact have an impressive phenomenological method. We would submit that this is precisely why Eliade is a methodological improvement over the other phenomenologists of religion we have examined. As one studies a major classic in the field, say, Gerardus van der Leeuw's *Religion in Essence and Manifestation*, she or he cannot help but be impressed by the vast amount of data which have been collected and classified. What invariably disturbs the philosophical phenomenologist is that van der Leeuw and his colleagues never appear to have formulated a critical methodology. On what basis do they make their comparisons and generalizations, guard agains subjectivity in their interpretations, defend their specific classifications and typologies? What we shall attempt to show is that underlying Eliade's approach is a certain methodological framework which allows him to deal with many of the central phenomenological concerns.

MIRCEA ELIADE AS PHENOMENOLOGIST

Throughout this study, we have referred to Mircea Eliade as a

4. In conversation, Eliade presented an interesting autobiographical explanation for his avoidance of a comprehensive methodological analysis. While in India, he began reading the literature in the History of Religions and was struck by a pervasive dilettantism. In order to avoid superficial, premature conclusions, he would pour himself into all the religious documents and not get involved in methodology. Nevertheless, such an explanation will not do. Methodology is not the kind of thing that one can postpone. Pouring oneself into the documents necessarily entails the adoption of some type of methodology. One of our primary tasks is to render explicit the methodological assumptions and principles which are often implicit in Eliade's phenomenology.

'phenomenologist' and to his approach as 'phenomenological' without really justifying the identification of his History of Religions with these terms. It must be stated that such an identification is controversial. Neither Eliade nor his interpreters usually identify his approach with phenomenology. We are aware of no interpreter who has shown a relationship between Eliade's methodology and philosophical phenomenology.

Chapter 5 is intended to lay the hermeneutical framework for Eliade's phenomenological method, and Chapter 6 attempts to relate Eliade's approach to specific notions and concerns of philosophical phenomenology. For now, we may begin to present some evidence to substantiate our controversial claim that Mircea Eliade is a phenomenologist.

Recall that we have discussed the present nature of *Religionswissenschaft* as disclosing a certain methodological tension between approaches tending toward either specialization or synthesis and generality. Phenomenological approaches were viewed as one of the tendencies toward generality.

In previous chapters, we have clearly established that Mircea Eliade is a *generalist*. One of Eliade's consistent themes has been the need for contemporary Historians of Religions to go beyond the self-imposed limitations of specialization and to attempt creative generalizations and syntheses. In fact, Eliade frequently identifies being a Historian of Religions with being a generalist: 'It is not a question, for the historian of religions [Historian of Religions], of substituting himself for the various specialists, that is to say, of mastering their respective philologies. . . . One is a historian of religions [Historian of Religions] not by virtue of mastering a certain number of philologies, but because one is able to integrate religious data into a general perspective.'[5]

In describing Eliade's generalist approach as phenomenological, we should note a distinction which was made in Chapter 2 in our introduction to phenomenological approaches. 'The term phenomenology of religion can be used in a double sense': 'It means both a scientific method and an independent science, creating monographs and more

5. 'Methodological Remarks in the Study of Religious Symbolism', *The History of Religions: Essays in Methodology*, pp. 90, 91. Cited hereafter as 'Methodological Remarks'.

or less extensive handbooks.'[6] Eliade's *Patterns in Comparative Religion* illustrates this second sense of phenomenology of religion.

Our paramount concern is with Eliade's methodology, and we shall not present a comprehensive exposition of his categorization of religious phenomena. Thus, we shall not formulate Eliade's analysis of sacred space, sacred time, myth, ritual, and other major categories for organizing and analyzing religious phenomena. If there is any resemblance between philosophical phenomenology and the phenomenology of religion as a branch of the History of Religions, this is because of the adoption of a *phenomenological method*.

Not only do Mircea Eliade's interpreters usually fail to associate his History of Religions with phenomenology, but they sometimes even distinguish his approach from the phenomenology of religion. For example, in the discussion of a paper given by Ugo Bianchi, Professor Bolgiani remarks that he has the impression that 'Bianchi used such expressions as "typology" and "phenomenology" rather indiscriminately, when it seems to me that in the current state of "religious sciences" we cannot purely and simply equate them. To set the bounds of the problem correctly it strikes me that we ought to distinguish between "typology", "morphology" and even "phenomenology" of religions. To reduce religious phenomenology simply to a "typology" of religions does not seem to me to be entirely right. . . .'

Professor Bianchi replies that 'some historians of religions [Historians of Religions] have a certain tendency to use such terms as "typology", "phenomenology" and "morphology" with a promiscuous meaning'. 'When we mention phenomenology we especially think of scholars such as Wach, Van der Leeuw and Bleeker; when we mention morphology then our mind goes especially to Eliade.'[7]

6. C. J. Bleeker, 'The Future Task of the History of Religions', *Numen* 7, fasc. 3 (1960): 228. See Bleeker, 'The Contribution of the Phenomenology of Religion', pp. 39–40.

7. Ugo Bianchi, 'The Definition of Religion', pp. 26–29. A good illustration of this lack of identification of Eliade with the phenomenology of religion may be seen in *Religion, Culture and Methodology*, ed. T. P. van Baaren and H. J. W. Drijvers. Although these 'Papers of the Groningen Working-group' repeatedly express their dissatisfaction with the phenomenology of religion, and a phenomenologist such as van der Leeuw is repeatedly cited for criticism, Eliade is not even listed in the index. See especially the articles by T. P. van Baaren (pp. 35–56), L. Leertouwer (pp. 79–98), and the Epilogue by H. J. W. Drijvers and L. Leertouwer (pp. 159–168).

Our position is that although morphology may be distinguished from phenomenology and most morphologists are not phenomenologists, in the case of Professor Eliade, morphology is an integral part of his phenomenological method. In Chapter 5, we shall see that a morphological analysis provides the foundation for Eliade's phenomenological method, primarily by allowing him to reintegrate the particular manifestation within its structural system of symbolic assocations. At the same time, we would submit that most interpreters who identify Eliade as a morphologist have simply taken his morphology at face value; as if by some mysterious process, the data simply revealed those essential structures. In Chapter 6, we shall analyze how Eliade proceeds, and we shall elucidate some of the phenomenological principles that allow for his morphological analysis.

At one point, Mircea Eliade specifically dissociates himself from phenomenology: '[the phenomenologist], in principle, rejects any work of comparison; confronted with one religious phenomenon or another, he confines himself to "approaching" it and divining its meaning. Whereas the historian of religions [Historian of Religions] does not reach a comprehension of a phenomenon until after he has compared it with thousands of similar or dissimilar phenomena, until he has situated it among them.'[8]

It seems that this reject on of phenomenology is based on a popular interpretation of Husserl's phenomenological reduction and eidetic intuition.[9] On the basis of one example and through reflection, reductions, and imaginative variation, one may gain insight into the structure and meaning of a phenomenon. The phenomenologist may arrive at this pure vision without the collection of historical examples and factual comparisons. We should note that contemporary phenomenologists (and apparently Husserl himself in some of his last works) reject this view of phenomenology.

8. Mircea Eliade, *Shamanism: Archaic Techniques of Ecstacy*, p. xv. Cited hereafter as *Shamanism*.

9. This is often classified as the position of the 'early' Husserl. In 'Phenomenologies and Psychologies', *Review of Existential Psychology and Psychiatry* 5, no. 1 (1965): 80–105, Stephan Strasser points out that there are several types of phenomenology. Eliade's rejection of phenomenology is directed primarily at what Strasser labels 'transcendental phenomenology'.

In terms of the historical-phenomenological 'tension', which Eliade and other scholars often formulate as defining the nature of the History of Religions today, Eliade invariably emphasizes the phenomenological 'side'. Professor Eliade may state that the Historian of Religions 'is attracted to both the *meaning* of a religious phenomenon and to its *history*; he tries to do justice to both and not to sacrifice either one of them'.[10] Yet in most of his writings, Eliade seems to indicate that he will not attempt a detailed examination of historical differences, variations, disseminations, etc.; instead he will aim at a phenomenological analysis of the meaning of his data.[11] Eliade's position seems to be that the Historian of Religions only completes his or her task *as a phenomenologist*: 'Ultimately, what we desire to know is the meaning of the various historical modifications. . . .'[12]

In 'The Sacred in the Secular World', Eliade begins by describing himself 'as a historian and phenomenologist of religion' and claims that the Historian of Religions 'is also a phenomenologist because of his concern with meaning'. This meaning 'is given in the intentionality of the structure'.

So at some point the historian of religion [Historian of Religion] must become a phenomenologist of religion, because he tries to find meaning. Without hermeneutics, the history of religion [History of Religion] is just another history — bare facts, special classifications, and so on. With the problem of hermeneutics — meaning — we see that every manifestation of the sacred — symbol, myth, ritual — tells of something which is absolutely real, something which is meaningful for that culture, tribe, or religion in which the manifestation takes place. Once the historian of religion [Historian of

10. 'Methodological Remarks', p. 88. See Eliade, 'Historical Events and Structural Meaning in Tension', pp. 29–31.

11. For example, see *The Myth of the Eternal Return*, pp. 73–74. In most of his books, Eliade refers us to more specialized works which treat these historical questions in greater detail. These historical approaches are meant to substantiate and complement his more phenomenological analysis.

12. 'On Understanding Primitive Religions', p. 501. This is a crucial methodological contention in such articles as 'History of Religions and a New Humanism', and 'Crisis and Renewal in History of Religions', and in the methodological sections of most of Eliade's books.

Religion] takes on the search for meaning, he can, following the phenomenological principle of suspension of judgment, assume the structure of synchronicity, and, therefore, as I have said before, bring together the meanings evident in many different cultures and eras.[13]

The extent to which we can show that Mircea Eliade is a phenomenologist, that his approach can be related to the concerns and notions of philosophical phenomenology, will finally rest on an analysis of what he has done. In short, we must determine whether Eliade approaches the central task of hermeneutics, whether he interprets the meaning of the religious manifestations, on the basis of some phenomenological method.

Before elucidating Eliade's key methodological notions, let us recall from Chapter 3 that religion presupposes religious experience. Investigators begin with religious expressions and attempt to interpret the nature of the experiences expressed in their data. 'The greatest claim to merit of the history of religions [History of Religions] is precisely its effort to decipher in a "fact," conditioned as it is by the historical moment and the cultural style of the epoch, the existential situation that made it possible.'[14]

Over and over again, Eliade argues that the paramount concern of the Historian of Religions is hermeneutics. 'For the ultimate goal of the historian of religions [Historian of Religions] is not to point out that there exist a certain number of types of patterns of religious behavior, with their specific symbologies and theologies, but rather to *understand their meanings.* . . . Ultimately, the historian of religions [Historian of Religions] cannot renounce hermeneutics.'[15]

As we have seen on several occasions, Eliade believes that the History of Religions has tended to be cautious and inhibited; the task of interpretation has been left to the various 'reductionist' approaches. Yet the 'hermeneutical work ought to be done by the historian of

13. Mircea Eliade, 'The Sacred in the Secular World', *Cultural Hermeneutics* 1, no. 1 (1973): 101, 103, 106–107.

14. 'Methodological Remarks', p. 89. *The Sacred*, p. 162: 'The ultimate aim of the historian of religions [Historian of Religions] is to understand, and to make understandable to others, religious man's behavior and mental universe.'

15. 'Australian Religions, Part V', pp. 267–268.

religions [Historian of Religions] himself, for only he is prepared to understand and appreciate the semantic complexity of his documents'.[16]

According to Eliade, the Historian of Religions 'uses an empirical method of approach' and begins by collecting religious documents which need to be interpreted. Unlike Müller, Tylor, Frazer, and other early investigators, the modern scholar realizes that she or he works 'exclusively with historical documents'.[17] Consequently, Eliade's point of departure is the historical data which express the religious experiences of humanity. Through his phenomenological approach, Eliade attempts to decipher these data, to describe the religious phenomena which constitute the *Lebenswelt* of *homo religiosus* and to interpret their religious meaning.

We have asserted that Mircea Eliade collects *religious* documents which need to be interpreted, attempts to describe the *religious* phenomena, etc. But how does one know which documents to collect, which phenomena to describe and interpret? To answer these and similar questions, we need to introduce several methodological principles in terms of which Eliade can distinguish the religious manifestations.

THE IRREDUCIBILITY OF THE SACRED

The methodological assumption of the irreducibility of the sacred can be seen as arising from Eliade's criticism of past reductionist positions. In fact, this antireductionism is the predominant reason for Eliade's rejection of previous approaches. We need not repeat Eliade's detailed criticisms. One recalls that scholars of 'the first period', utilizing certain assumed norms (rationalist, positivist, etc.), usually forced their data into unilinear evolutionary schemes. The sociologist and the psychologist of 'the second period' opened up new dimensions of the

16. 'Crisis and Renewal in the History of Religions', p. 9. On this same page, Eliade writes that 'we do not doubt that the "creative hermeneutics" will finally be recognized as the royal road of the History of Religions'.

17. 'Methodological Remarks', p. 88; 'The Quest for the "Origins" of Religion', p. 169. See *The Myth of the Eternal Return*, pp. 5–6; and *Patterns*, pp. xiv–xvi, 2–3.

sacred, but Eliade criticized them for reducing the meaning of the religious to its sociological or psychological analysis. Similarly, Eliade readily acknowledged his debt to the diffusionist and the functionalist, but tracing the diffusion or determining the function of a religious phenomenon does not exhaust its meaning.

The upshot of Eliade's criticism may be expressed by the following antireductionist claim which we have frequently cited: the Historian of Religions must attempt to grasp the religious phenomena 'on their own plane of reference', as something religious. To reduce our interpretation of the religious phenomena to some other plane of reference (sociological, psychological, etc.) is to neglect their full intentionality and to fail to grasp their unique and irreducible 'element' — the sacred.

Over and over again, Eliade expresses his antireductionist stance in terms of the following principle: 'the scale creates the phenomenon'. He quotes the following ironical query of Henri Poincaré: 'Would a naturalist who had never studied the elephant except through the microscope consider that he had an adequate knowledge of the creature?' 'The microscope reveals the structure and mechanism of cells, which structure and mechanism are exactly the same in all multicellular organisms. The elephant is certainly a multicellular organism, but is that all that it is? On the microscopic scale, we might hesitate to answer. On the scale of human vision, which at least has the advantage of presenting the elephant as a zoological phenomenon, there can be no doubt about the reply.'[18]

Eliade's methodological assumption of the irreducibility of the sacred can be seen as arising from his view of the role of the Historian of Religions. His justification for such an assumption seems to be that the task of the phenomenologist, at least in the beginning, is to follow and attempt to understand an experience as it is for the person who has had that experience. Unlike earlier investigators who superimposed their own normative standards upon their data, Eliade wants to deal faithfully with his phenomena as phenomena, to see just what his data reveal. What his data reveal is that certain people have had experiences

18. Mircea Eliade, 'Comparative Religion: Its Past and Future', *Knowledge and the Future of Man*, ed. Walter J. Ong, S. J., p. 251. See *Patterns*, p. xiii; and *Myths, Dreams and Mysteries*, p. 131.

which they have considered religious. Thus, the phenomenologist must first of all respect the original intentionality expressed by the data; he must attempt to understand such phenomena as something religious.

In short, Eliade's methodological principle of irreducibility is really an insistence upon a phenomenological *epoché*. One recalls that Husserl's phenomenological *epoché* was directed against reductionism. By 'bracketing' or suspending the interpretations we normally place on phenomena, the phenomenologist attempts to consider phenomena 'just as phenomena', 'to disclose and clarify the meaning of phenomena, that is of whatever presents itself'.[19]

The above discussion may be seen as relevant to one of our central methodological points in Chapter 3: if Historians of Religions are to understand religious phenomena 'on their own plane of reference', they must attempt to place themselves within the perspective of *homo religiosus*, and such a capacity for participation must be grounded in a sympathetic attitude. By means of the *epoché*, phenomenologists attempt sympathetically to grasp the meaning of the experiences of the other. By insisting on the irreducibility of the sacred, Eliade attempts sympathetically to place himself within the perspective of *homo religiosus* and to grasp the meaning of the religious phenomena.

We may formulate Eliade's methodological principle in the following terms. As we observed in Chapter 3, our approach must be commensurate with the nature of our subject matter. *Homo religiosus* experiences the sacred as something *sui generis*. If we are to participate in and sympathetically understand the religious phenomena of the other, our scale must be commensurate with the scale of the other. Consequently, Eliade insists on an irreducibly religious scale of understanding in order to have an adequate knowledge of the irreducibly religious phenomena.

To illustrate the paramount significance of this hermeneutical principle, consider the following question: How are we to understand the enormous prestige and the various functions and duties of the

19. Nathaniel Lawrence and Daniel O'Connor, 'The Primary Phenomenon: Human Existence', *Readings in Existential Phenomenology*, ed. Nathaniel Lawrence and Daniel O'Connor, p. 7.

Australian medicine man? Various reductionists from numerous disciplines have offered a wide range of interpretations. Our data, such as the initiation rituals for becoming a medicine man, reveal that the Australians have placed these experiences within a religious context. Eliade's 'religious scale' attempts to understand these phenomena on their own plane of reference. He finds that 'only the medicine man succeeds in surpassing his human condition, and consequently he is able to behave like the spiritual beings, or, in other words, to partake of the modality of a spiritual being'. It is because of his 'transmutation', his 'singular existential condition', that the medicine man can cure the sick, be a rainmaker, and defend his tribe against magical aggression. In short, his 'social prestige, his cultural role, and his political supremacy derive ultimately from his magico-religious "power" '.[20]

A second illustration of the significance of this hermeneutical principle can be seen in terms of the following question: How are we to understand the shaman's strange imitation of animal cries? It has been customary to interpret this phenomenon as manifesting a pathological 'possession', clear evidence of the shaman's mental aberration. However, suppose we suspend our normative judgments and first attempt to understand the religious meaning which such experiences have had for the other.[21]

Understood in terms of such a scale, Eliade finds that the shaman's friendship with animals and knowledge of their language reveal a 'paradisal' syndrome. Communication and friendship with animals is one means of partially recovering the 'paradisal' situation of primordial man; this blessedness and spontaneity existed in *illo tempore*, before the 'fall', and is inaccessible to our profane state. From this

20. Mircea Eliade, 'Australian Religions, Part IV: The Medicine Men and Their Supernatural Models', *History of Religions* 7, no. 2 (1967): pp. 160, 178–179. This article is reproduced as chapter 4 in Eliade's *Australian Religions: An Introduction*.

21. Eliade does go on to deny that shamanism can be assimilated to a kind of psychopathological condition: 'one becomes a shaman only if he can interpret his pathological crisis as a religious experience and succeeds in curing himself'; 'there is always a cure, a control, an equilibrium brought about by the actual practice of shamanism'; the shamanic initiation includes 'a course of theoretical and practical instruction too complicated to be within the grasp of a neurotic'; etc. See *Shamanism*, pp. 14, 23–32; *From Primitives to Zen*, pp. 423–424; 'Recent Works on Shamanism: a Review Article', *History of Religions* 1, no. 1 (1961): 155.

perspective, Eliade begins to understand that the 'strange behavior' is 'actually part of a coherent ideology, possessing great nobility'. In terms of this ideology, this 'yearning for Paradise', Eliade is able to interpret many shamanic phenomena and to relate the shaman's ecstatic experience to other religious phenomena.[22]

At the end of the last chapter, we submitted both that all approaches are reductionistic and that for some phenomena one might argue for the methodological primacy of some religious perspective. Especially for those phenomena which have been experienced by *homo religiosus* as something religious and which reveal a basic religious intentionality, the assumption of the irreducibility of the religious might be justified on phenomenological grounds.

This in no way should be taken as agreement with the frequently formulated antireductionist position that the religious must be interpreted as something religious and that all other positions are false. All knowledge is perspectival. Eliade is correct in arguing that the psychological or sociological perspective does not exhaust the meaning of certain religious phenomena, and, in some cases, may distort or overlook a basic structure of the sacred manifestation. But phenomenologists of religion cannot argue that their perspective and their perspective alone exhausts the total meaning of religious phenomena and does justice to all dimensions of the manifestations of the sacred.

After noting 'the amazing popularity of witchcraft in modern Western culture and its subcultures', Eliade undertakes an analysis of 'two highly controversial problems: (1) the "origins" of Western witchcraft, that is, the problem of its possible relation to pre-Christian beliefs and rituals; and (2) the so-called witches' orgies, which, from the moment witchcraft was assimilated to a heresy, were at the center of the charges brought against it'. Eliade then utilizes a religious scale from the perspective of the History of Religions, and this leads to many perceptive results.

Some of the most interesting 'openings' in the interpretation of witchcraft and various other religious phenomena have been formulated in the past few years by feminists. Yet one would never guess

22. Mircea Eliade, 'The Yearning for Paradise in Primitive Tradition', *Daedalus* 88 (1959): 258, 261–266.

from Eliade's treatment that androcentrism and a theologically misogynist tradition, that patriarchal structures of exploitation and oppression, were key notions in the interpretation of witchcraft.

Thus, Eliade writes that 'the decisive fact was that, imaginary or not, the witches' orgies, like those of the heretics, could endanger the social and theological institutions; indeed, they released nostalgias, hopes, and desires aiming at a mode of being different from the typical Christian existence'. Feminist interpreters— whether using a religious or nonreligious scale— would agree with this conclusion while qualifying and expanding it. From a feminist perspective, those 'endangered social and theological institutions' were patriarchal and oppressed and exploited women; and those 'released nostalgias, hopes, and desires' indeed aimed at a different (nonpatriarchal) mode of being from the 'typical Christian existence' ('typical' equals 'male-defined'), since that existence was sexist in its symbols, myths, rituals, and power-relations.[23]

In her 'Androcentrism in Religious Studies', Valerie Saiving uses Eliade's *Rites and Symbols of Initiation* as her case study. With a specific feminist sensitivity, she notes a common characteristic in Eliade's various 'metacultural aspects of male initiation': 'the element of aggression, conquest, domination'. She contends that what Eliade 'says about the *human* meaning of initiation corresponds almost exactly to what he says about *male* initiation, and that it contradicts in essential respects his understanding of *female* initiation'. 'It may be true, as Eliade asserts, that women have their own form of sacrality; but given his own conception of what "lies at the core of any genuine human life," it is a subhuman sacrality. From this viewpoint of women [and this author and many other men], this conclusion is scarcely trivial.'[24]

The above two illustrations are not so much intended to show that

23. Mircea Eliade, 'Some Observations on European Witchcraft', *Occultism, Witchcraft, and Cultural Fashions*, pp. 69–70, 90–91, and *passim*.

24. Valerie Saiving, 'Androcentrism in Religious Studies', *Journal of Religion* 56, no. 2 (1976): 183–184, 188, 189, 190; Eliade, *Rites and Symbols of Initiation*, p. 135. Prof. Saiving remarks that Eliade's study of initiation presents 'an especially difficult test' of her hypothesis concerning androcentrism in religious studies; 'if it embodies androcentric presuppositions, these are not immediately visible but exist at a very deep level'. We may note that Saiving assumes a religious perspective which is

Eliade's scale is explicitly androcentric, but rather that his perspective emphasizes certain notions and overlooks or de-emphasizes other dimensions of the phenomena which are central to other (in this case, feminist) perspectives. While granting a certain methodological primacy for assuming the irreducibility of the religious, we emphasize that no perspective does justice to all dimensions of religious phenomena.

Eliade has insisted on the irreducibility of the sacred but has not provided the hermeneutic framework for perceiving the irreducible manifestations. He must now recreate imaginatively the conditions for the manifestations of the sacred; in doing this, he seems to adopt a phenomenological approach by focusing upon the *intentionality* of his data.

In assuming the irreducibility of the sacred, we have recognized the need to participate in the life-world of *homo religiosus*, the sympathetic effort to understand the experiences of the other. Stephan Strasser remarks, 'In this authentically phenomenological attitude the world no longer appears to us as a whole of objective data, but as an "intentional configuration" [*Sinngebilde*] which is born and becomes meaningful in the course of an existential movement of orientation.'[25]

When Eliade examines his data, they do reveal a certain intentionality. He will attempt to recreate imaginatively the conditions for the 'intentional configuration' which expresses the specific existential orientation of *homo religiosus*. 'The attempt to understand the sacred as an irreducible form is accompanied by the technical attempt to capture its *intentional* mode. . . . Eliade's second hermeneutic principle, the dialectic of the sacred and the profane, is introduced precisely to capture this intentional characteristic of the sacred modality.'[26]

---

irreducibly feminist; many other feminists, of course, do not assume a religious perspective.

25. Stephen Strasser, *The Soul in Metaphysical and Empirical Psychology*, p. 3.

26. David Rasmussen, 'Mircea Eliade: Structural Hermeneutics and Philosophy', *Philosophy Today* 12, no. 2 (1968): 140. Rasmussen presents 'the irreducibility of the sacred' as Eliade's 'first hermeneutic principle'. Professor Rasmussen is one of the few interpreters who has uncovered some of the philosophical significance of Eliade's methodology.

RELIGION AND THE SACRED

In order to understand more fully the structure of the dialectic of the sacred, we shall first clarify Eliade's conception of religion and the sacred. Mircea Eliade tells us that 'in the title of the "history of religions" [History of Religions] the accent ought not to be upon the word *history*, but upon the word *religions*. For although there are numerous ways of practising *history* — from the history of technics to that of human thought — there is only one way of approaching *religion* — namely, to deal with the religious facts. Before making the *history* of anything, one must have a proper understanding of what it *is*, in and for itself.'[27]

Following Roger Caillois, Eliade begins by asserting that 'all the definitions given up till now of the religious phenomenon have one thing in common: each has its own way of showing that the sacred and the religious life are the opposite of the profane and the secular life'. Caillois admits that this sacred-profane distinction is not always sufficient to define the phenomenon of religion, but such an opposition is involved in every definition of religion.[28] 'The dichotomy of sacred and profane is the invariable par excellence in the religious life of man.'[29]

In Eliade's conception, religion 'does not necessarily imply belief in God, gods, or ghosts, but refers to the experience of the sacred'. The sacred and profane are 'two modes of being in the world, two existential situations assumed by man in the course of history'.[30] What is most characteristic of religion is its being occupied with the sacred, which it distinguishes from the profane. The sacred may be described as that which is experienced as 'power' (van der Leeuw), as 'wholly other'

27. *Images and Symbols*, p. 29.
28. *Patterns*, p. 1; *The Sacred*, p. 10; Roger Caillois, *Man and the Sacred*, pp. 13, 19.
29. Eliade, 'Structure and Changes in the History of Religion', p. 353. Winston L. King has written in his *Introduction to Religion: A Phenomenological Approach*, p. 32: 'Classically speaking what is not sacred is profane; but in our time "profane" connotes the antisacred rather than the merely nonsacred.' Although we must guard against this connotation of 'profane', we shall continue to use this term since it appears throughout the writings of Mircea Eliade.
30. Mircea Eliade, 'Preface', *The Quest: History and Meaning in Religion*, p. i; *The Sacred*, p. 14.

(Otto), as 'ultimate reality' (Wach). In other religious contexts, it is described by such terms as 'absolute reality', 'being', 'eternity', 'divine', 'metacultural and transhistorical', 'transhuman', 'transmundane', 'source of life and fecundity'.[31]

By citing several illustrations, we shall comprehend more fully the relationship between religion and the sacred. In interpreting experiences of 'mystic light', Eliade seems to feel that these experiences are religious because 'they bring a man out of his worldly Universe or historical situation, and project him into a Universe different in quality, an entirely different world, transcendent and holy'. Yoga preserves 'a religious value' by reacting against 'the "normal", "secular", and finally "human" inclination', by thirsting 'for the unconditioned, for freedom, for "power" — in a word, for one of the countless modalities of the sacred'. The myriad expressions of the '*coincidentia oppositorum*' reveal religious experiences because they may be deciphered as disclosing the human being's attempt to transcend his or her 'natural' or 'human' situation in the world by transcending 'the opposites' and thus reaching a mode of 'total' being.[32]

If we consider all of the descriptions of the sacred, Eliade seems to be indicating that religion always entails some aspect of *transcendence*. This sense of transcendence is expressed in such terms as absolute bliss and power, transhistorical and transmundane, etc. But Eliade intends this sense of transcendence to be viewed as a universal structure of religion: to restrict it to any particular description or content is to relativize it. All expressions are too specific. Eliade's universal characterization of religion in terms of this transcendent structure is meant to include, but not be exhausted by, the definitions offered by van der Leeuw, Otto, Wach, and others.

One immediately realizes that the above claim is not sufficient to define religion. Countless examples can be cited where a completely nonreligious individual, say, some scientist expounding her or his conception of space, presents us with a purely descriptive and secular sense of transcendence.

What differentiates the religious sense of transcendence is its special

31. For example, see *Rites and Symbols of Initiation*, p. 130; *Yoga*, p. 165; *The Sacred*, p. 28.
32. *Mephistopheles and the Androgyne*, pp. 76, 78–124; *Yoga*, p. 96.

normative basis for *homo religiosus*. This will become apparent in our treatment of the structure of 'evaluation and choice' in the dialectic of the sacred. At this point, let us simply note that religion involves a radical break with all of the secular or profane modalities. It invariably points us 'beyond' the relative, historical, 'natural' world of 'ordinary' experience. Indeed, Eliade goes so far as to assert that 'the principal function of religion' is to render human existence 'open' to a 'superhuman' world of 'transcendent' values.[33]

In a frequently quoted passage from *The Sacred and the Profane*, Eliade contrasts religion with the mode of being in the world of the nonreligious person:

> The nonreligious man refuses trancendence, accepts the relativity of 'reality,' and may even come to doubt the meaning of existence. . . . Modern nonreligious man assumes a new existential situation; he regards himself solely as the subject and agent of history, and he refuses all appeal to transcendence. In other words, he accepts no model for humanity outside the human condition as it can be seen in the various historical situations. Man *makes himself*, and he only makes himself completely in proportion as he desacralizes himself and the world. The sacred is the prime obstacle to his freedom. He will become himself only when he is totally demysticized. He will not be truly free until he has killed the last god.[34]

Eliade must not be confused with the numerous scholars who hold metaphysical positions concerning transcendence. He is not claiming that 'the value of the religious phenomena can be understood only if we keep in mind that religion is ultimately a realization of a transcendent truth'.[35] At this stage, his empirical approach is clearly descriptive. His religious documents reveal the sacred–profane dichotomy

33. 'Structure and Changes in the History of Religion', p. 366: 'the principal function of religion, that of maintaining an "opening" toward a world which is superhuman, the world of axiomatic spiritual values'.
34. *The Sacred*, pp. 202–203.
35. Bleeker, 'The Future Task of the History of Religions', p. 227. Bleeker's normative claim was rejected in a statement submitted by Professor Werblowsky, to which Eliade and many other Historians of Religions were willing to associate themselves. See 'Summary of Discussion' by Annemarie Schimmel, *Numen* 7, fasc. 3 (1960): 237.

and the attempt by *homo religiosus* to experience the sacred by transcending the profane.

It seems that Mircea Eliade's attempt to provide us with a universal structure of religion leads to a certain peculiarity. At the beginning of *Patterns in Comparative Religion*, he tells us that he will dispense 'from any a priori definition of the religious phenomenon; the reader can make his own reflections on the nature of the sacred as he goes'. Eliade will simply investigate his data in order to see 'just what things are religious in nature and what those things reveal'.[36] It would seem that a definition of religion arrived at in this manner would be open to modification; our conception of religion could change depending on the nature of the future documents we investigate.

Now Eliade appears to have given us a 'definition' of religion which is supposedly dependent on the nature of the religious documents he has investigated, but which is not in fact open to change.[37] What would it be like to falsify Eliade's definition? He cannot admit to coming up with a religious document not having the structure of transcendence.[38] Eliade's definition of religion has the peculiarity of any empirical definition which claims to be universal.

THE DIALECTIC OF THE SACRED

To recreate the conditions for the intentional mode of religious manifestations, we must carefully explicate the structure of the dialectic of

36. *Patterns*, pp. xvi, xiv.

37. This seems similar to the status of a phenomenological 'essence' as the concept is used by most philosophical phenomenologists. See our treatment of 'Phenomenological Method, Free Variation, and Induction' in chapter 6.

38. We may simply note that this is the source of Thomas Altizer's major criticism of Eliade. For Altizer, modern religiosity is defined by its very denial of transcendence. Hence Altizer argues that Eliade's conception of religion does justice to archaic but not to modern religion. Eliade would counter that such modern experiences are either not religious or do have a religious aura, because they reveal a transcendent structure which is not lived consciously. Much of Eliade's analysis is devoted to deciphering the transcendent structure which is expressed in the myths, rituals, ideologies, nostalgias, dreams, fantasies, and other unconscious or imaginary experiences of the modern person. For a discussion of how Eliade might respond to Altizer's criticisms, see Mac Linscott Ricketts, 'Mircea Eliade and the Death of God', *Religion in Life* (Spring, 1967): 40–52; Ricketts, 'Eliade and Altizer: Very Different Outlooks', *Christian Advocate* (October, 1967): 11–12.

the sacred. We shall divide our analysis into three parts: the separation of the hierophanic object and the sacred-profane distinction; the paradoxical relationship between the sacred and the profane; the evaluation and choice implied in the dialectic.

The separation and distinction

According to Eliade, the person who has the religious experience believes that something comes from somewhere else and shows itself to him or her. That which appears from somewhere else is the sacred; that through which it appears is the profane.

> To denote the act of manifestation of the sacred, we propose to use the term *hierophany*. This word is convenient because it requires no additional specification; it means nothing more than is implied by its etymological content— namely, that something sacred is shown to us, manifests itself. One may say that the history of religions — from the most elementary to the most developed — is constituted by a number of important hierophanies, manifestations of sacred realities.[39]

What interests *homo religiosus* are hierophanies. These manifestations of the sacred are never unmediated: the sacred is always revealed through something natural, historical, ordinarily profane. The profane alone has no significance for *homo religiosus*, but only insofar as it reveals the sacred.

The process of sacralization involves the 'radical ontological separation' of the thing which reveals the sacred from everything else. We find the singularization of a certain stone because of its size or shape or heavenly origin, because it protects the dead or is the site of a covenant, because it represents a theophany or is an image of the 'center'. A medicine man has been singularized because he has been chosen by gods or spirits, because of his heredity, because of various physical defects (an infirmity, nervous disorder, etc.), or because of an unusual accident or event (lightning, apparition, dream, etc.).[40]

---

39. *Myths, Dreams and Mysteries*, p. 124. See *Patterns*, pp. 7ff. Of course, we have already presented a partial analysis of the sacred-profane distinction in our discussion of Eliade's view of religion and the sacred.

What is important is that there is always something else, something other; that which is singularized is 'chosen' because it manifests the sacred. If a large rock is singled out, it is not simply because of its impressive natural dimensions, but rather because its imposing appearance reveals something transcendent: a permanence, a power, an absolute mode of being, which is different from the precariousness of human existence. If the medicine man is singled out, it is because his unusual accident or event is a 'sign' of something transcendent: he is a 'specialist of the sacred'; he has the capacity to transcend the human and profane, to have contact with and manipulate the sacred.

It is often difficult for the Historian of Religions to recognize hierophanies. We tend to see natural objects where our ancestors saw hierophanies. Eliade has observed that 'to the primitive, nature is never purely "natural" '. We may understand that the sky would reveal a sense of transcendence or infinity, but it often seems incomprehensible that a simple gesture, a normal physiological activity, or a dreary landscape would manifest the sacred. Yet we must be sensitive to the fact that all phenomena are potentially hierophanic.

We must get used to the idea of recognizing hierophanies everywhere, in every area of psychological, economic, spiritual and social life. Indeed, we cannot be sure that there is *anything* — object, movement, psychological function, being or even game — that has not at some time in human history been somewhere transformed into a hierophany. It is a very different matter to find out *why* that particular thing should have become a hierophany, or should have stopped being one at any given moment. But it is quite certain that anything man has ever handled, felt, come in contact with or loved *can* become a hierophany.[41]

40. *Patterns*, pp. 216–238; *The Myth of the Eternal Return*, p. 4; *Shamanism*, pp. 31–32 and *passim*.

41. *Patterns*, pp. 11, 38. In several contexts, Eliade has asserted that Judaeo-Christianity contributed greatly to the process by which we (modern, secular, Western, scientific) tend to see natural objects where 'archaic' religions saw hierophanies. The 'cosmic religiosity' of earlier religions was criticized: a rock was 'only' a rock and should not be worshipped. 'Emptied of every religious value or meaning, nature could become the "object" *par excellence* of scientific investigation.' 'The Sacred and the Modern Artist', *Criterion* 4, no. 2 (1965): 23.

At this point, we may note that Eliade's doctrine of hierophanies challenges the naturalistic interpretations of religious phenomena. Because we tend to see natural objects where *homo religiosus* saw hierophanies, there is the tendency to interpret the dialectic of the sacred as a 'natural' mode of manifestation. But to do this would be to fail to grasp the true intentionality of the sacred manifestation.

We must now examine the relationship which exists between the sacred and the profane as disclosed by the dialectic of hierophanies. This dialectical relationship has been the source of much confusion and misinterpretation.

The paradoxical relationship

Thomas J. J. Altizer seizes upon the point 'that the sacred is the opposite of the profane' as Eliade's 'cardinal principle' and the key to interpreting Eliade's phenomenological method. This opposition is taken to mean that the sacred and the profane are mutually exclusive or logically contradictory. From this 'cardinal principle', Altizer sees the key to Eliade's approach in terms of a 'negative dialectic': 'a single moment cannot be sacred and profane at once'. An understanding of religious myth, for example, is possible 'only through a negation of the language of the profane'. The 'meaning of the sacred is reached by inverting the reality created by modern man's profane choice'. In short, to observe the sacred one must totally negate the profane and vice versa.[42] Unfortunately, this interpretation destroys the dialectical complexity of the religious mode of manifestation and leads to an oversimplification and distortion of Eliade's phenomenological method.[43]

Eliade's religious data reveal that in the process of sacralization the sacred and the profane *coexist in a paradoxical relationship*. This process is the intention of the hierophany, an intention which constitutes the structure and lies at the foundation of the hierophany. A series of

42. Thomas J. J. Altizer, *Mircea Eliade and the Dialectic of the Sacred*, pp. 34, 39, 45, 65, and *passim*.

43. After completing this section, I came across a very similar criticism of Altizer's interpretation of Eliade's sacred–profane relationship in Ricketts's 'Mircea Eliade and the Death of God', *Religion in Life*; 43–48.

illustrations from Eliade will clarify this point.

'One must remember the dialectic of the sacred: any object whatever may paradoxically become a hierophany, a receptacle of the sacred, while still participating in its own cosmic environment.' 'One need only recall the dialectic of hierophany: an object becomes *sacred* while remaining just the same as it is.' The dialectic of the sacred consists of the fact that 'the sacred expresses itself through some thing other than itself', that 'in every case the sacred manifests itself limited and incarnate'. It is 'this paradox of incarnation which makes hierophanies possible at all'.[44]

In fact, this paradoxical coming-together of sacred and profane, being and non-being, absolute and relative, the eternal and the becoming, is what every hierophany, even the most elementary, reveals . . . every hierophany shows, makes manifest, the coexistence of contradictory essences: sacred and profane, spirit and matter, eternal and non-eternal, and so on. That the dialectic of hierophanies, of the manifestation of the sacred in material things, should be an object for even such complex theology as that of the Middle Ages seems to prove that it remains *the* cardinal problem of any religion. . . . In fact, what is paradoxical, what is beyond our understanding, is not that the sacred can be manifested in stones or in trees, but that it can be manifested at all, that it can thus become limited and relative.[45]

Thus we observe the paradoxical coexistence revealed by the dialectic of the sacred and the profane. What is paradoxical is that an ordinary, finite, historical thing, while remaining a natural thing, can at the same time manifest something which is not finite, not historical, not natural. What is paradoxical is that something transcendent, wholly other, infinite, transhistorical, limits itself by manifesting itself in some relative, finite, historical thing.

The evaluation and choice

Our religious data do not simply reveal a distinction between sacred and profane, as seen in their paradoxical coexistence in every

44. *Images and Symbols*, pp. 84, 178; *Patterns*, p. 26.
45. *Patterns*, pp. 29–30.

hierophany. The dialectic of hierophanies shows that *homo religiosus* is involved in an 'existential crisis': in experiencing a hierophany, he or she is called upon to *evaluate* the two orders of being and to make a *choice*. Charles Long describes this sense of evaluation in the following manner: 'The world of man exists as a limitation or qualification of his environment, and this qualification or limitation is at the same time a criticism. Man's world is an ordered world of meaning, but the organizing principle is interpreted as a revelation which comes from a source outside of his ordinary life. It is this source which is given (revealed) and (it) defines any future possibility of man's existence.'[46]

In experiencing the dialectic of hierophany, *homo religiosus* faces an 'existential crisis'; indeed, one's very existence is called into question. Because of the dichotomy of sacred and profane, as revealed in their paradoxical coexistence, distinction, differentiation, value, and even meaning are all introduced into one's existence.[47] In short, one dimension of being is seen as more significant, as 'wholly other' and 'powerful' and 'ultimate', as containing a surplus of meaning, as paradigmatic and normative in judging one's existence.

Eliade usually describes the person's choice and evaluation 'negatively'. The dialectic of hierophanies throws the realm of natural ordinary existence into sharp relief. After the 'rupture' of the sacred and the profane, the person evaluates her or his natural existence as a 'fall'. One feels separated from what is now evaluated as 'ultimate' and 'real'. One longs to transcend the 'natural' and 'historical' mode of being and to live permanently in the sacred.

The upshot of the above discussion seems to be the following. Through the dialectic of hierophanies, the profane is set off in sharp relief; *homo religiosus* 'chooses' the sacred and evaluates his or her 'ordinary' mode of existence negatively. At the same time, through

46. *Alpha*, pp. 10–11.
47. Eliade, *Myth and Reality*, p. 139; and G. Richard Welbon, 'Some Remarks on the Work of Mircea Eliade', *Acta Philosophica et Theologica* 2 (1964): 479. Langdon Gilkey, *Naming the Whirlwind: The Renewal of God-Language*, p. 293: 'if the sacred be the foundation of all of our profane life, then our relation to the sacred will determine the patterns of our behavior in every secular realm. For this reason, every religious symbol or myth entails "models" for our existence, patterns of sacrality by means of which man comprehends the forms of his human existence and so by which he patterns his life and that of his society.'

this evaluation and choice, the human being is given the possibility for meaningful judgments and creative human action and expression. The 'positive' religious value of the 'negative' evaluation of the profane, we would submit, is expressed in the intentionality toward meaningful communication with the sacred and toward religious action which now appears as a structure in the consciousness of *homo religiosus*.

At this point, a brief digression may be useful in clarifying one of the main sources of misconceptions in interpreting Eliade's phenomenology: most interpreters do not endeavor to understand Mircea Eliade on his own grounds. We may cite an example from our above discussion: *homo religiosus* evaluates his or her natural existence as a 'fall'.

Many interpreters have seized upon Eliade's personal doctrine of a 'fall' as being a pivotal notion in his thought. It is only because of Eliade's 'theological assumptions' that he considers modern secularization to be a 'fall'.[48] Eliade is a 'romantic' who believes that history is a 'fall' and who 'insists upon the reality of man's prefallen state'.[49]

The problem with these interpretations is that Altizer and Hamilton do not take Eliade seriously enough on his own grounds. They are theologians and criticize Eliade's theological position on a 'fall'. But Eliade at least purports to be a Historian of Religions; his claim is not that Mircea Eliade is committed to these diverse themes of a 'fall' but that *homo religiosus* has entertained such beliefs.

To give but one illustration, Eliade finds that 'the paradisiac myths' all speak of a 'paradisiac epoch' in which primordial beings enjoyed freedom, immortality, easy communication with the gods, etc. Unfortunately, they lost all of this because of 'the fall' — the primordial event which caused the 'rupture' of the sacred and the profane. These myths help *homo religiosus* to understand his or her present 'fallen' existence and express a 'nostalgia' for that 'prefallen'

48. See Kenneth Hamilton, '*Homo Religiosus* and Historical Faith', *Journal of Bible and Religion* 33, no. 3 (1965): 212, 214–215, 216. The following discussion would also apply to Eliade's point that 'from the Christian point of view' it could be said that modern nonreligion is equivalent to a new or second 'fall'. See *The Sacred*, p. 213; 'Archaic Myth and Historical Man', pp. 35–36.

49. See Altizer, *Mircea Eliade and the Dialectic of the Sacred*, pp. 84, 86, 88, 161; and Altizer, 'Mircea Eliade and the Recovery of the Sacred', *The Christian Scholar* 45, no. 4 (1962): 282–283. See Eliade, *Images and Symbols*, p. 173; *The Myth of the Eternal Return*, p. 162.

Paradise.[50] If history is a 'fall' for *homo religiosus*, it is because historical existence is seen as separated from and inferior to the 'transhistorical' (absolute, eternal, transcendent) realm of the sacred.

Summary

We may now summarize the structure of the process of sacralization which is revealed to us in the dialectic of hierophanies:

1. There is always the separation of the hierophanic object and the distinction between the sacred and the profane. From our earlier analysis, we recall that religion exists where the sacred-profane dichotomy has been made, and the sacred always entails some sense of transcendence.

2. This dichotomy is experienced in terms of a certain dialectical tension: the sacred and the profane coexist in a paradoxical relationship. What is paradoxical is that the sacred, which is transcendent (wholly other, ultimate, infinite, transhistorical), limits itself by incarnating itself in something profane (relative, finite, historical, natural). Or, we may express this paradoxical coexistence as follows: what is profane (finite, natural), while remaining a natural thing, at the same time manifests what is sacred (infinite, transcendent).

3. *Homo religiosus* does not simply distinguish the sacred and the profane, a distinction revealed through their paradoxical coexistence in every hierophany. Implied in the dialectic of the sacred is an evaluation and a choice. The sacred is experienced as powerful, ultimate, absolute, meaningful, paradigmatic, normative. It is in terms of the sacred that religious persons interpret their mode of being in the world and define the future possibilities of their existence.

FURTHER ANALYSIS OF THE SACRED MODALITY

Ambivalence in the religious experience

It is now possible to relate Eliade's analysis to several of the major concerns in earlier chapters. Our first common methodological point

50. *Myths, Dreams and Mysteries*, pp. 59 ff.

in Chapter 3 brought out the experiential basis of religion. Eliade has attempted to understand religion as a way that the human being is in the world; religion arises from existential crises and is understood as a mode of existence in the world. For *homo religiosus* the sacred 'is the category of *meaning* in the world. The *Sacred* is what is valid in the world, authentic, substantial, real, true, eternal. It is this and more. The *Sacred* is a dimension of being, a depth, or level, on which life is experienced.'[51] In our treatment of the dialectic of the sacred and the profane, we attempted to recreate the conditions for the sacred manifestation as experienced by *homo religiosus*.

In previous chapters, we have frequently elucidated a certain ambivalence in the religious experience, as exemplified by Marett's joining of taboo and mana in his minimum definition of religion or Otto's description of the numinous experience in terms of both the *tremendum* and the *fascinans*.

On the one hand, the religious experience is viewed in the most 'positive' terms. Mana, for example, characterizes whatever is 'real', efficacious, and creative. In addition, the religious experience is 'practical', soteriological. Thus we have found that the greatest hope of *homo religiosus* is to experience this 'ultimate reality' and attain salvation.

On the other hand, the religious experience is terrifying, dangerous, sometimes even fatal. A human being fears and is repelled by the religious; she or he conceives of it in terms of impurity, defilement, and death. To characterize a religious phenomenon as taboo is to signify that it is forbidden because any contact with it is extremely dangerous.

Eliade finds this same ambiguity of the sacred at the heart of the religious experience. He observes an ambivalence in the nature of the sacred and a corresponding ambiguity in the human reaction to the sacred. 'This ambivalence of the sacred is not only in the psychological order (in that it attracts or repels), but also in the order of values; the sacred is at once "sacred" and "defiled".' 'Man's ambivalent attitude towards the sacred, which at once attracts and repels him, is both

---

51. Ira Progoff, 'Culture and Being: Mircea Eliade's Studies in Religion', *International Journal of Parapsychology* 2 (1960): 53.

beneficent and dangerous, can be explained not only by the ambivalent nature of the sacred in itself, but also by man's natural reactions to this transcendent reality which attracts and terrifies him with equal intensity.'[52]

We recall that there is a difference in the order of being between the sacred and the profane: the sacred is transhuman, transhistorical, etc. That which is transcendent is taken as 'real', 'valid', eternal, authentic. *Homo religiosus* is drawn to the sacred reality, viewing it as the source and meaning of one's existence and as the hope of salvation.

However, we may recognize a quite different valuation of the sacred. How does one regard that which is not 'ordinary', not 'historical' or 'natural', not of the 'human' world of experience? Contact with something of a different order of being might produce 'an upheaval at the ontological level' which could prove disastrous. Should we not fear and attempt to avoid something absolutely powerful? Such a 'transhuman' power would seem terrifying and dangerous; it might result in defilement and pollution rather than sanctity and purity, destruction and death rather than salvation and immortality.

Awareness of this ambiguity of the sacred is often of great assistance in interpreting the religious. For instance, it helps us to understand the function and prestige of the 'experts' in religious matters. Consider the role of shamans as psychopomps: by means of their ecstatic experience, they transport souls to the other world.[53] The ambivalence of the sacred helps us to understand such matters as why it is only the 'specialist' who can undertake these trips, why the ecstatic journeys are so frequently fraught with perilous obstacles, and why it is so important for the society that the shaman succeeds as psychopomp.

G. Richard Welbon elucidates an important implication of this ambivalence of the sacred.

. . . if man really regarded the profane as non-being and his own existence is conditional — he surely would have 'nothing to lose' in deciding for the sacred.

The hesitation, the ambivalence can mean that the sacred is so wondrous that man is confused. And it can also mean that the

---

52. *Patterns*, pp. 14–15, 460.
53. *Shamanism*, pp. 182 ff., 205 ff., and *passim*.

'nothing' of man is worth something after all. Both these possibilities are true, the latter being more interesting in this context. There is something worse than the profane mode of existence; for it is possible that man may lose any and all his existential dimensions by trying to ascend to the sacred level. Apparently this fear is more immediate than the opposing desire.[54]

Does this evaluation of the profane contradict many of Eliade's descriptions? In various contexts, Eliade has characterized the profane as totally lacking reality, as being meaningless.

It seems that Welbon's interpretation is valuable but somewhat misleading. It must be qualified. The dialectic of hierophanies discloses that the human being faces an extreme existential crisis and is called upon to evaluate the two orders of being. Now if the profane were not 'worth something after all', there certainly would be no crisis and need to evaluate. Also, in terms of our rejection of Altizer's analysis of the dialectic of the sacred, it is clear that the profane has value: one could not realize the sacred without the profane through which it is revealed.

We would submit that Eliade, when he describes the profane as meaningless or nonbeing, is using a religious scale, is describing the profane *qua* profane,[55] and is presenting the view of *homo religiosus after* he or she has evaluated and chosen the sacred, *after* one has resolved his or her existential crisis. Our 'hesitation' does imply that the profane is worth something; but after we have chosen the sacred and evaluated the profane in terms of the sacred, then the profane is seen as meaningless and lacking reality.[56]

---

54. G. Richard Welbon, 'Some Remarks on the Work of Mircea Eliade', p. 488. Actually, Eliade makes a similar point (*Patterns*, pp. 17–18) when he describes one 'side' of this ambivalence in terms of one's fear that 'he may lose it [his own reality] completely if he is totally lifted to a plane of being higher than his natural profane state'.

55. We have written 'profane *qua* profane' because the profane does have meaning and value for *homo religiosus*, but only insofar as it reveals the sacred.

56. In some contexts, *homo religiosus* does not seem to describe that which is not sacred as 'nonbeing' or 'unreal'. For example, consider the case of Śankara Vedānta, which is particularly relevant since this school is most frequently criticized for its world-denying view. Advaita, it is claimed, regards the world as *māyā*, as mere 'illusion' and 'unreal'. What Advaita Vedānta in fact maintains is that the illusory

No purely religious phenomena and no self-sufficient approach

Eliade's 'first hermeneutic principle' necessitated a religious perspective which was commensurate with the specificity, complexity, and totality of the religious phenomena. To reduce the religious to a nonreligious scale is to negate the intentionality of the sacred manifestation.

But Mircea Eliade does not intend as a methodological implication of this principle of the irreducibility of the sacred a position which maintains that there are 'purely' religious phenomena.

> . . . a religious phenomenon cannot be understood outside of its 'history,' that is, outside of its cultural and socioeconomic contexts. There is no such thing outside of history as a 'pure' religious datum. For there is no such thing as a human datum that is not at the same time a historical datum. Every religious experience is expressed and transmitted in a particular historical context. But admitting the historicity of religious experiences does not imply that they are reducible to nonreligious forms of behavior. Stating that a religious datum is always a historical datum does not mean that it is reducible to a nonreligious history — for example, to an economic, social, or political history.[57]

By insisting on the irreducible nature of his approach, Eliade does not mean that *Religionswissenschaft* is a self-sufficient discipline. In his herculean effort at a phenomenological synthesis which can do justice to all dimensions of the sacred, Eliade depends heavily upon all the approaches we have previously considered.

To give some idea of the scope and diversity of Eliade's synthesis, we might simply enumerate a few of the perspectives which he integrates in his monumental work, *Shamanism: Archaic Techniques of Ecstasy*. The psychology of religion draws attention to the psychic

---

appearance is certainly not *sat* (being), but neither is it *asat* (nonbeing). The world of *māyā* is a kind of 'third category': it is 'indeterminable' (*anirvacanīya*), capable of being defined neither as 'real' nor as 'unreal'. Nevertheless, our main point still seems valid. The profane (*māyā*), even in those contexts in which it is not regarded in such terms as 'unreal' or 'nonbeing', has meaning and value for *homo religiosus* only to the extent that is reveals the sacred (*Brahman*).

57. 'Comparative Religion: Its Past and Future', pp. 250–251. See *Patterns*, p. xiii; 'History of Religions and a New Humanism', p. 6.

conditions of shamanism, especially the shaman's state of ecstasy. The psychological approaches help Eliade to understand his dialectic of hierophanies by describing the crisis within the psyche which gives rise to the shamanic vocation. Shamanism is not only a personal psychological experience but is also a societal institution. Consequently, Eliade looks to the sociology of religion in order to understand such topics as the social prestige of the shaman, his 'essential role in the defense of the psychic integrity of the community', etc. The ethnologist situates 'the shaman in his cultural milieu'. He or she establishes the 'history' of the constituent elements of shamanism and traces 'the circulation of the particular motif in time and space'. It is largely on the basis of ethnological studies that Eliade can conclude that Asiatic and Siberian shamanism is not a creation of southern Indian contributions. Eliade often uses the historico-ethnological perspective to distinguish specific shamanic characteristics from aspects of shamanism which either are later influences from other religious phenomena or are found in many phenomena and are not peculiar to shamanism.[58]

This dependence upon the contributions of other approaches is not meant to deny the unique perspective of *Religionswissenschaft*.

> The latter's [History of Religions'] mission is to integrate the results of ethnology, psychology, and sociology. Yet in doing so, it will not renounce its own method of investigation or the viewpoint that specifically defines it. . . . In the last analysis, it is for the historian of religions [Historian of Religions] to synthesize all the studies of particular aspects of shamanism and to present a comprehensive view which shall be at once a morphology and a history of this complex religious phenomenon.[59]

What Eliade maintains is that unless his hermeneutics can integrate the

---

58. *Shamanism*, pp. xi–xiii, 495 ff., 509; *Yoga*, pp. 318 ff.

59. *Shamanism*, p. xiii. We could go on to indicate that almost all of the approaches we have studied are utilized by Eliade in his investigation of shamanism. For example, he appeals to the evidence of philology to establish that 'the idea of "mystical heat" ("magical heat") is not an exclusive possession of shamanism; it belongs to magic in general.' *Shamanism*, pp. 474–477. Cf. *Rites and Symbols of Initiation*, pp. 85–87; *Myths, Dreams and Mysteries*, pp. 146–149; *The Forge and the Crucible*, pp. 79–86; *Yoga*, pp. 106–108, 330–334.

contributions of other approaches within his own unique approach, it will be guilty of the same type of reductionism of past approaches which did not realize that the sacred included, but was not exhaused by, the sociological, psychological, or some other perspective. At the same time Eliade knows that the scale makes the difference: he insists upon a specifically religious interpretation of his data. Therefore, Mircea Eliade's phenomenological approach claims to be autonomous but not self-sufficient.

In terms of our previous discussion of reductionism and the perspectival nature of all approaches, we may offer an observation about Eliade's task of synthesis and integration. In his integration of the contributions of other approaches, if Eliade thinks that he is doing justice to the ethnologist *qua* ethnologist or the Freudian *qua* Freudian, then he is mistaken. He presents us with a phenomenological synthesis. He selects those aspects of the contributions of various specialized approaches which are relevant to his phenomenological concerns; and in integrating the data within his own unique approach, he necessarily fails to respect the perspectival nature, the specific assumptions, and the self-imposed limitations of the ethnological, functionalist, psychological, sociological, and other particular approaches.[60]

This is similar to a central task in the history of philosophy. Philosophers examine the assumptions and contributions of various specialized approaches in order to determine whether they can be integrated within a broad philosophical framework. What do such findings tell us about the meaning of life and the nature of human existence, about the nature of the self, about questions of truth and morality, etc.? In realizing some philosophical synthesis, the philosopher goes beyond the perspectival limitations of the specialized approaches. Indeed, in Chapter 7, we shall submit that Mircea Eliade often raises significant philosophical questions, which involve ontological moves and take him beyond the perspectival limitations of the phenomenology and History of Religions.

60. Cf. Robert D. Baird, *Category Formation and the History of Religions*, pp. 30–31.

Religion as an 'opening'

We have seen that Eliade believes that the principal function of religion is to maintain an 'opening' toward a superhuman or transcendent world. 'On the one hand, the sacred is, supremely, the *other* than man — the transpersonal, the transcendent — and, on the other hand, the sacred is the exemplary in the sense that it establishes patterns to be followed: by being transcendent and exemplary it compels the religious man to come out of personal situations, to surpass the contingent and the particular and to comply with general values, with the universal.'[61]

Now we may understand how the dialectic of hierophanies helps to maintain this 'opening'. By means of this process of sacralization, the 'closed' profane world is 'burst open'. A natural object, such as a tree, while remaining a tree reveals something 'other'. 'No tree or plant is ever sacred simply as a tree or plant; they become so because they *share* in a transcendent reality, they become so because they *signify* that transcendent reality. By being consecrated, the individual, "profane" plant species is transubstantiated; in the dialectic of the sacred a part (a tree, a plant) has the value of the whole (the cosmos, life), a profane thing becomes a hierophany.'[62]

For example, a common ritual in shamanism is that of climbing a tree in which a certain number of notches have been cut. It is only because the 'natural' tree has the value of 'World Tree', the notches signifying the various heavens, that we can interpret the climbing of a particular natural tree as the celestial ascent of the shaman, an ecstatic journey beyond the heavens.[63] Without this sense of religious 'opening', the meaning of the shaman's experience of the sacred remains unintelligible.

If the process of sacralization depended entirely on the 'direct' consecration by hierophanies, the scope of religious phenomena

---

61. *Myths, Dreams and Mysteries*, p. 18. See *The Quest*, p. ii. In chapter 7, we shall suggest that this assertion that religion 'opens' us to the general and the universal has crucial methodological import for Eliade's phenomenology. It is largely on the basis of such methodological criteria as 'the most general' and 'the universal' that Eliade attempts to distinguish and to evaluate descriptively certain religious manifestations as 'elevated', 'mature', 'highest', and 'deepest'.

62. *Patterns*, p. 324.

63. *Shamanism*, pp. 117–127 and *passim*.

would be severely restricted. However, from the above illustration of celestial ascent, we may already detect the importance of symbolism in the process of sacralization. In Chapter 5, we shall see the primary role of symbolism in carrying further the dialectic of the sacred: through symbolism the profane is 'burst open' so that it reveals something 'other'.

TRANSITION

Our transition to Chapter 5 may be expressed in the following manner by David Rasmussen:

> It is one thing to construct an apparatus wherein the sacred may be perceived adequately; it is another to move from levels of perception to those of understanding. I regard Eliade's chief hermeneutic achievement as the movement from an initial acknowledgment of the sacred in its dialectical complexity and distinctive intentional modality to an understanding of its meaning. The problem is epistemological; its solution is structural.
>
> The doctrine of the irreducibility of the sacred and the dialectic of the sacred and the profane establish the conditions for the appearance of the sacred. They in no way provide the meaning of a particular sacred phenomenon.[64]

The above transition is helpful so long as we guard against a certain interpretation it seems to suggest. These are not two distinct temporal stages in Eliade's phenomenology: first he sets up the hermeneutical framework for 'perceiving' the religious phenomenon (Chapter 4); then his structural hermeneutics allows him to understand the meaning of that religious phenomenon (Chapter 5).

As we wrote in the beginning of this chapter, our order of analysis should not be interpreted as a temporal order in Mircea Eliade's methodology. Without the methodological framework we are about to analyze, Eliade could not possibly realize the hermeneutical principles we have just elucidated. Without his structuralism which is

---

64. Rasmussen, p. 141.

grounded in his interpretation of religious symbolism, the phenomenologist could not 'perceive' the religious phenomenon in its dialectical complexity. In short, all of the hermeneutical principles must be seen as functioning together in Eliade's methodology.

Interpreting the Meaning of Religious Phenomena

Symbolism and Religion

Now that we have analyzed the dialectic of the sacred and the profane, we may turn to the second of the key methodological notions in Eliade's phenomenological approach: the symbolism[1] or system of symbolic structures which provides the hermeneutical framework in terms of which Eliade interprets the meaning of the religious data.

There are other 'key notions' in Eliade's phenomenological approach, such as archetypes, images, patterns, function, and 'ideology'.[2] Our justification for focusing on symbolism is the following: Mircea Eliade is usually able to identify these other 'key notions' because there is a theoretical framework of symbolic structures underlying his hermeneutical approach. Thus, if Eliade is able to identify certain archetypes and patterns, this is primarily because he detects recurring, essential symbolic structures.

At the end of Chapter 4, we suggested a transition to our present discussion of religious symbolism. After elucidating the structure of the dialectic of hierophanies, we realized that the extent of the hierophanic process would be severely limited if all sacralization depended on 'direct' hierophanies. It was suggested that symbolism extends this process of sacralization by 'bursting open' the profane so that it reveals something other. Let us now begin to document this claim.

1. In reporting on the appearance of *Mephistopheles and the Androgyne* (also published under the title *The Two and the One*), *Time* magazine (February 11, 1966: pp. 68, 70) entitled its article 'Scientist of Symbols' and described Mircea Eliade as 'probably the world's foremost living interpreter of spiritual myths and symbolism'.
2. In some writings, Eliade has emphasized the methodological importance of identifying the 'center' of a religion: 'every religion has a "center," in other words, a central conception which informs the entire corpus of myths, rituals, and beliefs'; 'that is, a characteristic understanding of the sacred'. See 'South American High Gods: Part I', *History of Religions* 8, no. 4 (1969): 338–339; *The Quest*, pp. 10–11.

Eliade asserts that symbolism has played an important part 'in the magico-religious experience of mankind. . . . primarily because it [the symbol] is able to carry on the process of hierophanization and particularly because, on occasions, it is *itself* a hierophany — it itself reveals a sacred or cosmological reality which no other manifestation is capable of revealing'.[3] Symbolism 'carries further the dialectic of hierophanies by transforming things into *something other* than what they appear to profane experience to be'.[4]

To indicate the extent to which symbolism can extend the process of sacralization, consider what would appear to be an extremely 'limited' hierophany: a specific meteorite, such as the Ka'aba of Mecca. The meteorite has probably been experienced as a hierophany because of its celestial origins. In terms of the dialectic of the sacred, we can understand why the meteorite would be experienced as a sacred stone: while remaining a natural object, it has been singularized by *homo religiosus* because it reveals something 'beyond' the profane world, something transcendent.

Now consider one of many ways that symbolism can carry further this process of hierophanization.[5] In falling from the sky, the meteorite 'made a hole in it, and it was through this hole that a communication could be effected between heaven and earth. Through it passed the *Axis Mundi.*' The stone thus becomes a symbol for the 'center of the world', and the 'symbolism of the center' introduces countless possibilities for hierophanization. Because the meteorite is now seen as symbolizing a 'center', a sacred place where heaven, earth, and hell are

3. *Patterns*, pp. 446–447. On p. 448, Eliade states that 'the authentic nature and function of symbols can best be grasped by a closer study of symbols as a prolongation of hierophanies and an autonomous form of revelation'. This latter point, concerning the symbols as an *autonomous* form of sacred revelation, will be discussed later in this chapter.

4. *Ibid.*, p. 452. On p. 445, Eliade describes the symbol's 'function' as follows: 'it is to transform a thing or an action into *something other* than that thing or action appears to be in the eyes of profane experience.'

5. There are many obvious symbolic extensions of sacralization relevant to this hierophany, such as the numerous hierophanic possibilities relating to stone symbolism or to sky symbolism. Many of the symbolic extensions are not obvious. For example, in falling from the sky, the meteorite 'cleaved' the earth. This sacred stone (of 'heavenly, and hence masculine, essence') was experienced by some religious persons as symbolizing the sacred union between heaven and earth. See *The Forge and the Crucible*, pp. 20–21 and *passim*.

connected along one axis, an act (such as a 'ritual of ascension') taking place at this site will be seen as sacralized.[6]

From one perspective, the human being can be defined as *homo symbolicus*.[7] This conception of the human being is especially relevant to *homo religiosus* because religious facts are symbolic in nature.

> Since man is a *homo symbolicus*, and all his activities involve symbolism, it follows that all religious facts have a symbolic character. This is certainly true if we realize that every religious act and every cult aims at a meta-empirical reality. When a tree becomes a cult object, it is not as a *tree* that it is venerated, but as a *hierophany*, that is, a manifestation of the sacred. And every religious act, by the simple fact that it is *religious*, is endowed with a meaning which, in the last instance, is 'symbolic,' since it refers to supernatural values or beings.[8]

If there is one point that all writers on symbolism seem to accept, it is that the symbol 'points beyond' itself. As Paul Tillich states, 'First and most fundamental is the character of all symbols to point beyond themselves.' The symbol has a 'figurative quality'; it is an indirect means of communicating that which is not the 'usual', 'ordinary', 'literal' meaning.[9]

We recall that religion is always concerned with the sacred, that religious expressions always refer to 'something' transcendent, trans-

6. See *Patterns*, p. 227; *The Myth of the Eternal Return*, pp. 12–17; and 'Symbolism of the "Centre" ', *Images and Symbols*, pp. 27–56.

7. In *An Essay on Man*, p. 26, Ernst Cassirer writes that 'Reason is a very inadequate term with which to comprehend the forms of man's cultural life in all their richness and variety. But all these forms are symbolic forms. Hence, instead of defining man as an *animal rationale*, we should define him as an *animal symbolicum*.'

8. 'Methodological Remarks', p. 95. See *Mephistopheles and the Androgyne*, p. 199.

9. Paul Tillich, 'The Meaning and Justification of Religious Symbols', *Religious Experience and Truth*, ed. Sidney Hook, p. 4; and Paul Tillich, 'The Religious Symbol', *Religious Experience and Truth*, p. 301. See Paul Ricœur's analysis of the 'Criteriology of Symbols', *The Symbolism of Evil*, pp. 10–18. Perhaps the most illuminating aspect of Ricœur's 'direct eidetic analysis' is his analysis of the symbol's quality of 'pointing beyond' in terms of a 'double intentionality': a 'first, literal, obvious meaning itself points analogically to a second meaning which is not given otherwise than in it'. Ricœur then attempts to 'understand the analogical bond between the literal meaning and the symbolic meaning'. It seems that Eliade could accept Ricœur's analysis and that Eliade's phenomenology requires a more rigorous intentional analysis of this sort.

human, transhistorical. In nonreligious areas, one might maintain that we sometimes do not need to use a symbolic expression; this depends on the nature of the meaning we are attempting to communicate. However, *homo religiosus* has no such choice. Because of the nature of the sacred, and hence of all religious phenomena, he or she is forced to use symbolic expressions which 'point beyond' themselves and communicate meanings which are not direct, literal, ordinary.[10]

Thus far we have emphasized the need for symbolism arising from the fact that the *referent* of the religious expression is experienced as something transcendent. But how is it possible for us to relate to something 'other' than the human and natural? Here we must stress the *specificity* of the religious symbol, which enables it to serve as a type of *bridge*: the symbol uses specific, concrete, 'natural' phenomena in its expression and enables *homo religiosus* to relate that which is 'other' to his or her specific existential situation. Symbols 'render the reality of the other accessible and open to participation and communion'. 'The religious symbol because of its specificity takes into itself those realities which are a part of the religious man's local environment, but in the symbolic ordering the local ingredients take on meanings which are more than natural.'[11]

We shall conclude this initial discussion of religion and symbolism by citing a problem Eliade must encounter. As is well known, in addition to asserting that symbols 'point beyond' themselves, Paul Tillich claimed that symbols 'participate in the reality of that which they represent'. 'While the sign bears no necessary relation to that to which it points, the symbol participates in the reality of that for which it stands . . . the religious symbol, the symbol which points to the divine, can be a true symbol only if it participates in the power of the divine to which it points.'[12] This notion of 'participating in' has

10. Winston King, *Introduction to Religion: A Phenomenological Approach*, p. 134: '. . . precisely because man in religion seeks contact with that Other, or feels himself to be mysteriously apprehended by that invisible Otherness in the events and visibilities of his daily life, he is driven to use the symbolic to express meanings and aspirations not expressible in ordinary language.'

11. Long, *Alpha*, pp. 8, 10. See John E. Smith, *Reason and God*, p. 229. We shall return to this point when we discuss the *'existential value'* of the symbol.

12. Paul Tillich, *Systematic Theology*, Vol. I, p. 239; Tillich, 'The Meaning and Justification of Religious Symbols', p. 4.

been the source of much confusion and criticism of Tillich. One of the difficulties is that Tillich sometimes seems to go beyond a description of a psychological, subjective, personal experience of *homo religiosus*; at times he appears to claim that the religious symbol does in fact pierce through to the ultimate so that there is a realization of that ultimate reality.

In Chapter 4, we saw that Mircea Eliade does not intend to make this sort of normative claim. As a phenomenologist of religion, he wishes to avoid any metaphysical judgment as to whether *homo religiosus* does or does not in fact realize a transcendent reality. At the same time, we would submit that Eliade does not intend his descriptive analyses of religious meaning to be confined to a psychological account of certain subjective representations. To go beyond this psychological and subjective dimension and yet avoid uncritical normative judgments requires an objective hermeneutical framework in terms of which Eliade can describe meanings and make descriptive evaluations.

The key to understanding this hermeneutical framework lies in Eliade's view of the nature and function of religious symbolism. If Eliade can 'decipher in a religious fact the existential situation that made it possible', it is primarily because there is a theoretical framework underlying his hermeneutics. And this theoretical framework consists for the most part of objective systems of religious symbols.

SYMBOLISM AND STRUCTURALISM

We recall that Mircea Eliade's phenomenological *epoché* is directed against all forms of reductionism. By suspending all of his interpretations about what is 'real', the phenomenologist attempts sympathetically to reenact the experiences of *homo religiosus* and to describe the meaning of the religious phenomena.

Such a 'bracketing' by itself does not suffice to provide Eliade with insight into the fundamental structures and meanings of religious experience.[13] We saw that Franz Boas and other 'specialists' insisted on

13. Of course, in chapter 4, we did uncover certain essential religious structures. However, we must remember that Eliade could not possibly have arrived at those

cultural pluralism and relativity and were reluctant to allow for 'common structures'. Thus, a respect for the irreducibility of our data and an attempt to reenact the experience of the other might very well lead to the conclusion that there is an unlimited plurality of religious 'life-worlds', each having structures highly individualized and varying according to time and place.

If we are to understand how Mircea Eliade attempts to gain insight into the essential meanings of religious experience, we must now elucidate the structuralistic nature of his phenomenological approach. We may begin by summarizing David Rasmussen's interpretation.

Rasmussen submits that Eliade makes 'two claims' which allow the 'transition' from 'perceiving' the appearance of the sacred to understanding its meaning. First, Eliade 'suggests that phenomena of sacred manifestation will tend toward archetype', and by 'archetype' he means 'the initial structure of the sacred' and not the 'Jungian definition of archetype as the collective unconscious'. Second, Eliade 'suggests that phenomena of a given type or structure will tend toward system'. The 'initial structure tends toward a larger context of structural associations'.[14]

It does not seem that Rasmussen is justified in this interpretation of 'archetype' as 'initial structure of the sacred'. As we shall analyze in Chapter 7, Eliade is somewhat ambiguous, and there are two primary meanings of archetype found in his writings. In the 'Preface' to *Cosmos and History*, Eliade defines 'archetype' as 'exemplary model' or 'paradigm' and explicitly distinguishes this from the Jungian meaning. This is Eliade's main sense of archetype. However, in a few of his works, he uses the term in a manner quite similar to Jung's concept. As we shall see, this ambiguity is most significant, because each meaning of archetype has radically different methodological consequences for Eliade's phenomenology.[15]

---

results if his methodology were based solely upon the hermeneutic principles previously elucidated. All of those methodological conclusions, including the very possibility of some sort of phenomenological *epoché*, only make sense when seen as functioning together with the additional hermeneutical principles and framework which we are about to formulate.

14. Rasmussen, 'Mircea Eliade: Structural Hermeneutics and Philosophy', pp. 141–142.

15. *Cosmos and History*, pp. viii–ix. *Cosmos and History* is the same as *The Myth of the*

Morphological analysis is Eliade's 'hermeneutic alternative' to replace the 'historical-evolutionary hypothesis' we have previously considered. Through morphological analysis and classification, he attempts 'to separate those phenomena which have structural similarities from those which do not'. Rasmussen turns to structural linguistics and cites the diachronic-synchronic distinction found in Ferdinand de Saussure's *Course in General Linguistics* as providing the 'analogy which clarifies best a hermeneutic grounded in structuralism'. He submits that 'Eliade has asked the structural question regarding the place of a religious phenomenon within a total synchronic system. This leads to the basic judgment that religious phenomena tend toward system. This tendency is the intentional mode of every particular sacred manifestation. On this assumption morphological analysis is held to be necessary; its consequence is the transition from appearance to understanding.'

Rasmussen concludes that Mircea Eliade has a distinctive 'phenomenological procedure' which is grounded in structuralism: 'Understanding does not occur by the reconstruction of a particular phenomenon, but rather by the reintegration of that phenomenon within its system of associations through the use of morphology and structuralism.'[16]

Professor Rasmussen's interpretation of Eliade's methodology is basically correct, although initially it may not seem very convincing to some of Eliade's interpreters. What needs to be added and developed is the thesis that such a phenomenological approach has considerable support because of the very nature of religious phenomena, especially *religious symbolism*; such a procedure is not arbitrarily superimposed on

---

Eternal Return, except for the addition of the 'Preface to the Torchbook Edition'. Interesting interpretations of Eliade's concept of archetypes include the previously cited 'The Nature and Extent of Eliade's "Jungianism" ', by Ricketts; Wilson M. Hudson, 'Eliade's Contribution to the Study of Myth', *Tire Shrinker to Dragster*, p. 237; Ira Progoff, 'The Man Who Transforms Consciousness', *Eranos-Jahrbuch 1966*, Band 35 (1967): 126–130, 133. Progoff not only distinguishes Eliade's conception of archetypes from Jung's but also shows the similarity between Eliade's conception and Tillich's 'Method of Correlation'.

16. Rasmussen, p. 143. Cf. the section entitled 'Synchronicity' (pp. 104–106) in Eliade's 'The Sacred in the Secular World'.

the data but is largely derived from the nature of structural systems of religious symbols.

If Eliade finds this tendency toward system, toward systems of associations, this is primarily because of 'the function of symbols': the 'function of unification' of different zones and levels of experience, of enabling 'isolated fragments' to 'become part of a whole system'. His morphological analysis reveals that 'the various meanings of a symbol are linked together, interconnected in a system, as it were', and Eliade reserves the term 'symbolism' for such a 'structurally coherent ensemble'.[17] What Eliade finds is that

> we are faced with, respectively, a sky symbolism, or a symbolism of earth, of vegetation, of sun, of space, of time, and so on. We have good cause to look upon these various symbolisms as autonomous 'systems' in that they manifest more clearly, more fully, and with greater coherence what the hierophanies manifest in an individual, local and successive fashion. And I have tried, whenever the evidence in question allowed of it, to interpret a given hierophany in the light of its proper symbolism so as to discover its deepest significance.[18]

If understanding occurs when the phenomenon is 'reintegrated' into 'its systems of associations', this is possible because Mircea Eliade's hermeneutics is grounded in 'autonomous', 'coherent', 'universal' systems of symbolic associations.

Various interpreters, such as Edmund Leach, have criticized Eliade for emphasizing the individual symbol and not the structural relations between symbols.[19] Eliade is certainly inconsistent on this matter. However, if one considers all of Eliade's writings, it becomes clear that what is most important in his phenomenological approach is not the particular symbol but the structure of the whole symbolism; that the phenomenologist cannot grasp the meaning of the specific symbol

17. *Patterns*, pp. 451–453; *Images and Symbols*, p. 163; 'Methodological Remarks', p. 96. These cryptic remarks and the immediately ensuing observations will be analyzed in some detail either later in this chapter or in chapters 6 and 7.

18. *Patterns*, pp. 449–450.

19. See Edmund Leach, 'Sermons by a Man on a Ladder', *New York Review of Books*, October 20, 1966, pp. 30–31.

unless he or she sees the particular as one of many possible 'valorizations' of the structural system.[20]

According to Eliade, the symbol arises as a 'creation of the psyche', is constituted 'as the result of existential tensions', and must be regarded as an 'autonomous mode of cognition'. 'The phenomena of nature are freely transformed by the psyche in "an autonomous act of creation" into symbols of the power and holiness they reveal to the beholder.[21]

Eliade's primary concern is with determining how religious symbols function and what they reveal. In this regard he makes the following crucial assertions: symbolic thought is an autonomous mode of cognition which has its own structure; symbols have their own 'logic' and 'fit together' to make up coherent structural systems; every coherent symbolism is universal; the symbolic system will preserve its structure regardless of whether it is understood by the person who uses it.[22]

In order to understand some of the above assertions, we shall now examine a specific illustration: the snake or serpent as lunar symbols. Snake symbolism will be considered as one possible 'valorization' of a more comprehensive lunar symbolism. Then we shall elucidate various aspects of religious symbolism in general.

AN ILLUSTRATION: THE SNAKE AND LUNAR SYMBOLISM

Lunar symbolism, while being extremely complex, is one of those symbolisms most easily translatable into 'rational' terms. Hence, the general reader may find the following less 'mystifying' than an analysis of a different symbolism with a less 'rational' structure or

20. Cf. *Images and Symbols*, pp. 163–164: 'But it is not by "placing" a symbol in its own history that we can resolve the essential problem — namely, to know what is revealed to us, not by any "particular version" of a symbol but by the *whole* of a symbolism.' Eliade goes on to claim that the contradictions between particular versions of a symbol are usually 'resolved as soon as we consider the symbolism as a whole and discern its structure'.

21. *Images and Symbols*, pp. 9, 177; 'Methodological Remarks', p. 105; Luyster, 'The Study of Myth: Two Approaches', p. 235.

22. For example, see *Patterns*, p. 450; *Images and Symbols*, p. 168.

meaning. Our example of the snake or serpent as one possible valorization of lunar symbolism may prove especially interesting because Eliade's interpretation seems highly controversial. It is certainly not obvious that one ought to interpret snake or serpent symbols within a framework of lunar symbolism. Our purpose is not to defend Eliade's analysis — he probably overemphasizes the moon-snake relationship — but only to give some insight into the nature of his phenomenological approach.

The moon was a source of profound meaning for *homo religiosus*.[23] Unlike the sun with its sense of unchangeability, the moon is 'subject to the universal law of becoming, of birth and death'. But the moon's 'death' is never final; it is always 'reborn'. *Homo religiosus* 'intuitively perceived the moon's law of periodic change', 'life repeating itself rhythmically'. Lunar symbolism expresses the many valorizations deciphered in the moon's rhythms. Through lunar symbolism, *homo religiosus* was able to relate apparently unrelated phenomena from diverse 'spheres' which fell under the 'law of recurring cycles: water, rain, plant life, fertility'.

'Certain animals became symbols or even "presences" of the moon because their shape or their behaviour is reminiscent of the moon's.' 'The snake, because it appears and disappears, and because it has as many coils as the moon has days (this legend is also preserved in Greek Tradition); or because it is "the husband of all women," or because it sloughs its skin (that is to say, is periodically reborn, is "immortal"), and so on. The symbolism of the snake is somewhat confusing, but all the symbols are directed to the same central idea: it is immortal because it is continually reborn, and therefore it is a moon "force," and as such can bestow fecundity, knowledge (that is, prophecy) and even immortality.'[24]

Mircea Eliade now attempts to justify such an interpretation by providing us with numerous myths and symbols involving snakes or serpents, utilizing data which reveal their character as a lunar animal. We shall select two main types of data: the snake and erotic symbolism

23. The following introductory remarks about lunar symbolism are summarized from *The Sacred*, pp. 156–157, and *Patterns*, pp. 154–157.
24. *Patterns*, p. 164; Aristotle, *Historia Animalium* 2. 12; Pliny, *Historia Naturalis* 11. 82.

and the snake and initiatory symbolism. Each can be seen as a possible alternative to Eliade's lunar interpretation.

Alternatives: erotic and initiatory symbolism

The snake or serpent is often connected with women and fecundity.[25] Data from throughout the world illustrate the beliefs that snakes are the first object of sexual contact for women, are the cause of the menstrual cycle, copulate with women, and produce children.

The 'phallic character' of the snake is obvious, but Eliade claims that this phallic character 'far from excluding its [the snake's] connection with the moon, only confirms it'. He submits that the fundamental intuition is that of 'the moon as source of living reality and basis of all fertility and periodic regeneration'. 'There are a great many different women–snake relationships, but none of them can be fully explained by any purely erotic symbolism. The snake has a variety of meanings, and I think we must hold its "regeneration" to be one of the most important.'[26]

Let us examine why Mircea Eliade would consider an interpretation of the symbolism of snakes, which is based upon their phallic and erotic character, to be an unjustified reduction. The following analysis is in line with Eliade's hermeneutical orientation and helps to illuminate his phenomenological approach.

Our data reveal that not all snake symbolism has a special phallic structure. In analyzing an extant Australian secret cult, Kunapipi, Eliade describes the ritual swallowing by the snake as an initiatory pattern of return to the womb. In this context the snake is often described as female. Through the ritual swallowing by the snake, there is the idea of a new birth, of a complete regeneration of the initiate; but this is not because of the phallic character of the snake, but because of the initiate's return to the primordial Great Mother's womb, his gestation and birth by the Great Mother.[27]

25. The following illustrations are taken from *Patterns*, pp. 165–169. Eliade also provides examples illustrating the role of the moon as the source of fertility and as governing the menstrual cycle. These data strengthen the conclusion he will reach concerning the snake and lunar symbolism relationship.

26. *Ibid.*, p. 168.

27. *Rites and Symbols of Initiation*, pp. 47–51. See R. M. Berndt, *Kunapipi* (Mel-

In describing the Kunapipi and other similar Australian secret cults, Eliade indicates the 'sexual ambivalence' of the mythical snake and submits that 'these variations and apparent contradictions' probably 'point to an original bisexuality of the Snake'. One illustration is of the Rainbow Serpent, Angamunggi, who is described as an 'All-Father', but it is also 'suggested that he had a womb'.[28]

Eliade interprets this ambivalence and bisexuality as conforming to a familiar religious phenomenon: a Supreme Being becomes a 'totality' by uniting 'the opposites'. Thus, the mythical snake would not be satisfied with a completely 'phallic character' but has attempted to embrace within its symbolism both masculine and feminine structures and meanings.

If all snake symbolism cannot be reduced to a specific phallic structure, perhaps a more comprehensive erotic and sexual interpretation will suffice. We must recognize that when *homo religiosus* experiences phenomena in terms of such structures as 'bisexuality', he or she intends much more than the modern secular person understands by such structures. In *Mephistopheles and the Androgyne*, Mircea Eliade contends that the spiritual meaning of the androgyne — as an 'exemplary image of the perfect man', as perfection consisting of a 'unity-totality' — was reduced by many modern writers to a purely anatomico-physiological significance. Thus the androgyne was no longer understood in terms of a wholeness, 'a new type of humanity in which the fusion of the sexes produces a new unpolarized consciousness', but simply as a hermaphrodite 'with a superabundance of erotic possibilities'.[29]

Yet even such an enlarged notion of sexuality would not enable us to reduce all snake symbolism to an erotic interpretation. We shall

---

bourne, 1951), pp. 24 ff. In this secret cult, we may begin to notice the role of the snake as the 'master of initiation'.

28. Mircea Eliade, 'Australian Religions, Part III: Initiation Rites and Secret Cults', *History of Religions* 7, no. 1 (1967): 71–74, 80–81. This article is reproduced as chapter 3 in *Australian Religions: An Introduction*. Eliade bases his conclusion on the research of W. Lloyd Warner, *A Black Civilization. A Study of an Australian Tribe*; R. M. Berndt, *Kunapipi*; R. M. Berndt, ed., *Australian Aboriginal Art*; W. E. H. Stanner, *On Aboriginal Religion* (Oceania Monograph No. 11).

29. See 'Mephistopheles and the Androgyne or the Mystery of the Whole', *Mephistopheles and the Androgyne*, pp. 78–124, especially 98–100, 116–117.

soon consider data clearly not erotic. But even those snake and serpent symbols connected with fecundity are often not erotic. For example, snakes and serpents are water animals ('water symbolizes the whole of potentiality; it is *fons et origo*, the source of all possible existence') and 'bring rain, moisture, and floods, thus governing the fertility of the world'.[30]

It seems to be Eliade's position that the erotic symbolism of snakes really constitutes a *'secondary centre'* of a more comprehensive 'web' of lunar symbolism. Eliade admits that the erotic symbolism of snakes 'has in its turn "woven" a system of meanings and associations which in some cases at least push its lunar connections into the background'.[31] His position seems to be that the erotic is one of many possible valorizations of the inexhaustible lunar symbolism. Let us supply one more illustration[32] and then arrive at our methodological conclusions relevant to Eliade's analysis of the snake as a lunar symbol.

The snake or serpent plays a leading role in initiation ceremonies. We have already referred to the initiatory pattern of being ritually swallowed by a snake. There are many variations of this theme of initiation by being swallowed by a monster, the snake often functioning as the master of initiation, and the passage of the initiate through the snake being equivalent to an initiation.[33]

Eliade finds countless possibilities for initiatory symbolism in the rich structure of snake symbolism. In citing examples from Buddhism (*Majjhima-nikāya*, II, 17) and from Brahmanism (*Jaiminīya Brāhmaṇa*, II, 134, etc.), he shows that 'the image of the snake and its cast skin is

30. *Patterns*, pp. 188–189, 207–210.
31. *Ibid.*, p. 170. Mircea Eliade would probably attribute the apparent emphasis of modern persons on the sexual meaning of snake symbolism to our present existential situation. Not only do modern secular persons find it difficult to relate (consciously) to cosmic hierophanies, but Eliade maintains that human beings have always related to those valorizations of any symbolism which have the greatest existential relevance to their particular historical situation. This discussion leads us to the crucial importance of the historical–phenomenological 'tension' which we shall analyze in the next chapter.
32. An exhaustive treatment would involve analyzing the connections of the snake with aquatic symbolism, plant and vegetation symbolism, the symbolism of cosmic darkness and prenatal existence, and many other areas.
33. For several additional examples of this initiatory pattern, see *Shamanism*, p. 340; *Rites and Symbols of Initiation*, p. 35; and 'Australian Religions, Part IV', pp. 168–169.

one of the oldest symbols of mystical death and resurrection'.[34] Because snakes live underground, they symbolize darkness, 'the pre-formal modality of the universe', 'the primordial sacred force' concentrated in 'the depths of the earth'. They embody the souls of the dead, guide initiates into the bowels of the earth, and know all the hidden secrets which they can 'transmit through mysterious initiations'.[35] We may add that this structure of the snake or serpent symbolizing the preformal and the primordial is even more apparent in its role as a water animal connected with aquatic symbolism.

Without multiplying examples, we may now suggest the type of conclusion Mircea Eliade would arrive at concerning snakes and initiatory symbolism. If one examines all patterns of initiation — puberty rites, secret society cults, etc. — she or he finds the following essential structure: a ritual death followed by a 'rebirth', the initiate 'dying' to the old in order to be 'reborn' into a new mode of being. Now we recall the meaning which *homo religiosus* intuitively experienced in the moon's rhythms: the moon is subject to birth and death, but it is always 'reborn', etc. Eliade would submit that snakes appear in initiation ceremonies because of the 'symbolism of regeneration', and the most comprehensive and profound manifestation of this symbolism appears in the system of lunar symbols.[36]

Eliade's conclusion: lunar symbolism

After considering the numerous contexts of snake symbolism, Mircea Eliade arrives at the following conclusion: 'What emerges fairly clearly from all this varied symbolism of snakes is their lunar character

34. *Yoga*, p. 165. Cf. his analysis of 'to slough the skin' in *Mephistopheles and the Androgyne*, pp. 89–90.

35. *Yoga*, pp. 352, 428; *Shamanism*, p. 135. We may simply allude to one very familiar, highly complex initiatory pattern: to possess immortality (the Tree of Life, etc.), the primeval man (or hero) must do combat with and vanquish the monster (or serpent) guarding the tree. See *Patterns*, pp. 287 ff. Heinrich Zimmer claims that the antagonism of the hero-savior versus serpent symbolism, so frequent in the West, is resolved in India. ('The serpent and the savior are both manifestations of the one, all-containing, divine substance.') See Heinrich Zimmer, *Myths and Symbols in Indian Art and Civilization*, pp. 66, 75–76, 89–90.

36. See *Patterns*, pp. 169, 174–176.

— that is, their powers of fertility, of regeneration, of immortality through metamorphosis.'

Now it is tempting to conclude that *homo religiosus* arrived at such a position in 'an analytic and cumulative' manner, i.e., the various relationships between snake symbols and lunar symbolism gradually developed 'one from another by some method of logical analysis'. But this is the kind of reductionism of a religious system which Eliade vehemently opposes. 'In reality, all the meanings in a symbol are present together, even when it may look as if only some of them are effective. The intuition of the moon as the measure of rhythms, as the source of energy, of life, and of rebirth, has woven a sort of web between the various levels of the universe, producing parallels, similarities and unities among vastly differing kinds of phenomena.'[37]

The phenomenologist attempts to locate the 'centre' of such a 'web'. Sometimes a 'secondary centre' — such as the erotic symbolism of snakes — has 'woven' its own system of relationships and pushes the lunar relationships into the background. 'What in fact we are faced with is a series of threads running parallel to or across each other, all fitting together, some connected directly with the "centre" on which they all depend, others developing within their own systems.'[38]

The phenomenologist attempts to reconstruct the whole pattern: 'moon-rain-fertility-woman-serpent-death-periodic-regeneration'. But in certain contexts, the scholar may be dealing with 'one of the patterns within a pattern', such as serpent-woman-fertility.

It is true that Eliade does not always relate a particular snake symbol to a system of lunar symbols. For example, in analyzing a snake-water pattern, it may suffice to reintegrate a particular snake symbol within a system of aquatic symbolism.

Nevertheless, for the most comprehensive and profound interpretation, Mircea Eliade continually returns to the following type of claim: 'A lot of mythology has grown up around these secondary "centres," and if one does not realize this, it may overshadow the original pattern, though that pattern is, in fact, fully implicated in even the tiniest fragments.'[39]

37. *Ibid.*, pp. 169–170.
38. *Ibid.*, p. 170.
39. *Ibid.* This is the type of claim which Mircea Eliade makes when he asserts that

Let us attempt to relate the above analysis to several of our earlier methodological points. We recall that Mircea Eliade maintains that Historians of Religions must go beyond simply collecting religious documents; they must endeavor to understand the religious meaning revealed in their data. Through morphological analysis and classification, Eliade attempts to separate those phenomena which have structural similarities from those phenomena which do not. He then attempts to understand the religious meaning of a particular phenomenon by reintegrating it into its coherent, universal system of symbolic associations.

It seems that Eliade has assembled a variety of religious manifestations dealing with snakes or serpents and has attempted to gain insight into the 'invariant core' which constitutes their essential meaning. His approach, we would submit, is not unlike the phenomenological method of 'free variation'.[40] As we saw in Chapter 4, Eliade clearly rejects the phenomenological approach of the 'early' Husserl, where one may speak of an 'imaginative variation' and pure vision of the essential structure and meaning of a phenomenon, without the collection of historical examples and factual comparisons. Eliade is much closer to Merleau-Ponty and other existential phenomenologists, who in preparing for their eidetic reflection, seem to substitute for an imaginative variation an *actual variation* in the *historical data*.

Morphological analysis reveals that phenomena expressing snake or serpent symbolism in some contexts have structural similarities with phenomena expressing water symbolism, in some contexts with phenomena expressing phallic or erotic symbolism, in some contexts with phenomena expressing vegetation symbolism. There are various other types of religious phenomena which do not seem to share structural similarities with snake symbols and with which phenomena expressing snake symbolism are rarely associated.

---

every hierophany 'presupposes' an entire system of sacred manifestations. (For example, see *Patterns*, pp. 8–9.) Critics of Eliade have often cited this type of claim as showing that Eliade's approach is clearly normative. See Robert D. Baird, *Category Formation and the History of Religions*, pp. 75–77, 86–87. This analysis first appeared in Baird's 'Normative Elements in Eliade's Phenomenology of Symbolism', *Union Seminary Quarterly Review* 25, no. 4 (1970): 509–513.

40. The following methodological points will be discussed in greater detail in chapter 6.

Eliade now searches for the *invariant core*, the essential meaning which allows snake symbols to be related to and systematized with other religious symbols. In some cases, snake symbols have a phallic structure, but many other examples do not share this structure, and hence the essential structure of snake symbolism cannot be phallic. Through morphological analysis and variation of data, Eliade deciphers the essential meaning of snake symbolism as revealing inexhaustible life repeating itself rhythmically. And it is the moon as a sacred manifestation which is most able to reveal this profound religious meaning.

Thus, the invariant revealed by the diverse contexts of snake symbolism is seen in terms of a 'web' of lunar associations. The religious intuition of the moon and its rhythms is at the 'centre' of such a web and has 'woven' a sort of system of interdependent lunar relations.

In some contexts, phenomenological understanding occurs when a particular snake phenomenon is reintegrated within its aquatic system or erotic system of symbolic associations. But for the most comprehensive and profound understanding, which involves the reintegration of the particular phenomenon expressing snake symbolism within its *total system* of symbolic associations, Eliade usually grounds his hermeneutics in the framework of a coherent, universal system of lunar symbols. It is in terms of such a structural totality that Eliade attempts to understand the various relationships among snake, water, vegetation, and fertility symbols and what such structural relationships reveal about the meaning of religious phenomena.

We do not intend to evaluate Eliade's specific analysis, since our aim has simply been to convey some general sense of Eliade's phenomenological approach as grounded in coherent systems of symbolic associations. To realize how intricate and complex this hermeneutical foundation is, consider the fact that we have formulated only a partial analysis of only one symbolic valorization — and not one of the major lunar valorizations, at that — of the total lunar symbolism.

The reader may now have some initial sense of Eliade's structuralist approach and may grasp the essential (lunar) structure, but he or she probably finds the snake-lunar relationship rather 'forced'. Indeed, the 'modern' reader might find the interpretation more plausible if the lunar were analyzed as a 'secondary center' of a more comprehensive erotic symbolism.[41] Witness the persistent sexual symbolism in recent literature, as seen in the frequent theme of the search for the 'perfect' sexual orgasm as a self-transcending and liberating experience. Desacralized human beings seem much less likely to relate consciously to lunar or some other cosmic symbolism.

In all fairness to Eliade's specific analysis, we must recall his methodological principle: one must use a religious scale in order to interpret the meaning of religious phenomena. We know of the paramount importance cosmic phenomena have had in revealing the sacred to *homo religiosus*. It may be that on the plane of reference of the religious, and in terms of the dialectic of the sacred and other criteria we shall elucidate, that we shall be able to realize why a lunar symbolic structure would be much more relevant to the existential situation of *homo religiosus* than to the present situation of the nonreligious person.

In conveying some sense of Eliade's approach, we have suggested several methodological criteria, such as comprehensiveness and eidetic variation, which might serve to evaluate particular interpretations. In the next chapter, we shall analyze the phenomenological method for gaining insight into essential structures, free variation and induction, criteria for determining the essential structure or 'center' of a symbolic system, and other methodological topics relevant to the above analysis.

GENERAL FEATURES OF RELIGIOUS SYMBOLISM

Mircea Eliade describes the following characteristics and functions when analyzing religious symbolism. However, such a structural analysis usually can be taken as referring to *all* symbolism, religious

41. Eliade would never maintain that all erotic symbolism constitutes a 'secondary center' of a more comprehensive 'web' of lunar symbolism. Erotic symbolism is itself extremely complex, and, as a revelation of sacred meaning, it is far more comprehensive than its nonreligious (physiological, etc.) domain of meaning would seem to suggest. Eliade's point, if we interpret him correctly, is that the particular erotic symbolic structure, as illustrated by certain snake phenomena, constitutes a 'secondary center' of a more inclusive lunar 'web' of symbolic associations. Once again, this should indicate the complexity of Eliade's hermeneutical framework: not only has he formulated extremely complex (lunar, solar, aquatic) systems of symbolic structures, but he has found that these symbolic systems themselves interact and interpenetrate in numerous intricate ways.

and nonreligious. For example, it is only because there is a 'logic of symbols' operating on the levels of dreams, fantasies, imagination, aesthetic creativity, 'psychopathic' creativity, etc., that Eliade can 'homologize' the symbolic structures of religious phenomena with phenomena on other planes of manifestation. Or, to cite a second feature, we value poetic symbolism precisely because of such qualities as its 'multivalence'.

Our position is that these structural features refer, for the most part, to symbolism in general, but emerge as features of religious symbolism, when they are related to the structure of the dialectic of the sacred. In other words, symbols are religious symbols when they function within a religious context. And, we would submit, the crucial point of analysis in distinguishing religious from nonreligious symbolism concerns the nature of the symbolic referent. As we saw in the first section of this chapter, all symbols 'point beyond' themselves. But religious symbols, while using specific, concrete, 'natural' phenomena in their expressions, 'point beyond' themselves to 'something' transcendent, transhistorical, transhuman; in short, they point to sacred meanings.[42]

According to Eliade, the sacred 'speaks' or 'reveals' itself through symbols. But this revelation cannot be translated into a 'utilitarian and objective language'. In enumerating 'the different aspects of depths of this [symbolic] revelation', Eliade describes the nature and function of religious symbolism in general. His major points may be summarized in the following manner: religious symbols can reveal a structure of the world not evident on the level of immediate experience; religious symbolism is multivalent; because of this multivalence, the religious symbol can integrate diverse meanings into a whole or a system; because of this capacity for unification or systematization, the religious symbol can express paradoxical situations or other structures otherwise inexpressible; finally, we must recognize the 'existential value' of religious symbolism.[43]

---

42. Langdon Gilkey, relying heavily on Eliade's analysis, writes in *Naming the Whirlwind: The Renewal of God-Language*, p. 294, that 'The character of this [religious] language as referent to the unconditioned, the transcendent, the ultimate — or whatever in a given community's experience is taken to have these characteristics — has differentiated it from other types of discourse.'

43. 'Methodological Remarks', pp. 97–103.

Let us now discuss these characteristics and functions of religious symbolism in some detail. We shall supplement Eliade's treatment in 'Methodological Remarks on the Study of Religious Symbolism' with relevant observations from his other works and from earlier discussions of religious symbolism. We shall begin with that feature of symbolism which Eliade refers to as 'the logic of symbols', because, in our view, this is the key methodological concept in Eliade's interpretation of religious symbolism.

'The logic of symbols'

Our analysis of 'the logic of symbols' will be extremely brief, not only because we have already illustrated much of this concept in our discussion of Eliade's structuralist approach and his interpretation of the snake and lunar symbolism, but also because so much of our analysis in Chapter 7 (descriptive evaluations, levels of meaning, etc.) involves this methodological concept.

In Eliade's view, symbols are not arbitrary irresponsible creations of the psyche, but they function according to their own *'logical'* principles. It should be evident from the snake–lunar relationship that Eliade wishes to emphasize that various symbols can combine or 'fit together' to form coherent symbolic 'systems', that symbolism enables *homo religiosus* to bring heterogeneous phenomena into structurally interlocking relationships. In terms of the logic of symbols, Eliade submits that 'symbols of every kind, and at whatever level, are always consistent and systematic'. 'Certain groups of symbols, at least, prove to be coherent, logically connected with one another; in a word, they can be systematically formulated, translated into rational terms.'[44]

In *The Symbolism of Evil*, Paul Ricœur describes this concept as functioning on the 'first level' of analysis, and Ricoeur even cites Eliade as his major example of such 'purely comparative phenomenology'. This level of descriptive phenomenology 'limits

44. *Patterns*, p. 453; *Images and Symbols*, p. 37. In *The Comparative Study of Religion*, p. 25, Wach quotes Bleeker as identifying 'the *logos* with structure': 'This term [*logos*] again emphasizes this truth: that religion is not an uncontrollable, subjective secret of the soul but an objective entity shaped by strictly spiritual laws with its own altogether logical, that is, phenomenologically logical, structure.' Bleeker, *Revue d'histoire et philosophie religieuse* 21 (1951): 408.

itself to understanding symbols through symbols'. This analysis is on the 'horizontal' and 'panoramic' plane, in which the phenomenologist of religion attempts to describe the *internal coherence* of the world of symbols and to place symbols in a whole 'which forms a system on the plane of the symbols themselves'.[45]

Ricoeur has not captured the full significance of Eliade's logic of symbols. It is true that this logic functions on the horizontal plane of internal coherence. But, as we shall contend in Chapter 7, this logic of symbols is manifested on higher and higher levels of reality, and it is in terms of the 'highest' or most 'elevated' manifestations that the logic is best revealed and the 'center' of the symbolic system is understood. The logic of symbols enables Eliade not only to differentiate planes of manifestation, but also to evaluate certain levels as 'higher', 'deeper', 'mature', and 'elevated'. Whether Eliade can render such judgments on a descriptive basis remains to be seen. At this time, we simply wish to propose that Eliade's concept of the logic of symbols functions not only on the horizontal plane, where one appeals to some criterion of internal coherence, but also involves a 'vertical' appeal to some criterion of *adequacy*. It is this latter type of appeal which many critics of Eliade find so objectionable, since they argue that it takes him far beyond the descriptive and involves highly normative judgments based on an assumed ontological position. It is this type of methodological issue which will concern us in the concluding chapter.

We take 'the logic of symbols' to be the key methodological concept in Eliade's view of symbolism, because almost every other significant feature in Eliade's analysis of symbolism seems to depend on the validity of this concept. It is only because of such a 'logic of symbols' that Eliade can speak of the symbol's 'autonomous' mode of cognition and can maintain that symbols 'preserve their structure' and reveal a sense of continuity and universality, regardless of the particular historical and temporal conditionings. Only on the basis of such a concept can Eliade analyze symbolism as being 'multivalent' and comprehend the unification of structurally coherent meanings into symbolic wholes or 'systems'. We shall see that without such a logic of symbols, it would be impossible for the phenomenologist to dis-

45. Ricœur, *The Symbolism of Evil*, p. 353.

tinguish different levels of religious manifestations and to evaluate certain levels as 'higher' or 'elevated'. In short, without such a logic of symbols, Eliade's hermeneutical foundation, consisting of autonomous, coherent, structural systems of symbolic associations, would completely collapse; it might then be at best a highly imaginative and creative formulation, but one devoid of the methodological rigor and sense of objectivity demanded of a phenomenological approach.

The multivalence

Eliade's observation that 'religious symbols are capable of revealing a modality of the real or a structure of the world that is not evident on the level of immediate experience',[46] should be clear from his analysis of the snake as a lunar symbol. The snake symbol reveals the world as a living totality, as inexhaustible life repeating itself rhythmically. Such a revelation is not a matter of purely rational or reflective knowledge, but of an immediate intuition of a 'cipher' of the world. The world 'speaks' through the religious symbol; by such 'graspings' the religious world is constituted.

What allows such a revelation is the essential characteristic of symbolism which Eliade refers to as its 'multivalence': 'its capacity to express simultaneously a number of meanings whose continuity is not evident on the plane of immediate experience'. In his analysis of lunar symbolism, Eliade has shown that this religious symbolism is able 'to reveal a multitude of structurally coherent meanings': the lunar rhythms, 'the law of universal becoming', the death and rebirth or regeneration, rain and waters, vegetation and plant life, fertility, 'the female principle', human destiny, weaving, etc. 'In the final analysis, the symbolism of the moon reveals a correspondence of mystical order between the various levels of cosmic reality and certain modalities of human existence. Let us note that this correspondence becomes evident neither spontaneously in immediate experience nor through critical reflection. It is the result of a certain mode of "being present" in the world.'[47]

This emphasis on the multivalence of religious symbolism reaffirms

46. 'Methodological Remarks', p. 98.
47. *Ibid.*, p. 99.

one of Eliade's foremost phenomenological concerns: the criticism of all forms of modern methodological reductionism. The meaning of lunar symbolism cannot be reduced to some 'rational' interpretation, even though certain of its aspects, such as the relationship between the lunar cycle and menstruation, may seem to have developed by some method of 'logical' or 'rational' analysis. The meaning of lunar symbolism cannot be reduced to one of its many frames of reference, such as the erotic or sexual, even though the erotic is indeed one of its many valorizations. As we saw in Chapters 1, 2, and 3, Historians of Religions have consistently produced 'unilateral and therefore aberrant interpretations of symbols'. Such a reductionism is necessarily 'false', because it is a 'partial' and 'incomplete' interpretation of a religious symbolism. Such reductionism annihilates symbolism as 'an autonomous mode of cognition'. It is the symbolism as multivalent, as a totality of structurally coherent meanings, that is 'true'.[48]

Eliade illustrates such a 'unilateral' reduction of religious symbolism in his analysis of 'ritual caves'. 'Now the cave represents the otherworld, but also the entire Universe. It is not the immediate, "natural" valorization of the cave as a dark — and hence subterranean — place that enables us to perceive its symbolism and its religious function, but the experience caused by entering a place whose sacredness makes it "total", that is, a place that *constitutes a world-in-itself.*' After providing several examples of the religious meaning of ritual caves, Eliade offers this final observation: 'It is only since the "naturalistic" interpretation imposed by nineteenth-century scholars, who reduced religious symbolism to their concrete, physical expressions, that the cosmic meaning of caves and underground cult dwellings have been reduced to a single value, that is, the abode of the dead and the source of telluric fertility.'[49]

48. See *Images and Symbols*, pp. 15–16. In 'The Problem of the Double-Sense as Hermeneutic Problem and as Semantic Problem', *Myths and Symbolism: Studies in Honor of Mircea Eliade*, ed. Joseph M. Kitagawa and Charles H. Long, p. 68, Paul Ricœur writes that 'the sole philosophic interest in symbolism is that it reveals, by its structure of double-sense [multiple or double-meaning], the ambiguity of being: "Being speaks in many ways." It is the *raison d'être* of symbolism to disclose the multiplicity of meaning out of the ambiguity of being.'
49. Mircea Eliade, 'Zalmoxis', *Zalmoxis: The Vanishing God*, pp. 29, 30. This chapter is reproduced as 'Zalmoxis', *History of Religions* 11, no. 3 (1972): 257–302.

The function of unification

'This capacity of religious symbolism to reveal a multitude of structurally coherent meanings has an important consequence': 'The symbol is thus able to reveal a perspective in which heterogeneous realities are susceptible of articulation into a whole, or even of integration into a "system". In other words, the religious symbol allows man to discover a certain unity of the World and, at the same time, to disclose to himself his proper destiny as an integrating part of the World.'[59]

In *Yoga: Immortality and Freedom*, Mircea Eliade tells us that this 'tendency to homologize the different planes of reality is of the essence of every archaic and traditional spirituality'.[51] And religious symbolism plays the most important role in this process of homologization. One need only think of the snake, first as a purely natural and historical object and then as a religious lunar symbol, in order to understand how the snake as a symbol can be homologized with heterogeneous realities which reveal the fundamental structure deciphered in the lunar rhythms.

In this regard, Eliade's phenomenological method adheres closely to his understanding of the very activity of *homo religiosus* and the nature of his subject matter. That is, he attempts to empathize with and derive his method from the very nature of the religious life-world. The phenomenologist 'should strive to grasp the symbolic meaning of the religious facts in their heterogeneous, yet structurally interlocking appearances'.

Such a procedure does not imply the reduction of all meaning to a common denominator. One cannot insist strongly enough that the search for symbolic structures is not a work of reduction but of integration. We compare or contrast two expressions of a symbol not in order to reduce them to a single, pre-existent expression, but

---

50. 'Methodological Remarks', pp. 99–100.
51. *Yoga*, p. 123. In this section (pp. 117–124), Eliade indicates the tremendous Indian capacity for synthesis. The *Māṇḍūkya Upaniṣad* 'offers a system of homologies among the states of consciousness, the mystical letters, and . . . the four *yugas*'. The *Māṇḍūkya* presents 'the integration of several levels of reference: Upaniṣadic, yogic, "mystical," cosmological.'

in order to discover the process whereby a structure is likely to assume enriched meanings.[52]

Returning to our illustration, we observed how the lunar symbols revealed a perspective in which heterogeneous realities were integrated into a 'system'. We were able to speak of a 'logic of symbols' and observed how structurally coherent meanings were fitted together to form a lunar 'web'. The spiritual graspings of the religious meaning of the lunar rhythms allowed many different levels (cosmological, anthropological, etc.) of existence to be homologized. As a result, *homo religiosus* not only experienced a certain unity of the world, but also understood how his or her mode of being participated in the constitution and destiny of the world.

The expression of paradoxical and contradictory aspects of reality[53]

We have already noted the capacity of religious symbolism to reveal structures of the world not evident on the level of immediate experience. Eliade often develops this observation by asserting that symbols reveal 'the deepest aspects' of reality 'which defy any other means of knowledge'. Symbols 'respond to a need and fulfill a function, that of bringing to light the most hidden modalities of being'.[54]

52. 'Methodological Remarks', p. 97. Cf. John E. Smith's analysis in 'The Structure of Religion', *Religious Studies* 1, no. 1 (1965): 65–66. The emphasis upon universal religious structures need not reduce or compromise that which is singular. Citing a point made by Cassirer in *Substance and Form*, Smith argues that 'it is only through the use of universal conceptions making possible significant critical comparisons between singulars of the same kind that we are able to discover and express clearly what is distinctive of the singular phenomenon'.

53. This feature of symbolism could easily be subsumed under our previous discussion of the function of unification. It is the process of homologization and systematization, based upon a logic and multivalence of symbols, that allows symbolism to integrate phenomena which appear to be contradictory or paradoxical into a coherent structural whole. We have singled out this particular type of symbolic expression because of its special significance for *homo religiosus* and for Mircea Eliade.

54. *Images and Symbols*, p. 12. These assertions and other similar claims are a major source of criticism of Eliade's phenomenology: Eliade 'reads' all types of meaning into his data; his interpretations are highly subjective and normative. He usually presents such observations as if they are on the same level, and have the same degree of support, as his hermeneutical efforts to describe the characteristics of some myth or ritual. Yet many of his assertions are on a different level of analysis and involve unacknowledged

One notes the similar types of observations Paul Tillich often made when describing the general nature of all symbols. 'They [symbols] make accessible to our minds levels of experience from which we otherwise would be shut off; we would not be aware of them. This is the great function of symbols, to point beyond themselves in the power of that to which they point, to open up levels of reality which otherwise are closed, and to open up levels of the human mind of which we otherwise are not aware.'[55]

In this regard, Robert Luyster summarizes some of Eliade's discussion of symbolic revelation:

> The symbol successfully brings to expression, furthermore, those aspects of reality to which the conceptualizing consciousness has been most insensible and which it has been most unable to articulate. It is in fact just these contradictory and mysterious features of the universe for which the very ambivalence (or, more properly, multivalence) of a symbol is most highly suited. A symbol is an image charged with many meanings simultaneously. And it is this very indeterminacy — whatever the logical or scientific disadvantages it may possess — that renders it uniquely able to preserve the richness and the paradox of experienced reality.[56]

Now it is just these features of reality—paradoxical, contradictory, mysterious—which have most impressed *homo religiosus* (and hence, Eliade) and which have led Eliade to emphasize a special revelatory capacity of religious symbolism. 'Perhaps the most important function of religious symbolism—important above all because of the role which it will play in later philosophical speculations—is its capacity for expressing paradoxical situations, or certain structures of ultimate reality, otherwise quite inexpressible.'[57] What Eliade wishes to emphasize here is such symbolism as those of the 'Symplegades' and the *coincidentia oppositorum*. He believes that such expressions reveal

---

ontological moves. In chapter 7, we shall attempt to differentiate several levels of analysis in Eliade's phenomenological approach.

55. 'Theology and Symbolism', *Religious Symbolism*, ed. by F. Ernest Johnson, p. 109. See Tillich's 'The Meaning and Justification of Religious Symbols', pp. 4–5.
56. 'The Study of Myth: Two Approaches', pp. 235–236.
57. 'Methodological Remarks', p. 101.

the most creative spiritual experiences and the highest religious attainments of *homo religiosus*.

Let us cite an illustration which is relevant to the detailed analysis we have recently presented: the conjunction of the serpent and the eagle in various myths. In these myths, the serpent is usually a symbol of chthonian darkness, of the nonmanifest, of the fertilizing powers of Mother Earth, 'the female principle', and the terrestrial waters. The eagle is usually a symbol of solar light, of the manifest, of the powers of Father Heaven and the masculine celestial order. The serpent and the eagle are 'an archetypal pair of symbolical antagonists'.

In some myths, the opposition of the eagle and the serpent is emphasized.[58] In many other myths found throughout the world, these symbolical antagonists or polar principles paradoxically coexist. Through the paradoxical conjunction of the serpent and the eagle, *homo religiosus* has attempted to express the mystery and unity of the 'totality', the divinity, or the absolute.

Another illustration, extremely relevant to our analysis and interpreted at great length by Eliade, concerns the attempt by *homo religiosus* to unify the sun and the moon. One identifies all his or her experience with the valorizations of the solar and lunar rhythms; then the person endeavors to homologize these levels of experience and unify the solar and the lunar rhythms in his or her living body; finally, through such a unification, he or she aims at transcending the cosmos by realizing a primordial state of nondifferentiation, the primal unity, the original totality.[59]

In accepting his presence in the world, precisely as man found himself before the 'cipher' or 'word' of the world, he came to encounter the mystery of the contradictory aspects of a reality or of a 'sacrality' that he was led to consider compact and homogeneous. One of the most important discoveries of the human spirit was naively anticipated when, through certain religious symbols, man

58. See Heinrich Zimmer, 'The Serpent and the Bird', *Myths and Symbols in Indian Art and Civilization*, pp. 72–76. In citing one scene from Homer's *Iliad*, Zimmer observes that the 'heavenly bird [an eagle] ravaging the serpent symbolized to him [Kalchas, the priest-soothsayer] the victory of the patriarchal, masculine, heavenly order of Greece over the female principle of Asia and Troy'.

59. See *Yoga*, pp. 236–241, 253–254, 267–273; *Patterns*, pp. 178–181, 419–420.

guessed that the polarities and the antinomies could be articulated as a unity. Since then, the negative and sinister aspects of the cosmos and of the gods have not only found a justification, but have revealed themselves as an integral part of all reality or sacrality.[60]

The 'existential value'

Finally, we shall discuss 'the *existential value* of religious symbolism, that is, the fact that a symbol always aims at a *reality or a situation in which human existence is engaged*'. 'The religious symbol not only unveils a structure of reality or a dimension of existence; by the same stroke it brings a *meaning* into human existence. This is why even symbols aiming at the ultimate reality conjointly constitute existential revelations for the man who deciphers their message.'[61]

To understand this existential dimension of religious symbolism, we must recall how symbolism 'bursts open' the immediate reality of a particular, natural, profane, existential situation. The symbol is experienced as a 'cipher' which points beyond itself and reveals hidden levels of reality or structures of the world. The religious symbol is experienced as a 'cipher' of the sacred, relating the human and natural dimensions of existence to a mode of being 'beyond' or 'other than' the profane. 'In general, symbolism brings about a universal "porousness," "opening" beings and things to transobjective meanings.'[62]

Eliade claims that lunar symbolism adds new values and meanings to the snake without denying its immediate value. This symbolic transformation of the world can be related to our previous analysis of the dialectic of hierophanies. The snake, while remaining a natural profane phenomenon, 'explodes' or 'bursts' under the force of lunar symbolism to reveal many levels of profound existential meaning. The snake is no longer experienced as an isolated phenomenon in a completely fragmented universe; it is experienced as one of the countless valorizations of the moon and can be homologized with other phenomena revealing the structure of the lunar rhythms. 'In application to objects or actions, symbolism renders them "open"; symbolic

60. 'Methodological Remarks', p. 102.
61. *Ibid.*, pp. 102–103.
62. *Yoga*, pp. 250–251.

thinking "breaks open" the immediate reality without any minimizing or undervaluing of it: in such a perspective this is not a closed Universe, no object exists for itself in isolation; everything is held together by a compact system of correspondences and likenesses.'[63]

We have really uncovered two stages in this 'bursting open' of natural phenomena by religious symbolism. First, lunar symbolism may be seen as an extension of the dialectic of hierophanies. Snakes are transformed into 'something other' than what they appear to profane experience to be; as religious lunar symbols they reveal sacred meanings. Then, by becoming symbols of a sacred transcendent reality, snakes 'abolish their material limits, and instead of being isolated fragments become part of a whole [lunar] system; or, better, despite their precarious and fragmentary nature, they embody in themselves the whole of the system in question'.[64]

In this double process of symbolic transformation, we observe the fundamental structure of the symbolic existential revelation. First, individual profane situations are transformed into spiritual experiences. Then, what was experienced as an 'isolated', 'subjective', particular mode of existence now 'opens out' to a world which is unified and 'familiar', to a system of structures which is 'objective' and universal.

TRANSITION

Throughout our analysis of the general features of symbolism, as well as our analyses in earlier sections of this chapter, one may notice the extreme relevance of the historical–phenomenological 'tension' which was seen to define the nature of the History of Religions today. To cite our most recent symbolic feature, religious symbolism has existential value for *homo religiosus only if* it can 'burst open' the natural profane phenomenon, thus revealing a universal religious (transcendent,

---

63. *Images and Symbols*, p. 178. There seems no need to reiterate the obvious dependency of these and similar assertions on the methodological concept of the logic of symbols. See *Patterns*, p. 455.

64. *Patterns*, p. 452. This distinction of two stages is simply for the sake of analysis and is not intended to indicate a temporal sequence.

transhistorical) structure; and, *at the same time*, bring that universal structure into a dynamic relationship with those specific, concrete, historical, temporal conditions which define the existential situation of the natural profane phenomenon. Without such a dynamic relationship between the historical particular and the universal structure, the religious symbolism would have little existential value for *homo religiosus*.

We have refrained from continually relating our analysis to the historical-phenomenological 'tension', because an examination of this relationship constitutes our primary task in Chapter 6. Indeed, the adequacy of not only Eliade's treatment of symbolism but of his entire phenomenological approach rests upon the extent to which his method is successful in dealing with the crucial methodological issues and difficulties raised by this historical-phenomenological 'tension'.

PART THREE

Eliade's Phenomenology and New Directions: Some Methodological Issues and Conclusions

6

The Historical-Phenomenological 'Tension'

It has been our thesis that if Mircea Eliade's phenomenological approach to religious phenomena is an improvement over previous approaches we have elucidated, this is primarily because his creative method is grounded in a hermeneutical framework which enables him to interpret the religious meaning of his data. The two key interacting notions in his phenomenological approach were formulated as the dialectic of the sacred, which allows Eliade to distinguish religious phenomena, and the coherent universal systems of religious symbols, which serve as the foundation in terms of which he interprets the specific meaning of a religious manifestation.

We shall now attempt to relate Eliade's phenomenological approach to the basic methodological 'tension' which was seen to define the present discipline of the History of Religions. We wish to discuss the basic concrete, particular, historical versus general, universal, phenomenological tension which we initially elucidated in our analysis of Pettazzoni's approach. At the beginning of Chapter 7, entitled 'Descriptive Evaluations and Levels of Meaning', we shall summarize our conclusions.

In describing the history-phenomenology tension, we have shown that Mircea Eliade is primarily a phenomenologist whose methodology is grounded in universal coherent systems of symbolic structures. He conceives of his task as the interpretation of religious '-meaning' and asserts that one interprets meaning through structure. How does the phenomenologist regard the unique historical conditionings of his data? How do the universal structures interact with the historical particular dimension of existence in yielding meaning? Is interpreting phenomenological 'meaning' something different from providing a historical (psychological, causal, etc.) 'explanation'? Is there a 'given' (perhaps a 'constituted given') revealed in the History of Religions? Does Eliade use some phenomenological method, such as the technique of free variation, in comprehending the structures and meanings of religious experience?

THE HISTORICAL PARTICULAR AND THE UNIVERSAL STRUCTURE

The importance of the historical and the particular

To interpret the actual meaning of any religious manifestation, phenomenologists of religion must be sensitive to the unique, specific, historico-cultural conditionings of all data. Unlike the early philologists and ethnologists, they acknowledge the irreducibility of history. Phenomenologists work with historical documents, historical expressions of the experiences of *homo religiosus*.

To assert that all religious phenomena are historical is to acknowledge that all religious phenomena are conditioned. There are no 'pure' religious phenomena. The sacred is always manifested in history; temporal, spatial, cultural, and other factors always condition the religious manifestation.

The extreme importance of the particular and the historical dimensions of experience should be evident from Eliade's analysis of the process of sacralization. In order to realize why one cannot grasp the religious without taking into consideration specific historical conditions, one need simply recall the following: that which is infinite, transhistorical, eternal, limits itself by incarnating itself in something finite, historical, temporal. A particular, finite, historical phenomenon, while remaining a 'natural' thing, manifests something universal, infinite, unconditioned. Each hierophany is a historical fact, is set in a specific historical situation, and reveals some attitude human beings have had toward the sacred. As Langdon Gilkey has noted, 'every experience of the Whole comes through some particular finite medium in some particular historical situation, and thus is given its particular form'.[1]

The significance of particular historical factors becomes even more evident when we emphasize a point made by Merleau-Ponty and

1. *Naming the Whirlwind: The Renewal of God-Language*, p. 42. Cf. *Patterns*, p. 2; and Tillich, *Systematic Theology*, vol. 1, p. 111.

other existential phenomenologists: our perception of the world is always *perspectival* and incomplete. Insight into meaning does depend on certain factual conditions.[2] Human beings tend to relate to those valorizations of a religious symbolism which have the greatest existential relevance to their particular historical situation. G. Richard Welbon writes that 'it is the disposition of man's mind and being which finally determines whether specific modalities of the sacred are discovered. And that disposition is historically conditioned—to some extent, at least.'[3] The fact that few of us can experience the snake as a 'cipher' of the sacred in one of its lunar valorizations attests to this importance of historical conditionings. Indeed, 'modern man' has difficulty experiencing the moon as hierophanic in any of its valorizations.

The phenomenologist recognizes that certain religious symbolisms were constituted at specific historical times and were dependent on specific historical situations. To illustrate this point, we may refer to one widespread symbolism which expresses the solidarity between the fertility of the land and the fertility of women. We find the identification of the snake with the phallus, of the seed with the *semen virile*, of the tilled field with woman, of ploughing with conjugal union and the hierogamous fertilization of the Earth — Mother.[4] Such anthropo-telluric homologies could not have been constituted before 'the discovery of agriculture'. They are dependent on some understanding of both agriculture and the cause of conception.

The status of universal structures

Recognizing the necessity of interpreting the unique, specific conditionings of religious data, a scholar may not be overly impressed by Mircea Eliade's sensitivity to these particular, historical aspects of

2. For several illustrations of this point, see Maurice Merleau-Ponty, 'Preface', *Phenomenology of Perception*, pp. vii–xxi; Maurice Merleau-Ponty, 'Phenomenology and the Sciences of Man', *The Primacy of Perception*, pp. 43–95; Paul Ricœur, 'Existential Phenomenology', *Husserl: An Analysis of His Phenomenology*', pp. 202–212.
3. Welbon, p. 469.
4. See *Patterns*, pp. 256–260; *The Sacred*, pp. 166–167; *The Forge and the Crucible*, p. 144.

experience. Rather what probably stands out is the significant status Eliade has granted the universal structures of religious experience.[5]

It is true that all hierophanies are historical manifestations, but what is most crucial for Eliade's methodology is that their *structures remain the same*. Only because there is a permanence and continuity of structure can we participate in the life-world of the other and interpret religious data with some sense of objectivity.

Eliade maintains[6] that fundamental religious structures are non-temporal and nonhistorical. We cannot show that religious structures are created by certain societies or historical moments. We can only establish that specific societies and historical moments furnish the *opportunity* for the manifestation or predominance of a particular nontemporal structure. Thus we find countless and multifarious revalorizations of the symbols of 'flight' throughout history. Yet despite the historical conditionings, there is a structural solidarity expressed by the symbolism of 'flight': transcendence and freedom, an ontological mutation or abolition of 'the human condition'.

History does not basically modify the structure of an archetypal symbolism. History does add new meanings; new valorizations of a symbolism are occasioned by particular historical situations. But the new valorization is conditioned by the basic structure of the symbolism.

Thus, the primary structure of the symbolism of the Cross was not created at a specific historical moment. There are numerous variants of the universal symbolism of the 'Centre', such as the mountain, the ladder, or the Cosmic Tree. What interests the phenomenologist is the

5. Baird, *Category Formation and the History of Religions*, pp. 152–153, contends that 'The search for structures may be a legitimate inquiry, but it is not an historical one, and when it enters historical study under the guise of offering the "religious dimension" of the data, it does violence to authentic historical investigation. Phenomenological structures are not historically falsifiable, and their method of verification is therefore more akin to theological verification than to historical verification.' Baird argues that Eliade's phenomenological approach is like this, since 'it is not historically falsifiable. Since it is an ahistorical approach, however legitimate that might be in itself, when it enters into historical deliberation it becomes a barrier to the attainment of authentic religio-historical understanding.'

6. Some of the ensuing analysis can be found in *Myths, Dreams and Mysteries*, pp. 107–108, 110, 178; *The Sacred*, p. 137; *Images and Symbols*, pp. 159–161.

basic structure through which the meaning of the symbolism of the 'Centre' is interpreted. Christianity brought about a new valorization of this symbolism by having the Cross take the place of the Tree of the World. This is not to deny that such a homologization took place in history. To interpret the actual meaning that the Cross had for *homo religiosus*, the phenomenologist must consider the unique, specific, historical conditionings and the originality of the Christian experience. But the historical manifestation of the Cross did not radically modify the universal symbolism of which it was a significant variant. In fact, the new valorization of the Cross was already conditioned by the archetypal symbolism of the Cosmic Tree standing at the 'Centre' of the universe.

Over and over again we see that religious structures, especially symbolic structures, are 'autonomous'. There is a logic and coherency of symbolic structures. Each coherent symbolism is universal. Eliade's hermeneutics is grounded in autonomous, coherent, universal systems of symbolic structures, which allows him to reintegrate a religious phenomenon into its system of associations. Through a structural analysis, the phenomenologist can interpret religious meanings even when a particular person or group is not consciously aware of the religious meaning of its experience.

HISTORICAL 'EXPLANATION' AND PHENOMENOLOGICAL 'MEANING'

In the 'Foreword' to *Shamanism*, in *Myths, Dreams and Mysteries*, in *Images and Symbols*, and in several other works, Mircea Eliade seems determined to differentiate what he is doing from historical (psychological, causal, etc.) explanation. A scholar may 'explain' the origin or the diffusion of a particular religious manifestation in terms of various historical, cultural, and temporal conditionings. But Eliade continually maintains that the task of the phenomenologist is not completed by his or her historical research: one still must interpret the *meaning* his or her data reveal.

At the minimum, Eliade is making a claim common to phenomenology: giving a historical (causal, psychological) explanation does not exhaust the meaning of one's data. Phenomenology, it is often stated, is concerned not with giving 'explanations' but with finding 'meanings'. In this sense, interpreting meaning is not tantamount to uncovering historical and temporal conditions.

But, we would submit, Eliade intends something far more controversial than this by his more-than-historical-explanation claim. He seems to be making definite *ontological claims* about the nature of the human being and experience. One might even contend that these judgments lay the foundation for a philosophical anthropology.

Since Eliade wishes to formulate a descriptive phenomenological approach and would be reluctant to accept any analysis which attributed to him ontological judgments, it is imperative that we provide some documentation to justify our interpretation, namely, that Eliade's more-than-historical-explanation claim involves ontological judgments about the nature of the human being and experience.[7] More documentation will be provided in the following sections on evaluating descriptively and on different levels of meaning in Eliade's approach.

This Historian of Religions acknowledges that he works with historical data, but he asserts that his documents disclose 'something more than the simple fact that they reflect historical situations'. Eliade maintains that 'they reveal to him important truths about man and man's relation to the sacred'.[8]

In 'Recent Works on Shamanism', Eliade describes 'ecstasy' as seeming 'to form an integral part of the human condition'. Hence, it is not necessary 'to look for its "origin" in a particular culture or in a particular historical moment'. 'As an *experience*, ecstasy is a nonhistorical phenomenon; it is a primordial phenomenon in the sense that it is coextensive with human nature. Only the religious *interpretation* given to ecstasy and the *techniques* designed to prepare it or facilitate it are historical data. That is to say, they are dependent on

7. Although an approach which claims to be 'purely' descriptive may regard such an interpretation as a criticism, all methodologies *necessarily* involve implicit presuppositions and judgments about human beings and the universe, and not all of these claims are ever entirely justified simply in terms of the data investigated. This is not to assert that we must accept all such assumptions and judgments uncritically. Once we have rendered them explicit, we may formulate various criteria (consistency, applicability, etc.) for evaluating them.

8. 'The Quest for the "Origins" of Religion', p. 169.

various cultural contexts, and they change in the course of the history.'[9]

In the 'Foreword' to *Images and Symbols*, Eliade discusses 'the nonhistorical portion of every human being'. In *Rites and Symbols of Initiation* (pp. 130–131), he analyzes the phenomenon of initiation as not only a historical fact but also an experience which 'exhibits a dimension that is metacultural and transhistorical', an 'existential experience that is basic in the human condition'.

Perhaps the most illuminating discussion of this more-than-historical-explanation claim, which illustrates several of Eliade's assertions about the human being and his or her existential situation, is contained in the 'Foreword' to *Shamanism*.

(Celestial ascent) appears to be a primordial phenomenon, that is, it belongs to man as such, not to man as a historical being; witness the dreams, hallucinations, and images of ascent found everywhere in the world, apart from any historical or other 'conditions.' All these dreams, myths, and nostalgias with a central theme of ascent or flight cannot be exhausted by a psychological explanation; there is always a kernel that remains refractory to explanation, and this indefinable, irreducible element perhaps reveals the real situation of man in the cosmos, a situation that, we shall never tire of repeating, is not solely 'historical.'[10]

9. 'Recent Works on Shamanism: A Review Article', p. 154. During a conversation, I cited this passage and asked Mircea Eliade whether he intended by this description of 'ecstasy' as 'nonhistorical' anything other than an analysis of the 'meaning' of this experience. While acknowledging that he is not entirely happy with such terms as 'transhistorical' and 'nonhistorical', Eliade stated that he intended to say something about the experience itself. The experience itself 'isn't conditioned'; 'only the values given to this experience are historical'. When Eliade examines such religious phenomena as the innumerable ecstatic experiences of 'flight' or of 'mystical light', he sees that they are 'not so much related through their particular historico-cultural contexts' of the hunter, the Eskimo, the Indian; Zen, Jewish, or Christian mysticism; etc. Rather they are structurally homologous because they constitute primordial 'experiences as such'.

10. *Shamanism*, p. xiv. In *Myths, Dreams and Mysteries*, p. 106, Eliade expands this analysis and makes various ontological assertions when discussing the structure of freedom revealed by this symbolism of 'flight'. The 'roots of freedom are to be sought in the depths of the psyche, and not in conditions brought about by certain historical moments'. The creation of 'countless imaginary universes' with this essential structure 'speaks volumes upon the true nature of the human being'. This 'longing' is 'not a

In asserting 'the ahistoricity of religious life', Eliade points to the spontaneity and the reversibility of religious positions.[11] Certain coherent mystical experiences 'are possible at any and every degree of civilization and of religious situation'. That is, 'for certain religious consciousnesses in crisis, there is always the possibility of a historical leap that enables them to attain otherwise inaccessible spiritual positions'.

In short, particular historical and cultural conditionings cannot account for these primordial existential experiences, for these primordial phenomena which are constitutive of the human condition as such. The phenomenologist must consider the particular historical and cultural influences, but not all of the experiences of *homo religiosus* are historically determined. Sometimes human beings transcend their specific historical context and have certain primordial experiences simply by virtue of their human mode of existence.[12]

We have confined our references to assertions about the historical nature of human beings and experience. Similar assertions can be found throughout Eliade's works. It seems clear that Eliade is asserting something 'more' than the view that interpreting 'meaning' is not the same as giving an 'explanation' by uncovering historical and cultural conditionings. It also seems clear that he is asserting something 'more' than the interpretation that *homo religiosus* experiences religious phenomena as having transhistorical meaning.

By means of the basic nontemporal and nonhistorical religious structures, especially the archetypal systems of religious symbols, Mircea Eliade is making significant claims about human beings and their existential situation, about the human mode of being in the world and the human condition.

Without evaluating such ontological assumptions and judgments at this time, we can submit one important criticism: Eliade usually fails to acknowledge that such claims are on a different level of analysis and have a lesser degree of support than the more clearly descriptive analyses we have previously elucidated. Deciphering an essential

---

result of cosmic pressures or of economic insecurity — it is constitutive of man. . . .'. 'Such a desire . . . must be ranked among the specific marks of man.'

11. *Shamanism*, pp. xvi–xix.
12. See Hudson, 'Eliade's Contribution to the Study of Myth', pp. 234–235.

structure of 'the human condition as such' is quite different from deciphering an essential structure of a particular cosmogonic myth. Eliade's failure to distinguish different levels of analysis and meaning in his approach has been a major source of dissatisfaction among his readers. It seems not unfair to say that a common initial reaction—which is often a final reaction—to Eliade's writings is that his approach is hopelessly uncritical; after all, how can a descriptive History of Religions make such ontological claims? By clarifying various levels of analysis, with varying degrees of support, Eliade would go some distance in meeting this type of criticism.

'GIVENNESS' AND CREATIVITY

Now if Mircea Eliade is correct in asserting that there are fundamental universal religious structures which are nontemporal and nonhistorical, then we may have a 'given' which reveals a sense of permanence and continuity and can function as a foundation for Eliade's methodology. If there are certain general structures of experience which are not completely determined by particular, relative, historical, temporal, and cultural conditionings, then we may have a 'given' which can serve as a hermeneutical framework in terms of which the phenomenologist can understand religious phenomena, make comparisons and generalizations, and evaluate descriptively.

One may notice a certain ambiguity throughout Eliade's phenomenological analysis of what is revealed in religious experience. On the one hand, Eliade usually interprets the revelatory experience by emphasizing a fundamental *'givenness'* in experience and a definite *passivity* on the part of *homo religiosus* (and a corresponding passivity on the part of the phenomenologist who is interpreting the religious experience). For example, the sacred reveals itself *to homo religiosus*. The emphasis here is on universal or general religious structures, which are nontemporal and nonhistorical and are 'given' or revealed to people in religious experiences.

On the other hand, Eliade sometimes analyzes the revelatory experience by emphasizing a sense of *activity* and *creativity* on the part of *homo religiosus* (and a corresponding sense of activity and creativity on the part of the phenomenologist). Thus, *homo religiosus* deciphers the sacred and constitutes her or his religious 'World'. Emphasized is the extreme importance of the particular and the historical conditionings of the revelatory experiences; the phenomenologist is sensitive to the specific linguistic, cultural, historical, and other influences of the particular *Lebenswelt* of *homo religiosus*.

We shall provide some elucidation of the more frequent analysis of a sense of 'givenness' and passivity; then we shall introduce some criticism of such analysis; finally we shall suggest some way of bringing into relationship the universal and the particular, the passive and the active, the 'given' and the constituted.

'Givenness' and passivity: structures revealed to homo religiosus

In different contexts, the universal structures which are given in religious experience are described in various ways. We have maintained that the two key methodological notions in Eliade's phenomenology are the dialectic of hierophanies and the structural systems of symbols. When these are taken together, we begin to perceive the underlying framework of Eliade's methodology. Now we would submit that the fundamental universal structures given in religious experience are most frequently revealed by the dialectic of the sacred and the coherent symbolisms.

In Chapter 4, we elucidated the universal structure of the process of sacralization which is revealed in the dialectic of hierophanies: the invariable separation of the hierophanic object, the sacred–profane dichotomy, the paradoxial coexistence of the sacred and the profane, etc.

The point we wish to emphasize is that this process of hierophanization is analyzed as a universal given in the sense that its structure exhibits an autonomy, permanence, and continuity. The 'sacred expresses itself according to the laws of its own dialectic and this expression comes to man from without'. The religious person does not actively create this basic structure. The person rather passively experiences that which reveals itself to him or her.[13]

---

13. See *Patterns*, pp. 368–369; *Shamanism*, p. xvii.

When we look at the structures given by religious symbolism, we find that 'No religious tradition understands itself as having invented or even discovered its fundamental symbols; rather, phenomenologically they are always seen to have been "given" to that tradition.'[14] In Chapter 5, we analyzed many senses in which symbolic structures could be said to be given or revealed in experience. We found that every coherent symbolism is universal. Such symbolic structures are 'autonomous' in the sense that the symbols have their own logic and interlock to form coherent structural systems. History does not basically modify the structure of such universal symbolisms.

Thus, to return to an illustration recently cited, the essential structure of freedom and transcendence is revealed through the universal, coherent symbolism of 'flight'. This structure has not been actively created by a specific culture at a certain historical moment. It is true that particular cultures and historical moments have provided the occasion for the manifestation of such an archetypal symbolic structure. But the structure itself is given in the sense that it is nonhistorical and nontemporal and exhibits an autonomy, continuity, and universality.

Mircea Eliade tells us that 'the World "speaks" or "reveals itself" through symbols'; religious symbols reveal fundamental structures of 'the World'.

The World 'speaks' to man, and to understand its language he needs only to know the myths and decipher the symbols. Through the myths and symbols of the Moon man grasps the mysterious solidarity among temporality, birth, death and resurrection, sexuality, fertility, rain, vegetation, and so on. . . . In the last analysis, *the World reveals itself as language*. It speaks to man through its own mode of being, through its structures and its rhythms.[15]

14. Gilkey, p. 446.
15. *Myth and Reality*, p. 141. It seems that Mircea Eliade has intentionally used the term 'the World' to distinguish its meaning from that of the 'external' universe alone. Whether he uses the term 'the World' or the more usual 'the world', he usually is referring to the total *Lebenswelt* of *homo religiosus*. Wilson M. Hudson ('Eliade's Contribution to the Study of Myth', p. 223) is correct in stating that 'The world, by which Eliade does not mean to indicate external nature alone but the whole existential situation of man, speaks to man in the language of symbols. . . .'

Very often, as we consider symbols of a 'cosmic structure', it appears that the universal structures are given-in-the-world. These seem to be structures which can be seen in the natural, temporal, secular universe and which can serve as an 'objective' basis for the religious revelation. If we wish to understand the sacredness and religious symbolism of the sky, it would seem that the basic structures can be grasped in the very nature of the sky itself: high, infinite, transcendent. Similarly, one might argue that the basic structure of lunar symbolism is given in the very nature of the moon's rhythms: the lunar cycle of periodic change, the moon endlessly repeating itself rhythmically.

The danger in locating structures in the universe itself is the temptation of a *naturalistic reduction* of religious meaning. As we saw in the first part of our study, many excellent scholars have succumbed to this temptation. We recall that *homo religiosus* has never viewed the natural as simply natural. It is obvious that a 'modern' secular person can observe, analyze, and calculate the basic structures of the lunar rhythms and find it absurd, or at least irrelevant, to suggest that this can serve as the basis for religious revelation. Therefore, while it may be possible to gain some insight into the nature of certain religious intuitions and sacred manifestations in terms of basic structures given-in-the-world, we must never reduce the total meaning of a sacred manifestation to such a 'natural' structure in the universe.

This becomes even more evident when we examine symbolic structures of 'the World' which are 'given' but could not possibly be 'given' in the 'natural' universe. Indeed, these structures often seem to be completely at odds with what is given-in-the-world. For example, if we consider the sun from a 'rational' and secular perspective, it seems unintelligible that solar symbolism would reveal connections between the sun and darkness, serpents, and the dead. The 'dark side' of the sun, its 'ophidian' ('dark' or 'indistinct') aspects, revealed in such documents as the myth of Helios, the *Ṛg Veda* and the *Brāhmaṇas*, would seem the complete opposite of its 'natural' meaning.[16] Such symbolisms as those of the 'Symplegades' (the paradoxical passing between two rocks that clash together continuously or the entering of a mountain which has no opening) and the *coincidentia oppositorum*,

16. See *Patterns*, pp. 142–147.

which Eliade seems to evaluate as the highest spiritual realizations, illustrate this same point.

Often the only way to begin to decipher the meaning of a symbolic structure is to examine the 'sacred history' preserved in myths and periodically reenacted in rituals. Thus, the World of the Australian has a structure because the myths reveal the creative acts of the Primordial Beings; this knowledge of what happened *in illo tempore* transforms a chaotic universe into a structured meaningful World.[17] *Homo religiosus* does not feel he or she actively created these sacred histories; phenomenologically, the myths are seen to have been revealed to the religious person.

Finally, the World reveals itself through religious symbols related to 'the human condition': symbols which 'refer to situations constitutive of all human existence, that is to say, to the fact that man is mortal, is a sexual being, and is seeking what today we call "ultimate reality" '.[18] Many of the symbolisms we have considered — flight and ecstasy and ascension, initiation, lunar, *coincidentia oppositorum* — illustrate such structures of 'the human condition' which are revealed to *homo religiosus* in religious experience.

We have delineated several of the kinds of general structures of 'the World' which are 'given' or revealed in religious experience: the structures given in the dialectic of the sacred; symbolic structures which have a 'cosmic structure' and are sometimes related to structures 'given-in-the-world'; symbolic structures related to the 'human condition' as such; etc. What all of these structures have in common is that they are 'given' to *homo religiosus*; the religious person does not actively constitute them, but in a rather passive manner experiences that which reveals itself to her or him.

'Givenness' and passivity: several criticisms

Many difficulties arise from this view of the givenness of universal structures which are passively experienced by *homo religiosus*. Several

17. See the following illustrations provided by Eliade: *Myth and Reality*, pp. 43–45; 'Cosmogonic Myth and "Sacred History" ', pp. 179–183; 'Australian Religions, Part II: An Introduction', pp. 208–235.
18. Eliade, 'Methodological Remarks', pp. 104–105.

difficulties will be cited here; others will be formulated later in this chapter.

It does not seem forced to contend that there is a definite similarity between Eliade's analysis of these universal religious structures and the claim by much of existential phenomenology that it can 'read off' the 'given' universal structures of the *Lebenswelt*. Richard F. Grabau[19] has stated that the primary feature of the phenomenological *Wesenschau* or intuition of essences is a 'passive receptiveness'. His criticisms of such a position are relevant to Eliade's phenomenology. There is no experience 'without symbolization (thematization)' and 'these symbols are created by men in concrete historical situations' in response to their particular existential concerns. Therefore, these symbols cannot be regarded as given structures to be 'read off'. Grabau's alternative to this view of consciousness as a passive receptiveness of universal given structures is to claim that consciousness is a 'creative interaction with and interpretation of a situation by means of mediating symbols'.

It also does not seem forced to propose a certain similarity between Eliade's 'empirical approach' and the methodology of 'classical' British empiricism. True, the foundation for David Hume's epistemology consists of discrete particular sense impressions and not Eliade's universal structures. Nevertheless, both seem to analyze experience in terms of a rather passive reception by the self of what is given to it.

In 'The Experiential Foundations of Religion', John E. Smith distinguishes two principal types of empiricism: he rejects 'the classical or British type which found its most incisive expression in the thought of David Hume' and opts for 'the broader, vaguer type sometimes called "radical" which characterizes, in different degrees, the thought of an entire group of critics of the classical type—Hegel, Bradley, Peirce, James, Dewey, Whitehead, and perhaps even Heidegger'. He claims that this latter 'reconstructed' conception 'is required if religion is to be made intelligible as experience'.

Smith delineates four of the features of this reconstructed conception, the first two of which directly challenge the above interpretation

19. Richard F. Grabau, 'Existential Universals', *An Invitation to Phenomenology*, ed. James M. Edie, pp. 150–153.

of givenness and passivity: experience is a 'reciprocal affair' involving an 'organic togetherness of the experiencing self and the experienced world'; therefore, experience cannot be taken as the 'passive reception' of 'bare' or 'given' data and is 'impossible without interpretation from the side of self'.[20]

What may seem astonishing at first is the assertion that Mircea Eliade would probably want to accept as valid most of the aforementioned 'criticisms'. Although he would reject much of Grabau's analysis, he would concur that religious consciousness is a 'creative interaction' and not merely a 'passive reception'. He might be in total agreement with Smith's 'reconstructed' conception of experience. But the above points were presented as criticisms of Eliade's analysis of experience. Consequently, it seems necessary to modify or reconstruct the view that religious experience consists of a passive reception of nontemporal and nonhistorical universal structures which are 'given' or revealed to *homo religiosus*.[21]

Creativity and the 'constituted given'

We recall from the dialectic of hierophanies that an essential aspect of the structure of sacralization consists of the evaluation and choice by *homo religiosus*. The religious person is called upon to respond to that which is given or revealed. Without such an evaluation and choice, *homo religiosus* could not overcome his or her existential crisis and realize a structured meaningful life-world. Without such an active response, there would be no religious experience.

In asserting that the fundamental symbolic structures are given in

20. John E. Smith, 'The Experiential Foundations of Religion', *Reason and God*, pp. 173–183. Eliade would unhesitantly concur with the third and fourth features, involving the presence of 'relation and directionality or purpose' within experience and the presence of the 'intensive quality of experience'.

21. The following attempt to relate the active and the passive, the particular and the universal, the historical and the structural, is nowhere to be found in Eliade's writings, although it may very well be consistent with much of his methodology. The following may be taken as a partial criticism of Eliade, or, as I prefer to view it, as an attempt to modify Eliade by dealing with issues he does not consider, thus rendering his phenomenological approach more adequate. In any case, we do not wish to minimize the paramount significance Eliade grants to the universal structures which are 'given' in experience and the criticisms relevant to such a position.

experience, it must be emphasized that our notion of this sense of givenness and passivity, which already involves the self's being situated in the world and dynamically open to symbolic structures, is considerably different from the self's 'bare' passive receptiveness of a David Hume. Whether these structures should be viewed as Platonic forms or Whiteheadian eternal objects or Jungian archetypes or in some other manner is another matter. But to analyze the general structures as we have is an abstraction, which, it is possible to argue, may be necessary for the sake of analysis. What must be insisted upon is that a passive reception of such structures does not constitute religious experience.

The actual religious experience consists of just what *homo religiosus* does with the symbolic structures. These structures function as an inexhaustible source of religious meaning and offer virtually infinite possibilities for actualization. Symbolism is not present initially as fully articulated, as 'fulfilled' meaning. Symbols are present initially as 'ciphers', usually manifested on the level of the prereflective, experienced through vague intuitions and as 'empty intentionalities', which 'key' into experience and provide inexhaustible possibilities for gradually experiencing fulfilled meanings and structuring a meaningful World.

Actual revalorization of a religious symbolism is the particular way *homo religiosus* 'uses' a symbolism to structure his or her World. And just what *homo religiosus* does with these structures must always be seen in terms of his or her specific existential situation. What we become aware of, how we respond to our 'discovery', what meaning it has for us, how we use it to structure our World, etc., depends largely upon our historical, cultural, and other particular conditions.

Phenomenologically, the religious experience has an initial emphasis upon a kind of passivity and then a creativity emerging from the passivity. True creativity emerges when we can decipher the fundamental givenness that is revealed to us. It emerges from what the particular and historical does with this givenness: how it constitutes or actualizes these inexhaustible possibilities by embodying them in a specific historico–cultural context, by providing them with a particular content and particular values.

This sense of an active creativity emerging from a passive givenness seems to be what Paul Ricœur intends by 'Le Symbole donne à penser.'

> This maxim that I find so appealing says two things. The symbol invites: I do not posit the meaning, the symbol gives it; but what it gives is something for thought, something to think about. First the giving, then the positing; the phrase suggests, therefore, both that all has already been said in enigma and yet that it is necessary ever to begin and re-begin everything in the dimension of thought.[22]

Perhaps the relationship between the passive givenness of universal structures and the active creativity which involves the historical and the particular can be viewed in terms of a 'constituted given', an 'in itself for us'. On the one hand, *homo religiosus* experiences a World of given structures, a World of meanings already constituted and simply revealed to him or her; on the other hand, the person experiences his or her World as still to be constituted, as given meaning by his or her active creativity.[23] The structural givenness expresses the horizon within which human beings orient themselves and constitute the specific meanings of their 'new' World. What emerges is a radical intentionality of human consciousness: universal structures are given but are always experienced as given for the perceiving consciousness.

Such a conception of religious experiences involves a sense of *organic mutuality and dynamic interaction between religious consciousness and its intended World*. The person simultaneously looks at the World and feels looked at by the World. *Homo religiosus* feels that not only other human beings, but also the moon and stones and trees 'look' at us and

22. Paul Ricœur, 'The Hermeneutics of Symbols and Philosophical Reflection', *International Philosophical Quarterly* 2, no. 2 (1962): 193. This same maxim provides the title for another article by Ricœur: 'The Symbol: Food for Thought', *Philosophy Today* 4, no. 3 (1960): 196–207. The 'Conclusion' of *The Symbolism of Evil*, pp. 347–357, is entitled 'The Symbol Gives Rise to Thought'.

23. Cf. Richard C. McCleary, Preface to Maurice Merleau-Ponty's *Signs*, p. xiv: 'The central problem, Merleau-Ponty once said . . ., is to understand how we can simultaneously constitute the meaning-structures of experience and find that it is always already constituted in terms of meanings we have not bestowed upon it.' Later on p. xiv, McCleary writes that 'This experiencing of the world as always still to be constituted by our active and spontaneous involvement in it is precisely what it means to him [Merleau-Ponty] to "exist," to "be present to the world" as an "existential field." '.

reveal to us the inexhaustible possibilities by which we can constitute their religious meaning. In such a conception of religious experience, the World is always *structurally given* and at the same time *dynamically alive* and continuously *open* to new valorizations and creative spiritual experiences.

Phenomenological Method, Free Variation, and Induction

At various points in our analysis, we have insisted on the necessity for bringing historical particulars and universal structures into some kind of dynamic relationship. Perhaps we can increase our understanding of this dynamic interaction by focusing on several aspects of the phenomenological method for gaining insight into meaning.

Phenomenological insight and free variation

Before considering a general phenomenological procedure, we shall offer an incisive criticism of the phenomenological method for intuiting existential universals and shall then consider two contrasting methodological passages. These preliminary considerations will shed light on different methodological tendencies.

According to Richard F. Grabau, phenomenologists admit that existential universals are always embodied in some particular person's 'lived experience'. But phenomenologists assert that their method enables them to 'read off' these universals from concrete experience. Such universals are then taken as constituting 'the universal structures of historical existence', 'an ontology of human existence', and 'the conditions of the possibility of ontic experience'. The aim of existential phenomenology is thus 'to comprehend existence by delineating a set of these universal structures, all "read off" immediate experience'.[24]

Grabau then criticizes such a general phenomenological approach: 'The point is this: ontic experience, in which ontological structures are said to be rooted, is concrete and of the particular. Universals just do

24. Grabau, pp. 147–148.

not appear at this level; hence they cannot be "read off."'. . . Universal structures, consequently, are never a matter of reading off; they are always a matter of *construction*.'[25] Although Grabau does not subscribe to some Humean conception of experience based on the perception of 'bare' particulars, the above emphasis of the concrete and particular nature of immediate experience and the 'later' construction of universals contrasts with much of the emphasis in phenomenology.[26]

We shall now simply paraphrase two methodological passages from 'Symbolisms of Ascension and "Waking Dreams" ', in which Mircea Eliade seems to emphasize two different tendencies in relating the historical particular and the universal structure.

The first passage calls attention to the paramount methodological status of universal structures and the hermeneutical movement from universal structures to the particular historical expressions.[27] It is only after phenomenologists have clarified the whole structure of the symbolism of 'flight' and grasped its essential meaning (as expressing 'the abolition of the human condition, transcendence and freedom') that they can then begin to understand the meaning of each particular historical manifestation.

The second passage formulates the hermeneutical movement from particular historical expressions to universal structures.[28] It is only after deciphering or 'decoding' each particular meaning in its own specific 'frame of reference' that phenomenologists can begin to see 'different but interconnected planes' (of the oneiric, of myth and of ritual, of metaphysical speculation, of ecstatic experience) and to discern that particular symbolic revalorizations of ascension express a structural solidarity. From the diverse, particular contexts,

25. *Ibid.*, p. 148.
26. For the moment, we may simply note the different emphasis in the following assertion by Merleau-Ponty ('Phenomenology and the Sciences of Man', *The Primacy of Perception*, p. 72) which is characteristic of much of the present orientation of existential phenomenology: 'any knowledge of fact always involves an *a priori* understanding of essence'. At the same time, we must not confuse this emphasis in existential phenomenology with the 'early' Husserlian position in which knowledge of essences seems completely independent of all knowledge of particular, historical, contingent facts. Cf. Edmund Husserl, *Ideas*, pp. 57–58; and Husserl, 'Philosophy as Rigorous Science', *Phenomenology and the Crisis of Philosophy*, p. 112.
27. *Myths, Dreams and Mysteries*, p. 110.
28. *Ibid.*, p. 118.

phenomenologists begin to grasp 'structurally indissoluble meanings which fall into a *pattern*'. They attempt to integrate all of the particular meanings into a whole, to interpret each symbolism as a 'system' which 'can only be really understood so far as we study it in the totality of its particular applications'.

It may be possible to relate several of the above methodological emphases in terms of a general phenomenological procedure for gaining insight into meaning. Since our procedural outline is of a very general nature, we shall not document the following analysis.[29] It is imperative that we acknowledge the impossibility of outlining a linear temporal procedure in which the phenomenologist moves from particular facts to universal essences or vice versa. The particular and the universal must be seen in constant interaction and must be brought into some dialectical relationship.

In the phenomenological *Wesenschau*, the phenomenologist of religion attempts to disengage the essential structure embodied in the particular religious fact. His or her starting point is a specific perceptual experience of *homo religiosus*, a particular datum of religious experience. This does not mean that one can collect and describe particular religious facts and then generalize to universal religious structures. The particular *qua* particular is unintelligible. Experience always involves the unity of fact and essence.

Our above analysis is not confined to some 'mystical' or supersensible experience but expresses a precondition of any experience. Either consciously or unconsciously we make a distinction between the fact that we have an experience and what is experienced. It is in terms of this 'whatness' of an experience that we can distinguish, compare, and relate it to other experiences; that we can classify it as an experience of a certain kind.

Now the central aim of the phenomenological method is to disclose the essential 'whatness' or structure embodied in the particular facts,

29. In addition to the primary sources (various works of Husserl, Merleau-Ponty, etc.), see Lawrence and O'Connor, 'The Primary Phenomenon: Human Existence', *Readings in Existential Phenomenology*, pp. 8–10; Jules Bednarski, 'The Eidetic Reduction', *Philosophy Today* 6, no. 1 (1962): 15–18; Remy C. Kwant, 'Merleau-Ponty's Criticism of Husserl's Eidetic Reduction', *Phenomenology: The Philosophy of Edmund Husserl and Its Interpretation*, ed. Joseph J. Kockelmans, pp. 402–408. (The latter is a selection from Kwant's *From Phenomenology to Metaphysics*.)

to gain insight into the essential meaning which constitutes the facts as facts of a certain kind. This is not to say that one begins with a clear understanding of the universal structure embodied in a particular datum. Rather the phenomenologist begins with a vague intuition of what is revealed in the particular fact. Without such a vague eidetic intuition, the phenomenologist could not even begin to distinguish, describe, and classify the particular datum.

If we turn to a frequently cited illustration, a particular religious datum expressing snake symbolism, one phenomenologist of religion may see what is revealed in terms confined entirely to other snake phenomena; a second scholar may vaguely intuit an essential erotic structure; someone like Eliade may initially grasp the essential meaning of that same datum in terms of a lunar structure. This diversity in the initial eidetic intuition, as well as in the completed or 'fulfilled' *Wesenschau*, is attributable in large part to the diversity in the particular *Lebenswelts* of different phenomenologists. Although Husserl might be unhappy with such an introduction of contingency into phenomenological insight into meaning, this is a way of accounting for the fact that different phenomenologists, while considering the same phenomena and claiming to be using the same method, have continually come up with different eidetic intuitions.

The usual way to gain insight into meaning is by the method of 'free variation'. In certain cases, such as some mathematical phenomenon, one may be able to grasp an essential structure by reflecting on one example only. However, in the case of religious phenomena, the phenomenologist of religion must compile and compare a great variety of examples before she or he can gain insight into the essential meaning of the data. There must be not simply a purely imaginative variation but also a *factual variation* of one's data.

By the 'method of invariance', the phenomenologist of religion searches for the *invariant core* which constitutes the essential meaning of the religious phenomena. The snake example, which is already presumed to be a variation of a certain type (erotic, lunar, etc.), is subjected to a process of free variation. A variety of snake phenomena assume certain forms which can be considered 'accidental', in the sense that the phenomenologist can go 'beyond' the 'limits' imposed by such structures and not destroy the basic character of his or her data. For example, a particular aquatic or earth structure disclosed by some examples of snake hierophanies does not reveal the invariable meaning of snake phenomena.

Through free variation, the phenomenologist gradually sees that snake phenomena assume forms which can be regarded as 'essential', in the sense that such structures impose certain 'limits' beyond which one changes the basic 'whatness' of the data under investigation; one cannot 'remove' such 'elements' without destroying the basic nature of the data.

Such essential insight is not instantaneous. What Husserl calls an 'empty intention' is the vague appearance of certain permanence within the variations. Amidst the diverse revalorizations, one gradually deciphers a certain *structural identity*.

When the phenomenologist of religion has grasped the invariant core which constitutes the essential meaning of the data, he or she then has 'achieved' the eidetic intuition. For Eliade, the invariant core which constitutes the essential meaning of the snake phenomena was understood in terms of a structural 'web' of lunar symbolism. The essential structure embodied in the particular snake examples was grasped as inexhaustible life repeating itself rhythmically.

It is now possible to bring Eliade's two methodological passages into dynamic relationship. In actual religious experience, fact and essence are inseparable; although in analysis, the phenomenologist of religion can distinguish them and disengage or abstract the embodied universal structure.

In phenomenological analysis, especially by the method of free variation, there is a hermeneutical 'movement' from the historical particular to the universal structure. This is not to deny that there is a continual universal-particular interaction and that we could never even begin to distinguish and describe the particular unless we had already presumed some eidetic structure. However, once we have delineated a variety of such particular (snake) examples, we can then subject the particulars to free variation; begin to decipher certain structural similarities (erotic, initiation, etc.) and dissimilarities; and finally, ideally, grasp the invariant as a definite (lunar) structure.

Phenomenological analysis also involves a hermeneutical 'movement' from the universal structure to the historical particular. The invariant (the lunar 'web') serves as the hermeneutical framework in terms of which we can understand the meaning of a particular (snake) datum. Phenomenological understanding of the religious meaning of the particular phenomenon (expressing snake symbolism) involves reintegrating that phenomenon within its coherent universal (lunar) system of symbolic associations, within that totality which constitutes its universal (lunar) structure.

Uncritical inductive generalizations

By focusing on what is probably the most frequent criticism of Eliade's phenomenological approach, it may be possible to deepen our analysis of how the phenomenologist of religion gains insight into universal structures of meaning. As we observed on several occasions, this general criticism usually contends that Mircea Eliade, while investigating particular religious manifestations, arrives at his universal structures by means of highly subjective, uncritical, hasty generalizations; thus, he 'reads into' his specific religious data all kinds of 'sophisticated' universal structures and meanings.

Underlying most of these methodological criticisms is the assumption that Eliade proceeds by some kind of *inductive inference*. Critics submit that they cannot repeat Eliade's inductive process: they do not find it possible to generalize from the particular examples to Eliade's 'profound' universal structures of religious experience.

Such criticisms have considerable merit. Eliade never formulates a comprehensive and critical methodological analysis in which he clarifies and justifies his phenomenological grasping of universal religious structures. The impression he often conveys is that his procedure is not unlike the 'classical' formulations of inductive inference found in John Stuart Mill and other philosophers.

How did Mircea Eliade arrive at the universal structure of religious experience revealed in his analysis of the dialectic of the sacred? Did Eliade examine many particular religious examples and then detect certain common characteristics found in each particular phenomenon: a sacred–profane dichotomy, a sense of transcendence, etc.? It would then seem that Eliade might be able to claim varying degrees of *probability* for his generalized conclusions.

But Eliade has granted these universal structures of religious experience a sense of *necessity*, as if they had some synthetic a priori status. His generalized conclusions are supposedly dependent on the nature of the religious documents he had investigated, but they are not open to falsification: in the future, one could not investigate a religious datum which was without any of these structures. It does not seem possible for Eliade to grant these structures such a universal necessary status if they are arrived at by some inductive process of generalization.

Turning to Eliade's analysis of snake symbolism, it often seemed that he studied many snake examples, deciphered common characteristics in each datum, and then inductively generalized to his conclusion asserting their universal lunar structure. But then why don't other scholars discern in each of these particular facts that 'inexhaustible life is repeating itself rhythmically'?

Without multiplying our examples, the above should suffice to establish our conclusion: if Eliade insists that he has inductively generalized from the particular religious facts to his universal religious structures, then many of the aforementioned criticisms of his methodology seem justified.

Phenomenological induction

But perhaps the phenomenologist of religion does not arrive at his fundamental structures through some 'classical' (Mill, etc.) inductive inference.[30] We would like to suggest that if one can formulate universal religious structures, such as those of the sacred and the profane, sacred space, sacred time, initiation, ascension, etc., he or she may grasp such meanings through a kind of induction which bears some similarity to the phenomenological *Wesenschau*.[31] Our suggestion is

30. Once again, the interpretation which follows is not what Mircea Eliade ever claims he is doing. As was just stated, Eliade tends to convey the impression of some 'classical' inductive method generalization, and such an approach is not commensurate with the status he grants his conclusions. Our interpretation is intended to suggest an alternate approach which might render the phenomenological insight into universal religious structures more acceptable.

31. The following suggestion is very similar to the analysis of induction found in 'Phenomenology and the Sciences of Man', pp. 66–72. We might add that whereas Merleau-Ponty argues for such an analysis in *The Primacy of Perception*, defending an interpretation which he takes to be implicit in Husserl's phenomenology, he later appears to reject much of this position in *The Visible and the Invisible*.

submitted as one possible means to supplement, and not to negate, the recently elucidated general analysis of the phenomenological method and its use of eidetic variation.

The phenomenologist of religion proceeds by means of various 'idealizing fictions' which are based on the particular facts. One recalls that there are no 'pure' religious phenomena; the religious manifestation is viewed as spatial, temporal, conditioned, relative, 'limited'. By reflecting on the particular, contingent, 'imperfect' manifestations, the phenomenologist of religion attempts to disengage an *ideal religious structure*, to 'read off' a conception of a 'pure case'. This ideal structure is actively constructed by the phenomenologist.

A key point in this analysis is the contention that such a conceived ideal structure or pure case is *founded on* the particular facts but is *not found in* the facts. In examining different expressions of flight and ascension symbols, the phenomenologist of religion conceives the ideal structure: transcendence and freedom, an ontological abolition of the human condition. Now a critic of Eliade's phenomenology analyzes the ascension phenomena and does not find such an ideal meaning expressed in each manifestation. Hence she or he assumes that Eliade is guilty of a highly subjective, uncritical inductive generalization; that Eliade has 'read into' his data 'pure', 'sophisticated' religious meaning.

Our position concedes that 'transcendence and freedom . . .' is not a generalized structure which is found in each particular, historical fact. Rather it, like other atemporal and ahistorical universal structures, is a 'pure' or 'perfect' structure which has been actively conceived or constructed by the phenomenologist. It is founded on the particular, historical, 'imperfect' facts, but is not found fully in any of them.

The phenomenologist of religion may attempt to analyze 'the difference' between the ideal structure of ascension and any specific ascension datum in terms of the particular, historical, cultural, and other relevant conditionings of the existential situation within which the ascension manifestation is experienced. Perhaps this is one clue to Eliade's frequent evaluations of a phenomenon as a 'higher' or 'more perfect' religious manifestation. The Indian yogi, for instance, may achieve a 'higher' spiritual realization in the sense that the experience is 'closer' (is less conditioned, etc.) to the ideal meaning or 'pure case' of ascension symbolism.

The phenomenologist of religion attempts to verify the ideal structure by showing how it illuminates the meaning of the particular empirical facts. According to Merleau-Ponty,

> That which gives its probable value to the induction and which finally shows that it is truly founded on things is not the number of facts involved to justify it. No! It is rather the intrinsic clarity which these ideas shed on the phenomena we seek to understand. . . . [Induction is] a process of intellectual analysis whose verification consists in the total, or at least sufficient, clarity which the group of concepts worked out in this way bring to the given phenomena.[32]

The above view of induction can be compared with the phenomenological *Wesenschau*. Both are based on facts; both involve a 'reading' of universal. But they can be 'differentiated with respect to their elaboration': (Husserl's) *Wesenschau* 'moves on the plane of the imaginary', involving an imaginary variation of certain facts; induction moves 'on the level of actual facts', involving 'effective variations in considering the different cases that are actually realized'.[33]

In light of this inductive approach, it would seem that Grabau's criticism has some justification if the phenomenologist of religion maintains that he or she simply 'reads off' universal structures which are found in the particular facts. The atemporal and ahistorical essential structures are 'a matter of construction'.

We may also recall Altizer's broad criticism of Eliade's method as being 'mystical', brilliantly intuitive, but completely divorced from any 'rational' and 'scientific' approach. If the paradigm for a 'rational' and 'scientific' empirical approach entails some form of 'classical' inductive generalization, then this criticism seems justified. But Husserl argued that intuiting essences is not something 'mystical' or 'supersensible', but something we all do with varying degrees of insight. If our suggested inductive approach has any value, then certainly a tremendously creative phenomenologist such as Eliade, who

32. *The Primacy of Perception*, pp. 69–70.
33. See Bednarski, 'The Eidetic Reduction', p. 22; Merleau-Ponty, *The Primacy of Perception*, p. 70.

can formulate ideal universal structures of religious meaning, would have to be 'brilliantly intuitive'.

The crucial methodological point is that such a brilliant intuitive conception of essential religious structures is not completely arbitrary and subjective. Such a phenomenological procedure is not arbitrarily superimposed on the religious data but is largely *derived* from the nature of the religious facts. Thus, Eliade analyzes the specific snake examples, subjects them to an 'actual variation', begins to decipher structural similarities, etc.[34] What emerges is some sense of a hermeneutical foundation derived from the religious phenomena, a structural 'web' of religious symbols. Now by reflecting on this foundation, Eliade is able actively and creatively to conceive an ideal lunar structure, which then helps to illuminate the meaning of the particular manifestations. This is not to minimize the brilliant creativity in gaining insight into such ideal meanings, but rather to indicate that such insights are founded on the facts and are not simply arbitrarily imposed.

Phenomenological insight and the dialectic of the sacred

We may conclude this section by taking note of a remarkable similarity between the (philosophical) phenomenological method for gaining insight into meaning, especially the inductive procedure for 'reading off' essences, and Mircea Eliade's analysis of the nature of religious experience. Indeed, it was largely because this similarity struck us as so remarkable that we felt that an elucidation of various aspects of the philosophical phenomenological method might have considerable relevance for *Religionswissenschaft*.

In the dialectic of hierophanies, *homo religiosus* intuits that which is paradigmatic, 'perfect', the ideal structure, 'the pure case'. The ideal religious structure is not found in the particular, spatial, temporal, historical, conditioned facts. We have analyzed those methodological approaches which attempt to find the religious structure in the 'natural' profane facts as naturalistic reductions which negate the basic

---

34. This is not to deny our previous methodological point that there must be some eidetic intuiting, at least at the level of an indistinct 'empty intentionality', even to begin this procedure.

intentionality of religious phenomena. What 'verifies' the sacred model, the paradigmatic structure, for *homo religiosus* is that he or she can use it to illuminate the nature of the particular existential situation; to give meaning to the chaotic, isolated, finite, 'impure', 'imperfect' facts of his or her profane existence.

We should note that for Eliade the ideal religious structures, such as those of ascension or of the moon, do not constitute 'original' constructions by the phenomenologist. Eliade's position seems to be that the ideal religious structure is actually experienced by *homo religiosus* in at least a few cases. The religious structure is not revealed in the profane facts *qua* profane facts. And it is not revealed fully in the vast majority of religious phenomena. But at certain highly creative moments in the history of humankind, *homo religiosus* did conceive fully the 'pure case', the ideal religious meaning of ascension, of agriculture, of the moon, etc. Hence, in 'reading off' these ideal structures, the phenomenologist of religion is attempting to empathize with, participate in, and reenact within his or her own experience the ideal meanings which *homo religiosus* has experienced.

7

Descriptive Evaluations and
Levels of Meaning

Throughout Chapter 6, we attempted to relate Eliade's phenomenological approach to the basic 'tension' which was seen to define
the contemporary field of *Religionswissenschaft*: the historical and the
particular versus the phenomenological and the universal. The historical and the particular were analyzed as playing an indispensable role in
Eliade's hermeneutics, but his primary methodological emphasis was
placed on the lofty status of nontemporal and nonhistorical universal
structures. Eliade's methodology was seen as addressing itself to the
task of finding phenomenological 'meanings' rather than formulating
historical (psychological, causal) 'explanations'. In his more-than-
historical-explanation claim, we submitted that Eliade often seemed
to be making normative judgments about human nature, our mode of
being in the world, and the 'human condition as such'.

In further analyzing the historical-phenomenological relationship,
we attempted to show that the universal structures of religious experience revealed by the dialectic of hierophanies and the religious symbolisms could be analyzed in terms of a fundamental 'givenness',
which served as a foundation for Eliade's phenomenology. At the
same time, we maintained that actual religious experience and creativity always entailed the dynamic interaction between the historical
particular and the 'given' universal structures, and that it might be
fruitful to conceive of such a relationship in terms of a 'constituted
given'.

Finally, we attempted to deepen our analysis of Eliade's methodology, with its hermeneutical framework and historical-
phenomenological relationship, by formulating a general approach
for intuiting essences from philosophical phenomenology. We submitted that in interpreting the data and uncovering universal structures of religious experience, the approach of the phenomenologist of
religion was not unrelated to the phenomenological *Wesenschau*, the

relating of fact and essence, and the method of 'free variation'. We then acknowledged with many of Eliade's critics that the conclusions Eliade reaches concerning the profound meaning of his essential universal structures are not commensurate with some 'classical' empirical method of inductive generalization. Our methodological alternative was to suggest that the phenomenologist of religion may decipher and verify these universal structures by some phenomenological method of induction, involving eidetic variation and the construction of the ideal structure or 'pure case', which is founded on but not found in the particular facts. We concluded by noticing a remarkable similarity between the philosophical analysis of the phenomenological *Wesenschau*, eidetic variation, and induction, on the one hand, and Mircea Eliade's analysis of the nature of religious experience, on the other.

Although we have never intended our study to be restricted to an exposition of Mircea Eliade's writings and have continually strived for original and creative interpretations of his phenomenology, one might argue with some justification that much of our analysis in Chapter 6 simply goes too far beyond anything Eliade has written to be taken as an interpretation of his methodology. It is true that we have felt free to go beyond Eliade's thought and to analyze how his phenomenological approach could be used, and in some cases modified, to deal with significant methodological issues. However, it could be argued that we are not simply broadening and deepening Eliade's phenomenological approach but are in fact *criticizing* it; i.e. we are exposing the fact that Eliade has not dealt adequately with many of the methodological questions implicit in his approach.

Mircea Eliade would probably agree that he has not devoted sufficient attention to these methodological issues, but he would contend that, as a descriptive phenomenologist and Historian of Religions, such questions usually do not fall within the domain of his particular field of investigation. Indeed, it is a proper role for the philosopher to reflect on and go beyond Eliade's descriptive analyses and to deal with many of the methodological questions we have been raising.

Such a response has considerable merit, but it would have even greater force, save for one telling observation: as we have occasionally seen, Mircea Eliade *himself* goes far beyond the limits of analysis set by almost all descriptive phenomenologists and other Historians of Religions. This renders his phenomenology open to frequent criticisms. If Eliade is to make assertions, which at least seem to be normative and to entail ontological judgments, then he must deal with the methodological questions raised by such assertions.

In this concluding chapter, under the general topic of 'Descriptive Evaluations and Levels of Meaning', we shall discuss several of the most important of these methodological issues implicit in Mircea Eliade's phenomenology. In rather schematic fashion, we shall suggest ways that Eliade's methodological approach could be employed or modified in order to deal with such questions.

EVALUATING RELIGIOUS PHENOMENA

A major source of much of the criticism of Mircea Eliade's phenomenology centers around the various types of evaluative judgments found throughout his works. That this would arouse considerable criticism should be obvious if one recalls our elucidation of previous methodological approaches.

The initial effort by Max Müller to define a new, autonomous, scientific discipline known as *Religionswissenschaft* was largely motivated by his desire to remain descriptive and avoid the normative judgments of philosophy of religion and theology. Past Historians of Religions usually insisted on this sharp descriptive-normative distinction. Phenomenology, according to Kristensen, is 'purely descriptive' and avoids all evaluative questions. No statement can be taken to be valid, according to Wilfred Smith, unless it is acknowledged by the believer. At the end of Chapter 3, we indicated that most contemporary Historians of Religions reject the past ideal of being 'purely descriptive'; but it is not clear whether scholars can provide the objective basis for their comparisons, classifications, and other interpretations.

The problem confronting Eliade is whether he can make his frequent evaluations of religious phenomena without committing himself to some highly normative and subjective approach, which, in the manner of Hendrik Kraemer, seems to distort the basic intentionality and meaning of the data under investigation; which does not do justice to the experience of 'the other'.

It has been our thesis that if Mircea Eliade is able to describe religious meanings and to deal with comparative and evaluative questions, he is able to do so on the basis of the hermeneutical framework underlying his phenomenological approach. In this regard, we have often suggested that the sharp descriptive-normative distinction may not be adequate and that one ought to entertain the possibility of evaluating descriptively or phenomenologically.

This does not mean that all of Eliade's evaluations of religious phenomena are on the same 'level' of analysis, nor that all can be subsumed under the classification of 'descriptive evaluations'. It seems possible to make an initial differentiation of at least three general 'senses' of evaluation in Mircea Eliade's phenomenology.

First, there is the sense in which the religious person *her or himself* makes normative judgments concerning what is meaningful, valid, and real. As we saw in Chapter 4, the very structure of the process of sacralization always entails evaluations and choices by *homo religiosus*. All past Historians of Religions have agreed that the description of such judgments is a necessary part of their discipline.

Second, there is a sense of evaluation which involves such criteria as *authentic, genuine*, and *true*. This level of evaluating is more controversial since Eliade often goes *beyond* the descriptions and affirmations of *homo religiosus*.

Third, there is a sense of evaluation which seems least descriptive and appears based on an *assumed ontological stance*. Illustrations of such judgments might be Mircea Eliade's assertions about the nature of the human being and the human condition as such.

Evaluations of 'authentic' and 'genuine'

When Mircea Eliade continually distinguishes authentic from inauthentic religious phenomena, genuine from nongenuine religious experience, his evaluations raise a crucial methodological problem: he seems to be making normative judgments and not simply describing just what appears or manifests itself. Our suggestion is that the phenomenologist of religion may *evaluate descriptively*. We do not contend that Mircea Eliade consistently adheres to the following suggestion, but only that this is a possible means for dealing with some of the methodological difficulties raised by such evaluations as authentic and genuine.

For the phenomenologist of religion, the authentic–inauthentic distinction is not tantamount to distinguishing 'the real' from 'the unreal'. In terms of the phenomenological *epoché*, the scholar suspends her or his judgment concerning the reality or unreality of the particular phenomenon. If the phenomenologist of religion wishes to use the term 'real', then we may say that all the phenomena are taken as 'real' in the sense that they 'appear' or manifest themselves as phenomena.[1]

Phenomenologists of religion attempt to uncover various structural differentiations within their data. Certain phenomena reveal an essential structure which we classify as *religious*. Thus, for Eliade, phenomena which disclose the general structure analyzed in the dialectic of the sacred are authentic religious manifestations.

Other phenomena exhibit a structure which can be classified as *nonreligious*. In terms of Eliade's phenomenology, an expression which clearly rejects any structures of 'transcendence' does not express a genuine religious experience.

Unfortunately, the structural differentiations are frequently not so clear-cut. Some phenomena appear similar to religious phenomena, but as phenomenologists continue to describe and analyze their data, they begin to detect various structural dissimilarities. Eliade often describes 'magico-religious' expressions, but usually concludes his analysis by differentiating the phenomena of magic as not authentically religious. He sometimes evaluates such movements as 'spiritism' and Theosophy and various developments in depth psychology and in modern art as 'parareligious', as having a religious 'aura', but not as genuinely religious.[2]

Our point is that the above distinctions of inauthentic and nongenuine are arrived at by evaluative judgments, but such evaluations do not have the usual normative sense of unreal or illusory. All of

1. Cf. *Myths, Dreams and Mysteries*, pp. 74, 75, 88, 89.
2. See 'History of Religions and a New Humanism', p. 3; 'The Quest for the "Origins" of Religion', p. 158; 'The Sacred and the Modern Artist', pp. 22–24; 'Cultural Fashions and the History of Religions', pp. 21–38.

the phenomena are real in the sense that they appear or manifest themselves, but the phenomenologist can descriptively evaluate some manifestations as not authentic or genuine religious expressions on the basis of a structural analysis.

Not all of Eliade's evaluations of authentic-inauthentic concern the above distinction between the religious and the nonreligious. He will often differentiate *different types* of religious experience in terms of their essential structures. Thus, he will evaluate certain phenomena as authentically shamanic because they reveal a certain essential structure of 'ecstasy'.[3] As we have frequently indicated, if Eliade can describe such essential structures and make these descriptive evaluations, he does so on the basis of his hermeneutical framework, which consists for the most part of coherent universal 'webs' of structures of religious symbols.

There is a third kind of evaluating as authentic which may be less descriptive than the religious–nonreligious distinction and the structural differentiation of essential types of religious phenomena. Eliade often distinguishes *different levels* of religious phenomena and evaluates certain levels as more authentic, in the sense that he evaluates certain religious experiences as 'elevated', as 'higher' or 'deeper' than religious experiences on 'lower' levels. Whether he can arrive at such hierarchical distinctions through a descriptive analysis remains to be seen.

Evaluations of 'true'

Related to, and sometimes synonymous with, the evaluations of authentic or genuine is Eliade's frequent judgment of religious phenomena in terms of 'true' or 'false'. Before delineating what seem to be two different levels of analysis in Eliade's evaluation, let us cite an ambiguity in his use of the term 'true'. Usually he evaluates the phenomena as true or false, and in this regard, true is often synonymous with authentic or genuine. Sometimes he evaluates a scholar's approach or interpretation as true or false.[4] These two uses of 'true' are

3. See *Yoga*, pp. 319–320; *Shamanism*, pp. 3–32.
4. We need not analyze the most descriptive sense in which Eliade describes what *homo religiosus* judges to be true.

not unrelated, because, as we have seen, Mircea Eliade attempts to derive his phenomenological approach from the nature of the religious data. Thus, the religious symbolism as a whole bundle of meanings is 'true', and a Freudian approach to religious symbolism is 'false', because it is 'partial' and interprets only one symbolic 'frame of reference'.

Eliade usually seems to evaluate the truth or falsity of a religious manifestation by some criterion of *coherency*. As we have seen, Eliade's phenomenological method is grounded in a hermeneutical framework of universal, structural, symbolic 'systems'; phenomenological understanding is usually achieved by reintegrating the particular datum within its coherent 'web' of symbolic associations. If the religious manifestation 'fits' into such a 'web', if it is consistent with its symbolic 'system', Eliade can evaluate it as a 'true' religious (lunar, etc.) manifestation. Conversely, when Eliade evaluates a phenomenon as 'aberrant' and 'false', this is often based on his judgment that the phenomenon cannot be reintegrated into, and is not consistent with, its 'proper' structural system. On this level of coherency, it seems that the phenomenologist of religion can evaluate descriptively.

There are serious methodological problems and hermeneutical limitations if we confine our evaluation of true or false to this level of analysis. One could have a very *consistent* and at the same time *false* system. For example, in times of severe existential crisis, certain archetypal escape mechanisms may be used in a very consistent manner. Thus, 'superstition', 'infantilism', and other 'aberrant' manifestations may reveal coherent structural systems of symbolic associations.

In addition, Paul Ricœur has pointed out that on this 'first' level of understanding, in which the phenomenologist of religion comprehends coherent symbolic systems or totalities, 'the question of truth has not yet been brought up'. If the phenomenologist gives the name truth to 'the internal consistency' of this symbolic world, 'such truth is truth without belief, truth at a distance'.[5]

Now when one examines Mircea Eliade's numerous evaluations of true, it appears that he does not remain on the 'horizontal and panoramic' level of coherency, but he supplements standards of con-

5. Ricœur, *The Symbolism of Evil*, pp. 353–354; 'The Symbol: Food for Thought', p. 203.

sistency with a 'vertical' appeal to some criterion of *adequacy*. For example, a symbol or image is described as 'true' in the sense of expressing a deep level of reality, a profound mode of being; a phenomenon is described as 'more true' in the sense that it is 'more adequate to the actual situation of man'.[6]

Without multiplying examples, it seems clear that Mircea Eliade is no longer evaluating on the 'horizontal' plane of coherency but is judging phenomena on a different level of analysis. We previously submitted that, in terms of an underlying framework of autonomous structural systems, it might be possible to evaluate descriptively if our standard for truth were coherency. But in terms of some criterion of adequacy, it may be more difficult to evaluate descriptively, and Eliade's evaluations may often be based on various ontological assumptions.

Meaning for homo religiosus *versus meaning for Eliade*

A crucial methodological difficulty, illustrated by Mircea Eliade's evaluation of phenomena as authentic, genuine, and true, arises from the fact that Eliade's interpretation often goes beyond, and even contradicts, what religious persons tell us about their phenomena. In reviewing *The Quest: History and Meaning in Religion*, Winston L. King poses the question: 'What meaning does he [Eliade] have in mind, and for whom?' The answer King finds in Eliade's writings is seen in the contrasting of 'Meaning for the investigator' and 'for the *homo religiosus in situ*'.[7]

Most scholars who have formulated such a dichotomy have intended it as a criticism of Eliade's methodology: the level of analysis of 'meaning for *homo religiosus*' is more descriptive and objective; 'meaning for Eliade' is highly subjective and normative, fails to do justice to the experience of 'the other', and is meaning which Eliade often 'reads into' his data.

The methodological difficulty seems to be the following: if Mircea

---

6. See 'The Sacred and the Modern Artist', p. 24; *The Forge and the Crucible*, p. 45; Luyster, 'The Study of Myth: Two Approaches', p. 243.

7. Winston L. King, Book Review of *The Quest: History and Meaning in Religion*, *Journal for the Scientific Study of Religion* 9, no. 1 (1970): 71.

Eliade interprets the religious meaning of a particular phenomenon and claims that *homo religiosus* has a false understanding of his or her own phenomenon, if he evaluates as inauthentic a phenomenon which the religious person regards as authentic, what kind of methodological check does Eliade have on these meanings and evaluations?

One possibility for checking such interpretations of meaning would be to suggest some kind of 'historical reconstruction': if the investigator reconstructed what was going on and if she or he brought this to the attention of the participant, *homo religiosus* would then recognize the interpretation to be true. But, unlike Wilfred Smith, Eliade could never accept such a methodological check. In some cases, there is no possibility that the participant would recognize the authentic religious meaning of her or his experience.

We may suggest one way of approaching the above methodological difficulty which partially undermines the 'for *homo religiosus*' — 'for Eliade' dichotomy. What needs to be challenged is that such a contrast illustrates a sharp distinction between the descriptive and objective versus the normative and subjective.

By the phrase 'meaning for *homo religiosus*', the phenomenologist of religion may be indicating those religious meanings of which the religious person is *conscious*. But, as we saw in Kristensen's descriptive phenomenology, limiting our domain of investigation to such 'conscious' meanings imposes severe restrictions on our phenomenological analysis. In addition, the psychological approaches of Freud and Jung clearly established that symbols and images convey their 'messages' even when they are not consciously understood.

Accordingly, by the phrase 'meaning for Eliade', we may be indicating the *total* religious meaning of some phenomenon, even if *homo religiosus* is not conscious of, or only partially understands, this meaning. We saw that religious experience concerns the whole person and does not limit itself to the plane of consciousness. Our analysis of 'meaning for Eliade' seems to gain greater support if we recall his views on the all-important function of religious symbolism: symbolism, as an autonomous mode of cognition and with its own 'logic', 'speaks to the whole person', and not just to the intellect; 'the validity' of the symbolism does not depend on its being understood; archetypal symbolisms preserve their structures and 'reappear spontaneously' even unconsciously in nonreligious phenomena; what matters to the phenomenologist is that the symbolic meanings 'are present' even if they are not consciously understood.[8]

The key methodological point in our above proposal is that 'meaning for Eliade' need not be taken as arbitrary, subjective, and normative if the analysis of the total religious meaning is based on some 'objective' hermeneutical framework. This would enable the phenomenologist of religion to go beyond the conscious understanding of *homo religiosus*, to analyze the full intentionality of a religious manifestation, and to evaluate descriptively.[9]

Of course, the very possibility for such phenomenological analyses depends on the lofty status granted to those structures which provide the foundation for Eliade's methodology. How can Eliade account for the remarkable sense of permanence, continuity, and universality he attributes to the archetypal symbolic structures? On what grounds can Eliade maintain that archetypal religious structures persist and preserve their structures, even when not consciously understood; that they can spontaneously reappear at any time and in any place? Mircea Eliade seems to provide us with two general kinds of explanation, one of which was suggested in our interpretation of his more-than-historical-explanation claim.[10]

Eliade's first explanation for the remarkable continuity, permanence, universality, and spontaneous reappearance, of the archetypal symbolic structures seems very *Jungian*: these are 'imprinted structures' or primordial 'memories' which persist in the *unconscious*. We noted Eliade's attempt in *Cosmos and History* to distinguish his sense of 'archetype' ('exemplary model' or 'paradigm') from Jung's meaning. It should also be acknowledged that Eliade never speaks of 'the collective unconscious' and that, in conversation, he claims never to have intended a Jungian account.

8. For example, see *The Sacred*, p. 129; *Patterns*, p. 450; *Images and Symbols*, pp. 24–25.
9. Eliade would submit that all of his analysis is at the level of 'meaning for *homo religiosus*'. Our dichotomy might be reformulated as '*conscious* meaning for *homo religiosus*' and '*total* meaning for *homo religiosus*'. Such a reformulation has considerable merit. Its major drawback, as we shall see, arises from the fact that Eliade sometimes goes beyond even this 'enlarged' descriptive level of interpreting the 'total meaning for *homo religiosus*' and bases his interpretations on an assumed ontological position.
10. See Ricketts, 'The Nature and Extent of Eliade's "Jungianism" ', pp. 216–224.

Nevertheless, there are many passages in Eliade's writings which seem to propose a rather Jungian explanation:

> . . . profane man is the descendent of *homo religiosus* and he cannot wipe out his own history — that is, the behavior of his religious ancestors which has made him what he is today. This is all the more true because a great part of his existence is fed by impulses that come to him from the depths of his being, from the zone that has been called the 'unconscious.'. . . Yet the contents and structures of the unconscious are the result of immemorial existential situations, especially of critical situations, and this is why the unconscious has a religious aura.[11]

Eliade's second explanation for the universality, permanence, and continuity of the essential religious structures is seen in his views of the *commonality* of certain 'primordial' existential situations, the human mode of being in the world, the human condition as such.

> The evolutionary view of man is prevalent today, but a historian of religion [Historian of Religion] generally works from a non-evolutionary view of human consciousness. When a man becomes aware of his mode of being, he has something in common with the so-called primitive and the modern philosopher. We know from letters and publications of anthropologists that what the philosopher calls 'angst', anxiety and death, was experienced by the primitives. I mean that *la grande situation humaine* has probably been the same in every era. I consider this a kind of basic universal.[12]

11. *The Sacred*, pp. 209, 210. Additional references cited by Ricketts as illustrating a rather Jungian account include: *Images and Symbols*, pp. 12–13; *Rites and Symbols of Initiation*, p. 128; *Myths, Dreams and Mysteries*, pp. 27, 28; *Mephistopheles and the Androgyne*, p. 10. Ricketts asserts ('The Nature and Extent of Eliade's "Jungianism" ', p. 223) that 'By not clearly distinguishing between his own idea of archetype and that of Jung, he [Eliade] has introduced confusion into his work; and by accepting what is widely considered to be the weakest point in Jung's hypothesis, he has created — unnecessarily, I believe — problems and enemies for himself.'

12. 'The Sacred in the Secular World', pp. 102–103. On page 101, Eliade writes 'that the sacred is an element in the structure of human consciousness, that it is a part of the human mode of being in the world'. 'If the sacred means being, the real, and the meaningful, as I hold it does, then the sacred is a part of the structure of human consciousness.' Such claims will be analyzed under 'ontological moves'.

We observed Eliade's interpretation of 'ecstasy' as forming 'an integral part of the human condition'; as a 'primordial phenomenon' in the sense that it is 'coextensive with human nature'; as revealing 'something of the human condition, regarded in its own right as a mode of existence in the universe'. Eliade also claimed that historical conditionings could not account for these 'primordial situations, of the human condition as such'.

This is Eliade's main explanation for the status of his universal structures: human beings, simply by their presence in the world, continually experience various 'primordial' existential situations; they continually encounter various archetypal kinds of existential crises, involving suffering, death, etc.; they continually utilize certain paradigmatic models for resolving these crises, as seen in such religious structures as those of ascension and initiation.

Whether Mircea Eliade can decipher all of this in his data or whether such an explanation entails certain ontological moves remains to be seen. We shall examine more closely his views about primordial existential situations and the human condition as such under 'levels of meaning'.

LEVELS OF MEANING

Evaluations of levels as 'elevated' and 'highest'

As we saw in Chapter 5, symbols are not arbitrary irresponsible creations of the psyche, but function according to their own 'logical' principles. It is because of such a 'logic of symbols' that Mircea Eliade can speak of structurally coherent meanings which 'fit together' to form symbolic wholes or 'systems'. In terms of such a logic, symbolism was seen to be 'multivalent': it has the capacity to reveal a multitude of structurally coherent meanings; it can reveal a perspective in which heterogeneous phenomena on different planes of reality are brought into structurally interlocking relationships.

Now Eliade not only distinguishes these different planes of reality, but he evaluates some levels as 'higher', as 'deeper', as more 'elevated'. Phenomena manifested on these higher levels are evaluated as 'more authentic', 'more true'. Such evaluations are of crucial methodological importance because it is primarily in terms of such 'elevated' meanings that Mircea Eliade is able to grasp the essential structure of the religious experience, to comprehend the 'center' of the symbolic 'web', to interpret and evaluate the meaning of 'lower' level religious manifestations.

Such evaluations by Eliade certainly appear to be the very kinds of normative judgments which Historians of Religions have traditionally avoided and have ascribed to such fields as philosophy and theology. For example, one expects the Christian theologian to evaluate the phenomenon of Jesus as the Christ as manifested on the 'highest' plane of reality, but such a judgment clearly rests on a normative basis.

If Eliade is to meet such a criticism, he must provide us with 'objective' criteria on the basis of which he can descriptively evaluate these levels of religious meaning. We shall begin with several hints from Eliade's writings and then develop an analysis which, it must be admitted, is nowhere explicitly propounded in Eliade's phenomenology.

Mircea Eliade begins the final paragraph of 'Methodological Remarks on the Study of Religious Symbolism' with this conclusion: 'In order to decipher a religious symbol, not only is it necessary to take into consideration all of its contexts, but one must above all reflect on the meanings that this symbol has had in what we might call its "maturity." ' Two sentences later, in what seems to be submitted as restatement of the above conclusion, Eliade writes: '. . . since the "cipher" constituted by this symbolism carries with it in its structure all the values that have been progressively revealed to man in the course of time, it is necessary in deciphering them to take into account their most general meaning, that is, the one meaning which can articulate all the other, particular meanings and which alone permits us to understand how the latter have formed a structure'.[13] It is this relationship between Eliade's evaluation of religious phenomena as '*mature*', '*elevated*', and '*highest*', on the one hand, and his use of criteria such as '*the most general*' and '*the universal*', on the other hand, which we wish to develop.

13. 'Methodological Remarks', p. 107. Cf. *Patterns*, pp. 6–8.

Let us recall only a few of the numerous illustrations, found throughout our study, which have clearly established the methodological emphasis on the universal and the general in Eliade's phenomenological approach. Eliade wishes to formulate a method which can 'integrate' the sociological, the psychological, the historical, etc., into the general perspective of the History of Religions. He interprets the meaning of the particular (snake) datum by reintegrating it into its universal (lunar) structural system of symbolic associations. In gaining insight into the essential structure of various (snake) phenomena, the phenomenologist of religion, through such methods as 'free variation', attempts to grasp the universal (lunar) 'invariant core' which constitutes the essential meaning of the particular (snake) phenomena.

That Mircea Eliade as a phenomenologist emphasizes the general and the universal is evident, but *why* should these standards be so relevant to religious phenomena and, more specifically, to evaluations of religious data as 'elevated', 'mature', 'highest', and 'deepest'? Our analyses of the dialectic of the sacred and the profane and of the nature of religious symbolism clearly established a *necessary* relationship between such criteria and the nature of religious experience.

In Chapter 4, it was seen that *homo religiosus* experiences the sacred as the transcendent, absolutely 'real' dimension of existence which provides him or her with universal exemplary models; in terms of such paradigmatic structures, the religious person can experience what were chaotic, isolated, profane phenomena as now part of a coherent, meaningful, spiritual *Lebenswelt*. Thus, when we discussed the nature of religion as an 'opening', we quoted Mircea Eliade as asserting that 'by being transcendent and exemplary it [the sacred] compels the religious man to come out of personal situations, to surpass the contingent and the particular and to comply with general values, with the universal'.[14]

In Chapter 5, it was seen that religious symbolism, as an 'extension' or 'prolongation' of the process of hierophanization, enables *homo religiosus* to experience and 'to live' the universal. Religious symbolism has an 'existential function': it 'bursts open' the immediate reality of

---

14. *Myths, Dreams and Mysteries*, p. 18.

the historical, 'natural', profane existential situation, 'opening' the particular beings and things to 'transobjective meanings'. What were experienced as 'fragmented', profane situations are transformed into spiritual experiences; what were experienced as 'isolated', 'subjective' particular modes of existence now 'open out' to universal systems of coherent structures.

Indeed, Eliade often uses these criteria of most general and universal to distinguish the religious from the nonreligious and to distinguish the authentically religious manifestations from 'parareligious' phenomena. For example, it is on such a basis that he can judge the distance separating the universe of the unconscious, which often has a 'religious aura', from the universe of religion. In terms of the symbolism of 'the Tree of the World', *homo religiosus* may experience a particular phenomenon as signifying 'the whole of the cosmos', and thus, as a total religious experience, he or she may succeed in 'living the universal'. A depth psychologist, such as Jung, may observe the image of the Tree functioning on the dream level, and this may reveal to him that the individual is now able 'to integrate a crisis in the depths and to recover his psychic balance'. But for Eliade this does not constitute a religious experience unless there is the revelation of the universal structure of the tree-symbolism: periodic and unending renewal, regeneration, immortality, absolute reality. 'But, not having been accepted in its symbolic sense, the image of the Tree [in dreams] has not succeeded in revealing the universal, and therefore has not lifted the man up to the plane of the Spirit, as religion, however rudimentary, always does.'[15]

We may now be able to relate Eliade's criteria to his evaluations of 'elevated' and 'highest'. As we have just seen, all religion 'opens out' to the universal. But it has been shown that not all religious expressions are equally successful in revealing the universal. A particular snake phenomenon, expressing one possible lunar valorization, may reveal very little of its universal lunar structure. It may be a very *limited* religious expression, in the sense that the manifestation hardly 'points beyond' the finite, contingent, historical conditionings of its profane existential situation, and *homo religiosus* is not even conscious of the

15. *Ibid.*, pp. 18–20.

essential lunar structure. Such a religious phenomenon is manifested on a 'low' level of reality, and, in some cases, that level may be evaluated as 'degenerate' or 'infantile'. At the other extreme, there are certain religious expressions, arising from archetypal intuitions of essential religious structures, which clearly reveal the universal. At various, highly creative moments in the history of humankind, *homo religiosus* actually grasped the essential lunar structure, and, in terms of this most general or universal structure, he or she was able to homologize the diverse planes of lunar valorization. Thus, the religious person was able to 'fit together' the heterogeneous phenomena manifested on different levels into a structurally coherent lunar 'system'. Such a religious phenomenon, *fully revealing* the universal lunar structure, is evaluated as on the most 'elevated', 'the highest', or 'the deepest' level of reality.

In our analysis of the phenomenological method for gaining insight into meaning and of a specific kind of induction, we suggested a possible 'clue' to Eliade's frequent evaluations of religious phenomena as 'higher'. In light of our present analysis, we may propose that *homo religiosus* achieves a 'higher' spiritual realization to the extent that his or her religious experience is *less limited* by the particular, finite, historical and cultural *conditionings* relevant to the existential situation within which the sacred is manifested; to the extent that the religious experience is 'closer' to, or more fully reveals, the essential religious structure and thus enables the person to 'live the universal'.

Identifying the 'highest' level: 'the transconscious'

Perhaps the best way to check such an interpretation would be to identify those specific religious experiences which Mircea Eliade evaluates as 'the highest' or most 'elevated' religious phenomena. If there is a logical principle in terms of which symbols point beyond themselves toward higher and higher levels of manifestation, what type of religious experience is expressed by the religious symbol in its 'maturity'? What type of religious experience best enables *homo religiosus* to intuit the essential religious structure and to 'live the universal'?

In answering these questions, we may return to the symbolism of ascension, which is probably that religious symbolism Eliade finds most capable of revealing the 'highest' religious experiences.

All this admitted, one cannot refrain from affirming that the symbolism of ascension reveals its deepest meanings when it is examined in relation to the most 'pure' activity of the spirit. It may be said to deliver its 'true message' upon the planes of metaphysics and mysticism. One might also say that it is thanks to the values that ascension stands for in the spiritual life (the lifting-up of the soul to God, mystic ecstasy, etc.) that is other significances, discernible on the levels of ritual, myth, dream-life or psychagogy, become fully intelligible and disclose their secret purport.[16]

A word of caution on Eliade's use of the term 'metaphysics' may be helpful. Although a philosopher, taking into consideration Eliade's criteria of the 'most general' and 'universal', could easily understand why Eliade would evaluate the metaphysical plane as elevated, the phenomenologist of religion does not restrict this term to the highly rational and systematic formulations of traditional philosophy. Thus, Eliade can speak of an archaic metaphysics because the symbols, myths, and rites express a 'complex system of coherent affirmations about the ultimate reality of things', a 'recognition of a certain situation in the cosmos'.[17] In this sense, the 'pure' mystical consciousness, which enables *homo religiosus* to homologize diverse planes of reality and experience in a unified coherent structural 'system', reveals a highly spiritual, metaphysical position.

Let us cite a second illustration: the final 'stage' recommended by Patañjali which enables the yogi to emancipate her or himself from one's human condition, to realize absolute freedom and the unconditioned. The act of transcendence, *samādhi*, is a 'paradoxical state', which can be related to other manifestations of 'the coincidence of opposites'. 'Like all paradoxical states, *samādhi* is equivalent to a rein-

16. *Ibid.*, pp. 118–119. *Ibid.*, p. 122: 'The images of "flight" and of "ascension", so frequently appearing in the worlds of dream and imagination, become perfectly intelligible only at the level of mysticism and metaphysics, where they clearly express the ideas of *freedom* and *transcendence*. But at all the other, "lower" levels of the psychic life, these images still stand for procedures that are homologous, in their tendency, to acts of "freedom" and "transcendence".'

17. See *The Myth of the Eternal Return*, p. 3; *Images and Symbols*, p. 176.

tegration of the different modalities of the real in a single modality—the undifferentiated completeness of precreation, the primordial Unity.' This 'supreme reintegration' is not a 'mere regression to primordial nondistinction', which is the case with various trances and other means of 'emptying consciousness'.

> One essential fact must always be borne in mind: the yogin works on all levels of consciousness and of the subconscious, for the purpose of opening the way to transconsciousness (knowledge-possession of the Self, the *puruṣa*) . . . the recovery, through *samādhi*, of the initial nonduality introduces a new element in comparison with the primordial situation. . . . That element is *knowledge* of unity and bliss. There is a 'return to the beginning,' but with the difference that the man 'liberated in life' recovers the original situation enriched by the dimensions of *freedom* and *transconsciousness.*[18]

Without multiplying examples, we may identify the 'highest' type of religious experience: it is the liberating experience of the 'pure', unifying consciousness, the mystical intuition of undifferentiated unity, of mystical union with the Ultimate, in which all finite, historical, 'limiting' conditions of human existence are transcended.

It seems to me that this identification of such a higher religious consciousness is consistent with Eliade's general *antireductionist* orientation, as illustrated by the methodological assumption of the *irreducibility* of the sacred. Mac Linscott Ricketts, in a section entitled 'The Religious a Priori', analyzes this concept of the transconscious as Eliade's attempt to render more adequate Rudolf Otto's a priori category of the Holy. 'Eliade wishes to designate a mental structure or capacity set apart from all others, one which comes into play only in religious experience': this is 'a higher logos', which involves trans-

---

18. *Yoga*, pp. 95–100. We shall adopt this term, '*transconsciousness*', as describing the most elevated or highest state of religious consciousness. Eliade, himself, rarely uses the term, and, his usage in several contexts is quite ambiguous. As we saw in the case of such terms as 'transhistorical' and 'transhuman', Mircea Eliade never appears entirely satisfied with any specific term when he describes this 'higher' religious experience. Ricketts cites the following places in which the expression, 'the transconscious', is employed: *Patterns*, pp. 450, 454; *The Forge and the Crucible*, p. 201; *Image. and Symbols*, pp. 17, 37, 119–120; *Yoga*, pp. 99, 226.

cending of both conscious and unconscious levels, as seen in the highest mystical experiences.[19]

This notion of transconsciousness may be related to our analysis of evaluating levels of meaning as elevated, highest, or deepest. In Chapter 3, we saw that most contemporary Historians of Religions, reacting against past reductionist approaches, claim that religious experience concerns the 'total person'. Accordingly, for Eliade, religious experience includes all levels of consciouness: the conscious, the unconscious, and the transconscious.

This may provide us with an additional criterion for distinguishing the authentically religious from the nonreligious and the 'parareligious'. Recall our recently formulated example from *Myths, Dreams and Mysteries* in which Eliade distinguished the image of 'the Tree of the World' as a 'psychic phenomenon' from its religious manifestation. The dream image of the Tree was not genuinely religious, because it was manifested *only* on the plane of the unconscious; the symbolism of the Tree of the World was evaluated as religious, because it was manifested on all levels of reality and thus included the transconscious, which was, in fact, that higher consciousness which enabled *homo religiosus* to *unify* the diverse levels of manifestation, thereby experiencing 'the totality' and 'living the universal'.

We may have uncovered a serious methodological difficulty. Mircea Eliade often employs this concept of the transconscious as a criterion for all genuine religious experience. Indeed, the very intentionality of the dialectic of hierophanies (experience of 'something' transhuman, transhistorical, not 'natural', not temporal) would seem to require a 'higher' or at least unique structure of consciousness. Thus, in terms of this irreducibly religious structure of consciousness, we can distinguish genuine religious phenomena from such pseudoreligious and parareligious phenomena as those of various forms of nationalism and of Marxism; certain science fiction stories, movies, and other aesthetic creations; secular rituals, such as most Western New Year's celebrations.

But Eliade usually describes the transconscious state in such a way that it appears to be a structure of only the 'highest', 'deepest', 'most

19. Ricketts, 'The Nature and Extent of Eliade's "Jungianism" ', pp. 228–230.

elevated' religious experiences. It is on such a basis that he often distinguishes the lower level phenomena of the masses from the higher consciousness of the 'religious specialist', who grasps the essential structure of the phenomena and may have the only 'correct' or 'genuine' understanding of the religious manifestations.

Our proposed solution to this methodological difficulty is the following. *All* genuine religious experience involves the *transconscious*; without such a unique, 'higher', religious consciousness there would be no experience of hierophanies. But the *degree* to which the transconscious functions in different societies and in different people within the same society varies considerably. Consequently, certain mystical religious experiences can be evaluated as 'the highest' because *homo religiosus* is fully aware of the essential structure revealed in the manifestation and thus his or her consciousness 'opens out' to the universal.

During several of our sessions, Mircea Eliade has agreed with the identification of this kind of mystical experience as the most elevated and has gone on to say that such 'complex' mystical experiences are 'related to elaborate symbolic constructions' and seem to be 'the most revealing' in terms of the meaning given to them. Eliade claimed that the *raptus mysticus* was 'considered in the religions as the highest attainment', i.e., this evaluation has been made by *homo religiosus*. Thus, in light of the above analysis, Eliade's claim is that *homo religiosus* has experienced and evaluated such a mystical 'pure' consciousness of undifferentiated unity as best revealing 'the most general', as best 'opening out' to the universal; in short, as the highest religious experience.

Such an evaluation would seem to be at least partially based on an assumed ontological position, much more characteristic of Eastern rather than Western religious traditions. Indeed, Eliade's general methodological orientation leans somewhat toward a more Eastern 'direction'. Arnold Toynbee, in *An Historian's Approach to Religion*, and many other scholars have suggested that the Western religions (Judaism, Islam, Christianity) tend toward 'exclusivism'. Thus, it would be a temptation for such a synthetic generalist as Mircea Eliade to derive much of his methodological framework from religious phenomena of the more 'inclusivistic' Eastern traditions. We shall cite only one illustration and then offer several general comments on the kind of religious experience Eliade evaluates as highest.

Thomas Altizer is probably correct in arguing that the *coincidentia oppositorum* is Eliade's 'favorite' symbolism. Eliade certainly regards 'the Symplegades', the *coincidentia oppositorum*, and other 'paradoxical' symbolisms so prevalent in mystical traditions as expressing the highest level of religious experience. Eliade is justified in stating that the symbolism of 'the coincidence of opposites' is universal, and he does cite such Western illustrations as Meister Eckhardt and Nicholas of Cusa.[20]

Nevertheless, such Western religious figures were never in the mainstream, but rather on the fringe, of their particular religious traditions. Christianity and the other Hebraic religions have been theistic and have usually attributed only 'positive' attributes to God. One need only recall that such Western mystics were usually suspect and often persecuted, excommunicated, or even put to death.

If one turns to Eastern religions, the situation is quite different. Here, in the more monistic traditions, symbolisms such as the *coincidentia oppositorum* abound and are often considered the best means for expressing ultimate reality. Eastern mystics who employ such symbolisms are often revered as having attained the highest spiritual realizations.

It seems possible to formulate two general 'models' of religious mysticism which differ with respect to their views of Ultimate Reality and of the mystical realization. First, there is the pattern we may call 'union with a remainder'. In this pattern, the mystical realization is of union with the Supreme Reality (usually expressed as God), but God is always transcendent and 'Other'. This pattern is union with a remainder, communion with God, union interpreted dualistically. This is the usual Western 'model', although all theistic religions tend to illustrate it.

Second, there is the pattern we may call 'union without a remainder'. In this religious pattern, the mystical realization is of complete unity and identity with the Ultimate Reality. Here we have the more typical Eastern 'model', although various Western mystics such as Eckhardt seem to exemplify it.

Now it is our contention that the types of experiences that Eliade

20. See Altizer, *Mircea Eliade and the Dialectic of the Sacred*, pp. 17–20, 81–104, and *passim; Patterns*, pp. 419–423; *Mephistopheles and the Androgyne*, pp. 78–124.

evaluates as the highest are much closer to the second, more typically Eastern, pattern of religious mysticism. Here we have the mystical intuition of a completely undifferentiated unity; the transconscious experience of the universal, in which all particular, historical, 'natural', 'limiting' conditionings are transcended.

Finally, we may comment on a point already suggested in our discussion of the *coincidentia oppositorum*. It seems that religious mysticism in general is most prevalent in Eastern religions. Salvation, as seen in the 'highest' forms of Hinduism and Buddhism, is identical with the ultimate mystical realization. But the Western religions, while manifesting religious mysticism, are not essentially mystical; their major sources, scriptures, and values are usually not mystical and are sometimes even at odds with mysticism. Christian mystics usually appear as the 'exceptions' and are often looked upon with suspicion by the traditional religion. Traditional Juadaism has not encouraged its mystical paths of Kabbalism and Hasidism. Islam subjected the Sufi mystics to considerable persecution; many Muslims consider these mystical strains to be an impure and insignificant Indian influence.

Therefore, I would conclude that Mircea Eliade has not simply described what *homo religiosus* has evaluated as 'most elevated'. In fact, Eliade has gone beyond a descriptive evaluation of what the data from each religious tradition revealed. His assessment is partially based on normative judgments: that the plane of mystical experience (in itself more characteristic of Eastern religious phenomena) is evaluated as the 'most elevated'; that the 'highest' or 'deepest' manifestations on the level of mystical experience have a structure more typical of Eastern mysticism.

Mircea Eliade could take the very bold step and claim that not he, but the religious data themselves— the structure of the dialectic of the sacred, the nature of the symbolic structural systems, the 'bursting open' of the particular and the revealing of the universal, etc. — establish the conclusion that the highest levels of spiritual realizations are more often expressed by Eastern rather than Western phenomena. And we suspect that this is precisely how Eliade feels about his religious data. Although Mircea Eliade has never explicitly made such a judgment, there are other equally bold, equally controversial claims found throughout his writings, and it is to several of these that we shall now turn.

Illustrations of normative judgments

Throughout this study, we have cited a number of controversial statements by Mircea Eliade, which seemed to be highly normative and which were often the source of considerable criticism of his phenomenology of religion. These assertions often involved judgments about the human mode of being in the world and 'the human condition, as such'; about what is 'true' and 'authentic' and 'the highest' aspect of reality.

In the vast majority of such assertions, it is our position that methodological difficulties can be resolved by inserting 'for *homo religiosus*' or 'from the perspective of the History of Religions' in the text. Eliade is describing normative judgments made by the religious person; evaluations arrived at on the basis of a 'religious scale'. As Ira Progoff writes: 'The question to which Eliade addresses himself is nothing less than the question of how man establishes his sense of what is real and ultimately valid in his life. This is not a philosophical question, but a matter of fact. It is a question of what individuals feel to be real with sufficient conviction so that they can base their conduct upon it.'[21]

Thus, we observed that many interpreters have criticized Mircea Eliade for his personal (theological) doctrine of a 'fall'. But in most of his statements about a 'fall', Eliade is describing the evaluations made by *homo religiosus*. In terms of the dialectic of hierophanies, in terms of the 'perfect', transhistorical, transcendent, exemplary models revealed through myths, the religious data disclose that religious people have evaluated their historical, temporal, 'natural', 'conditioned', profane mode of being in the world as a 'fall'. Similarly, most of the assertions about phenomena as 'real' and 'true' are made on the basis of a religious 'scale'; from the perspective of a nonreligious scale, such religious phenomena might be evaluated as 'unreal', 'illusory', or 'false'.

---

21. 'Culture and Being: Mircea Eliade's Studies in Religion', p. 51.

We have seen that many scholars, who might be sympathetic with such an effort at describing religious phenomena on the basis of a religious scale, have criticized Eliade's phenomenology precisely for not doing this. They contend that Eliade goes far beyond a description of meaning for *homo religiosus*; that he 'reads into' the religious data all kinds of meaning and is guilty of highly personal and subjective judgments.

To meet such criticisms, we suggested that Eliade's phenomenological approach often allows him to evaluate descriptively. We granted that Mircea Eliade often goes beyond a description of the (conscious) interpretations and evaluations of *homo religiosus*. But we submitted that, in terms of his hermeneutical framework, Eliade could evaluate religious phenomena as 'real', 'true', 'higher', etc., and that such judgments could be rendered on a descriptive level and from the religious perspective of the History of Religions.

Nevertheless, several of our previous illustrations seem to indicate that even such an 'enlarged' notion of the descriptive does not completely remove the impression that Eliade is sometimes very subjective and is just interjecting his own personal feelings. Before turning to a delineation of several such normative judgments, let us emphasize two points which must be kept in mind.

First, only a small part of Mircea Eliade's total scholarship is represented by such normative judgments; most of his analysis is on the level of descriptive hermeneutics. Eliade devotes far more of his scholarship to describing the particular historical and cultural conditionings and to interpreting the meaning of, say, some Australian cosmogonic myth than using that phenomenon to render a judgment about the human condition.

Nevertheless, even if they represent a small part of Eliade's total scholarship, these normative judgments are extremely important: they are the source of much dissatisfaction with Eliade's History of Religions; they reveal a level of creative speculation, synthesis, and generality which distinguishes Eliade from almost all other Historians of Religions; they illustrate the most philosophical level of Eliade's analysis.

Second, we would never claim that all of what follows, especially much of the analysis under 'Ontological Moves and Levels of Generality' and 'Primary Symbolic Structures and Verification', can be found in Eliade's writings. Much of the following, although never formulated by Eliade, does seem implicit in his phenomenological approach. Often our procedure takes the form of beginning with Eliade's significant normative judgments and then asking what assumptions he had to make and what principles he had to adopt in order to arrive at such conclusions. Sometimes our analysis goes beyond anything Eliade has written; this may be taken as an attempt to suggest some new directions and possible openings for future creative thought.

We shall not repeat our previous illustrations, such as assertions about the phenomena of ecstasy and ascension, which described primordial existential situations and the human condition as such. What follows are several other statements by Mircea Eliade which seem to be highly normative and the reactions of a few of his interpreters to this level of analysis.

In *Myths, Dreams and Mysteries*, Eliade submits that

> religion is the exemplary solution of every existential crisis. Religion 'begins' when and where there is a total revelation of reality; a revelation which is at once that of the sacred — of that which supremely *is*, of what is neither illusory nor evanescent — and of man's relationship to the sacred, a relationship which is multiple, changing, sometimes ambivalent, but which always places man at the heart of the real.[22]

On what basis can Eliade make these claims? He is not simply asserting that religion always presents a paradigmatic model in terms of which religious persons resolve their existential crises. 'Religion is the exemplary solution of *every* existential crisis.' On what basis can Eliade assert that the religious revelation is not 'illusory', is of 'reality', and 'always places man at the heart of the real'?

Eliade would probably claim that these are not his personal judgments, but are judgments made by *homo religiosus*, and that they are valid only in terms of such a religious perspective. Nevertheless, in this and in numerous other contexts, it does seem that Eliade has gone

22. *Myths, Dreams and Mysteries*, p. 18. *The Sacred*, p. 210: 'For religion is the paradigmatic solution for every existential crisis.'

beyond such a level of analysis and is presenting us with some very general, normative judgments about the nature of our mode of being in the world and our existential crises.

What Professer Eliade wishes to claim, as we shall see in the next two illustrations, is that it is *more authentically human* to live one's life in terms of transcendent exemplary models than to identify oneself fully with the temporal and historical dimension of existence; that the modern historical person, who refuses any 'religious solutions', *cannot* solve his or her most fundamental existential crises.

In *The Sacred and the Profane*, Eliade describes the religious perspective of archaic societies in which 'the whole of life is capable of being sanctified'. He then goes on to assert that 'For nonreligious man, all vital experiences — whether sex or eating, work or play — have been desacralized. This means that all these physiological acts are deprived of spiritual significance, hence deprived of their truly human dimension.'[23] As Ricketts has written, 'instead of choosing historicism, Eliade chooses the transhistorical or the religious mode of being as the more truly human'.[24]

One may question the grounds on which Eliade makes such a judgment, especially since Camus, Sartre, most other existentialists and historicists claim just the opposite. They would evaluate such religious appeals to transcendence as *escapes* from reality, as *negations* of authentic human existence. Only desacralized experience allows human beings to realize their 'truly human dimension' of existence. 'They [those in rebellion] choose, and give us as an example the only original rule of life today: to learn to live and to die, and, in order to be a man, to refuse to be a god.' The rebel rejects all appeals to divinity so that one might share in the struggles of humanity. Unless we assume the struggle and tension of the revolt, we betray our *true nature* as human beings.[25]

23. *The Sacred*, pp. 167, 168. Cf. 'The Sacred in the Secular World', p. 104: 'I cannot limit his [the modern person who claims not be religious] universe to that purely self-conscious, rationalistic universe which he pretends to inhabit, since that universe is not human.'

24. Ricketts, 'Mircea Eliade and the Death of God', p. 43.

25. Albert Camus, *The Rebel*, pp. 304–306 and *passim*. What makes a comparison of Sartre or Camus and Eliade especially interesting is that they seem to be in basic agreement as to the nature of religion and religious experience. It is their evaluations of religious phenomena which are so antithetical.

Illustrations of such normative claims may be found throughout the final chapter of *The Myth of the Eternal Return*, which is entitled 'The Terror of History'. For example, Eliade contends that 'Whatever be the truth in respect to the freedom and the creative virtualities of historical man, it is certain that none of the historicistic philosophies is able to defend him from the terror of history.' When the modern person confronts Nazi concentration camps, U.S. atrocities in Vietnam, and other historical 'tragedies', Eliade submits that 'the terror of history' must lead to nihilism or despair if the person completely makes her or himself through one's historical situations. Eliade claims that 'the man who has left the horizon of archetypes and repetition can no longer defend himself against that terror except through the idea of God'. 'Any other situation of modern man leads, in the end, to despair.'[26]

From various comments about the peasants and history of his native Romania, it is evident that Mircea Eliade identifies with the above analysis in a very personal manner. He concludes his essay on the most popular Romanian ballad, the 'Mioritza', by telling us that the Romanians and other peoples of eastern Europe became conscious of 'the terror of history':

Despite all that they are ready to accomplish, despite all sacrifices and all heroism, they are condemned by history, because they are situated at the very crossroads of invasions . . . or in the immediate neighborhood of military powers dynamized by imperialistic fanaticism. There is no effective military or political defense against the 'terror of history,' simply because of the crushing inequality between the invaders and the invaded peoples. To be sure, this does not mean that the latter did not defend themselves, militarily and politically, and often with success. But in the end the situation could not be changed. Small political groups of peasants could not long resist the masses of the invaders.[27]

Mao Tse-tung told the Chinese peasants and Ho Chi Minh told the Vietnamese peasants that despite the past successes of outside invaders, and despite the military and imperialistic forces that oppressed

26. *The Myth of the Eternal Return*, pp. 159, 161–162.
27. 'The Clairvoyant Lamb', *Zalmoxis: The Vanishing God*, p. 254.

and exploited them, the situation could be changed. Feudalism, colonialism, capitalism, and neocolonialism were specific structures that were manifested at different stages of history and hence were not inevitable or eternal. If the peasants were divided into small groups, they must unite with other peasants and other anti-imperialist forces so that they could free themselves from the invaders and in the process change history.

Eliade, immediately following the above quotation, submits that 'To despair and nihilism the only response is a religious interpretation of the terror of history.' As in his interpretation of the Romanian ballad, the 'essential element' in overcoming the terror of history 'lies in *the capacity to annul the apparently irremediable consequences of a tragic event by charging them with previously unsuspected [religious] values'*. [28]

Certainly, the history of peasants in Romania and India may lend considerable support to Eliade's interpretation. Certainly, the successes of peasants and workers in China and Vietnam may lend considerable support to the interpretations by Mao and Ho. As we have previously submitted, the 'scale' makes the difference, and all interpretations are perspectival. Under 'verification', we shall suggest how one might begin to verify such perspectives.

Let us cite another illustration from Albert Camus, his 'experiment with nihilism', but this time, instead of indicating how the existentialist might disagree with Eliade's judgment, we shall indicate how Eliade might defend his above judgments. In *The Myth of Sisyphus*, Camus describes the total absurdity and meaninglessness of the world. Then in *The Plague*, and especially in *The Rebel*, he finds value in the human protest against one's absurd conditions. But if all is meaningless, what does it matter if others suffer and protest against the conditions that oppress you? Camus bases his social dimension and theory

---

28. *Ibid.*, pp. 254–255. Although our study is not intended to be a biographical study of Mircea Eliade, we may mention that there is a considerable documentation, especially in Romanian, which clearly establishes how deeply Eliade identifies both himself and his native Romania with such a position. The most comprehensive documentation in English of such views is Dennis A. Doeing, 'A Biography of Mircea Eliade's Spiritual and Intellectual Development from 1917 to 1940' (Ph.D. diss., University of Ottawa, 1975). Several of the selections in *Myths and Symbols: Studies in Honor of Mircea Eliade*, ed. Joseph M. Kitagawa and Charles H. Long, especially the essay by Virgil Ierunca, make clear this personal identification.

of revolt on the value of solidarity revealed in rebellion. Without this sense of complicity, we are still in the world of Sisyphus's solitary defiance. But it seems possible to contend that in a universe of the absurd, this affirmation of solidarity is just another manifestation of our curtailing lucid reason and attempting to escape nihilism through 'hope' and 'philosophical suicide'.[29]

Our point has not been to show that Mircea Eliade's judgment may be correct: that human beings, who completely make themselves through history, may not be able to overcome nihilism and despair. Our point is that such judgments, as well as our previous illustrations, involve a very different level of analysis from, say, an analysis of the meaning of some myth or ritual for *homo religiosus*. And Eliade has left himself open to considerable criticism by not distinguishing these different levels of analysis.

The above illustrations are typical of hundreds of similar statements found throughout Eliade's writings in which he makes judgments about the 'true' nature of the human being and one's 'actual' situation in the world, the nature of the modern Western human being and his or her alienated mode of being in the world, the present need for a 'new humanism' based on the modern person's encounter with the primordial religious symbolisms, etc.[30]

The point we wish to stress is that such assertions are not simply on the descriptive level of 'for *homo religiosus*'. Eliade has gone beyond what the religious data *directly* reveal. It is evident that he wishes to make such observations about modern human beings, Western so-

29. Even in *The Myth of Sisyphus and Other Essays*, in which Camus is so determined to uphold this *raisonnement absurde*, he encounters this same kind of difficulty. He argues that it is better to live like Sisyphus, with a consciousness of the absurd, than to live under religious or other illusions. But, to be consistent with his analysis of the absurd, it seems that Camus should maintain that it makes no difference whether one is aware of the absurd or blind to the human condition.

30. Such claims form the basis of 'History of Religions and a New Humanism', 'Crisis and Renewal in History of Religions', and various other articles by Mircea Eliade. Many of these articles have been revised and reproduced in *The Quest: History and Meaning in Religion*. Such claims are also emphasized in Eliade's collections of essays and articles: *Images and Symbols, Myths, Dreams and Mysteries*, and *Mephistopheles and the Androgyne* or *The Two and the One*. Most significantly, in our opinion, is the fact that such normative assertions can be found in those works which we consider Eliade's most scholarly books: *Shamanism, Yoga, Patterns*, and *The Myth of the Eternal Return*.

ciety, and the future of humankind from the perspective of the History of Religions. But it is equally evident that he is claiming something very different from a descriptive interpretation of the meaning of religious phenomena. Why are these claims different from the normative judgments of such disciplines as theology and philosophy of religion?

Robert D. Baird argues that Eliade's phenomenology of symbolism is 'as normative as theology because it is based on an assumed ontology which is neither historically derived nor descriptively verifiable'. In discussing Eliade's use of archaic man as a 'model of authentic existence', Baird writes as follows: 'Once one sees "the sacred" or "religion" as an ontological reality and once one operates as though its structures are also ontologically real, having identified these structures one has discovered reality. It then follows that those whose lives are lived in the sacred as completely as possible are the most authentic since they exist closest to reality.'[31]

In a similar manner, Thomas Altizer contends that Eliade's analysis (in 'Methodological Remarks') 'assumes an essential continuity between the religious symbol and the structure of the world: it assumes an ultimate identity between *reality* and the *sacred*'. Eliade 'believes that the religious symbol opens man to the real as such — to Being itself'.

According to Ricketts, Eliade 'is convinced that the study of religious data as such (and not as psychological data, for example) is the best way to understand not only the symbols and images, but also the nature of man himself'. In Eliade's differences with Jung, it 'is the nature of man and the reality of the religious experience that are at stake'.[32]

Our purpose in citing these illustrations has been neither to argue for or against Eliade's judgments nor to agree or disagree with his interpreters. Our purpose has been to substantiate the fact that Eliade's phenomenology functions on different planes of analysis and that at

31. Baird, *Category Formation and the History of Religions*, pp. 86–87. It is our position that Eliade is not nearly as normative as Baird and, to a lesser extent, Altizer seem to think. This is because they do not acknowledge Eliade's hermeneutical framework, which allows him to describe much of what they deem to be obviously normative.

32. Altizer, 'The Religious Meaning of Myth and Symbol', p. 89; Ricketts, 'The Nature and Extent of Eliade's "Jungianism" ', p. 232.

least some levels of his analysis seem to consist of highly normative judgments.

Now we recall that Mircea Eliade, in arguing against various reductionist approaches, has insisted on the religious perspective of the History of Religions. In terms of such a scale, the phenomenologist of religion can distinguish religious phenomena, interpret their religious meaning and evaluate them as 'higher' or 'lower' religious manifestations. To avoid being guilty of the same kind of reductionism he so vehemently opposes, Professor Eliade must grant that from a different (sociological, psychological, anthropological, economic) perspective, an investigator would interpret different meanings and make different evaluations.

But from the above and similar illustrations, it seems that Mircea Eliade is attempting to go *beyond such a perspectival orientation*. He has not limited his approach to participating sympathetically in the religious experiences of *homo religiosus* and to describing the structures of the religious life-world. He is presenting us with claims about the highest and deepest aspects of reality, about the true nature of the human being.

Are Eliade's normative judgments about, say, our modern secular modes of being in the world and about the human condition in general simply arbitrary and subjective? Has Eliade completely divorced himself from the proper domain of the phenomenology of religion and from any perspective within the History of Religions? It is the endeavor to answer such questions, especially by relating Eliade's normative judgments to his descriptive phenomenology, to which we now turn.

Ontological moves and levels of generality

In trying to analyze the status of such normative judgments, we would submit that Mircea Eliade's analysis moves to *greater and greater levels of generality* and that such a methodological procedure reveals an *ontological* stance. Our position is that such an approach, involving ontological moves which allow for analyses on greater levels of generality, can be seen in the works of most major philosophical phenomenologists.

For example, Merleau-Ponty describes the structures of perceptual consciousness in order to gain insight into the fundamental structures of human consciousness generally. And the assumption is that perception will in some way reveal this. This is an ontological move. This is not to say that such moves to greater levels of generality are simply arbitrary and subjective. Merleau-Ponty and other phenomenologists are concerned with verifying or justifying such moves in light of the greater clarity, coherency, etc., they bring to our understanding of the phenomena.

This is how we interpret Eliade's methodological procedure when, after describing the nature of some religious phenomenon in terms of its particular historical and cultural conditionings, he frequently asks whether that phenomenon 'might not reveal something of the human condition regarded in its own right as a mode of existence in the universe'. Thus, Eliade describes a variety of examples expressing 'ecstasy' and finally deciphers the essential structure of religious ecstasy. He then seems to *assume* that the structure of ecstasy, as a fundamental religious phenomenon, will reveal something essential about the human mode of being and the structure of consciousness; about our 'real' situation in the world and 'the human condition, as such'.

A crucial methodological difficulty in Eliade's phenomenology arises from the fact that he usually presents his interpretations as if they are all on the same level of analysis, arrived at by the same method, and having the same degree of support. He does not acknowledge that a judgment about an essential structure of the human condition is arrived at in a manner different from, say, a description of an essential structure of some cosmogonic myth; it is on a less descriptive level of analysis, is far more difficult to verify, and does not have the same degree of certainty.

Consider our illustration of the snake and lunar symbolism. At a certain stage in his analysis, Eliade detects various structural similarities between certain phenomena. Finally, he is able to grasp the total lunar 'web' and can then interpret the religious meaning of the particular snake datum by reintegrating it within its coherent, lunar, structural 'system' of symbolic associations.

This hermeneutical movement to greater and greater levels of generality has led many critics to charge that such interpretations are highly normative. However, we attempted to show the possibility of formulating such a general perspective through a descriptive level of analysis. But Mircea Eliade proceeds to even greater levels of generality, and, in this regard, it seems unlikely that he can avoid assuming some ontological position.

Eliade attempts to formulate a 'general picture' of what all the lunar hierophanies reveal; to determine whether they 'fit together' to form a 'theory', expressing a series of 'truths' which constitute a 'system'.[33] By grouping the lunar hierophanies around four central themes, Eliade grasps 'the dominant idea' in all these themes as 'one of *rhythm* carried out by a succession of contraries, of "becoming" through the succession of opposing modalities'. Nothing in the sublunar world can be 'eternal'; no change is final, since 'every change is merely part of a cyclic pattern'.

Mircea Eliade now moves to an even greater level of generality. He wishes to understand what this most 'general picture' of the structure disclosed by all of the lunar hierophanies reveals to us about the human mode of being in the world and about the nature of the human condition.

It might be said that the moon shows man his true human condition. . . . Though the modality of the moon is supremely one of change, of rhythm, it is equally one of periodic returning; and this pattern of existence is disturbing and consoling at the same time — for though the manifestations of life are so frail that they can suddenly disappear altogether, they are restored in the 'eternal returning' regulated by the moon. Such is the law of the whole sublunary universe.

On this general level of analysis, Eliade submits that the infinite variations of the universal 'myth of reintegration' express man's 'thirst to abolish dualisms, endless returnings and fragmentary existences'. According to Eliade, this universal expression reveals that man, 'from the time when he first realized his position in the universe', sought to pass beyond 'his human status ("reflected" so exactly by the moon's)'.[34]

Once again, the interpretations of the nature of 'the human condi-

33. See the section in *Patterns*, pp. 182–185, entitled 'Lunar Metaphysics'.
34. *Ibid.*, pp. 184–185.

tion' and religious experience formulated by Camus and Eliade seem remarkably similar. Indeed, the nature of the human mode of being in the world, which Eliade deciphers in the 'sublunary law' of the universe, is quite similar to Camus's understanding of the existential situation of Sisyphus. In addition, Camus concurs fully with Eliade's interpretation of the 'myth of reintegration': the human being, in experiencing 'his position in the universe', has an intense desire and 'nostalgia' for a more meaningful, coherent, unified existence; for a mode of being beyond 'his human status'.

Their differences in analysis arise from radically different evaluations of such phenomena. For Camus, an authentically human existence necessitates that one does not 'escape' from or negate her or his 'human condition'. The 'myth of reintegration' thus reveals a religious 'leap' which leads to 'existential suicide', to an inauthentic and illusory existence which negates what is 'truly human'.

Let us now consider a recently cited illustration: Eliade's analysis of 'the terror of history'. We shall then propose several methodological conclusions regarding the status of the lunar judgments, the following claims, and other similar interpretations.

At the beginning of *The Myth of the Eternal Return*, Mircea Eliade states the purpose of this book: 'to study certain aspects of archaic ontology — more precisely, the conceptions of being and reality that can be read from the behavior of the man of the premodern societies'. By studying multifarious 'facts' drawn from many different cultures, Eliade gains insight into 'the mechanism of traditional thought': 'how and why, for the man of the premodern societies, certain things become real'. In this manner, he hopes 'to identify the structure of this archaic ontology'.

After investigating the particular facts, Eliade submits the following conclusion about 'the same "primitive" ontological conception: an object or an act becomes real only insofar as it imitates or repeats an archetype. Thus, reality is acquired solely through repetition or participation; everything which lacks an exemplary model is "meaningless," i.e., it lacks reality.'[35]

---

35. *The Myth of the Eternal Return*, pp. 3–6, 34. One can understand why Eliade asserts that this 'primitive' ontology might be viewed as having 'a Platonic structure'. On p. 35, Eliade formulates 'a second aspect of this primitive ontology': the 'abolition

Mircea Eliade proceeds to an even more general level of interpretation, in which he seeks to analyze just what such an ontological conception reveals about the nature of the 'traditional' or 'premodern' person. He claims that the person's desire 'to refuse history, and to confine himself to an indefinite repetition of archetypes [probably] testifies to his thirst for the real and his terror of "losing" himself by letting himself be overwhelmed by the meaninglessness of profane existence.'[36]

In the last chapter of *The Myth of the Eternal Return*, Eliade attempts to confront the modern historical person with the archaic conception, which is 'archetypal and ahistorical'; more specifically, he wishes to analyze 'the solutions offered by the historicistic view to enable modern man to tolerate the increasingly powerful pressure of contemporary history' within the horizon of the archaic ontology. He concludes with the judgments we have previously described: none of the historicistic philosophies succeeds in defending a person from the terror of history; any solution to this terror which rejects the idea of God must lead to nihilism and despair. 'Justification of a historical event by the simple fact that it is a historical event' cannot free humanity 'from the terror that the event inspires'. 'Only such a freedom', grounded in the Judaeo-Christian 'category of faith' — 'for God everything is possible' — can defend the modern Western person 'from the terror of history'. 'Every other modern freedom . . . is powerless to justify history.'[37]

---

of profane time, of duration, of "history" ', through 'the imitation of archetypes and the repetition of paradigmatic gestures'.

36. *Ibid.*, pp. 91–92. On p. 91, Eliade describes this as the traditional person's 'thirst for the "ontic", his will to be. . .' Kirk (*Myth: Its Meaning and Functions in Ancient and Other Cultures*, p. 255 n) submits that Eliade's assumption that such traditional persons 'must in all likelihood have possessed concepts of "being", "non-being", "real", and "becoming", even if they did not have the words for them. . . . [and other] such extravagances, together with a marked repetitiousness, have made Eliade unpopular with many anthropologists and sociologists.' Eliade's position, as we have seen, is that when investigators uncover and interpret the meaning of the basic structures expressed in their data, they find that there are fundamental structures of human consciousness and of the human mode of being in the world; and these structures, which at their most essential level are constitutive of the human condition, transcend the historical and cultural conditionings of their particular religious manifestation.

37. *The Myth of the Eternal Return*, pp. 141, 150, 159–162. It may surprise the reader that Eliade uses the term 'God', rather than a more general term such as 'the sacred';

What concerns us is not the adequacy of Eliade's particular interpretation, but rather the fact that Mircea Eliade is no longer defining his analysis simply in terms of the perspective of *homo religiosus*. He seems to have moved to a level of generality beyond such perspectival limitations. In other words, Eliade is not claiming the following: from a religious perspective, no historicistic 'solution' can defend us from 'the terror of history'; but from some nonreligious perspective, there may be a 'solution' which can 'justify' history and overcome nihilism and despair. He is making general judgments about the human mode of being in the world and the human condition as such; and, on the basis of such judgments, he is claiming that the 'historicistic philosophies' of Hegel, Marx, Dilthey, and others cannot defend the modern Western human being from the terror of history.

Now such a procedure clearly involves an ontological stance. On what basis can Mircea Eliade proceed beyond his perspectival limitations? Isn't he guilty of the same *reductionism* he attacked when he formulated his methodological principle that 'the scale creates the phenomenon'? It would appear that Eliade *assumes* that the structures of religious experience, as seen in the religious person's refusal to identify her or himself with the temporal and historical dimension of existence, reveal fundamental structures of the human mode of being generally.

How does one arrive at such judgments? How does the phenomenologist justify them? Do such judgments simply express subjective, personal 'feelings'? Are they related in any way to more descriptive, phenomenological analysis?

Primary Symbolic Structures and Verification

We interpret the nature of most of Eliade's highly normative claims in light of the *ontological status* he grants the *archetypal symbolic structures*. As we have seen, Eliade views these universal, autonomous, coherent

---

such a choice is dictated by the specific context, involving an analysis of the modern, Western, historical person. Cf. Eliade's similar level of analysis in the last chapter of *Myths, Dreams and Mysteries*, 'Religious Symbolism and the Modern Man's Anxiety', pp. 231–245.

symbolisms as revealing the inexhaustible possibilities for expressing phenomena on all levels of reality. Such symbolisms allow for expressions on the 'lowest' and most 'aberrant' planes of manifestation and for expressions of the 'highest' and most creative metaphysical and mystical realizations. And the phenomenologist of religion, in gaining insight into the essential structure of a symbolism, can integrate the heterogeneous phenomena manifested on diverse planes of reality into a unified structural system. Often, in view of the particular historical and cultural conditionings and existential crises, the phenomenologist can understand why we have expressed our experiences through certain of the infinite possibilites of symbolic valorizations.

It is our interpretation that Eliade's phenomenological analysis, *on all levels of generality*, is dependent on this primary symbolic foundation. Most of these levels of phenomenological analysis are descriptive. Thus, on the 'horizontal' plane of hermeneutics, Eliade describes symbols through other symbols; describes how symbols function according to their own 'logic' and interlock to form coherent structural 'webs'; and describes the meaning of a particular symbolic expression by reintegrating it within its 'proper' symbolic system. In addition, these 'logical' structural systems allow the phenomenologist of religion to distinguish different planes of symbolic expression and to evaluate descriptively certain phenomena as 'higher', 'deeper', or 'elevated' manifestations.

Without recalling all of the levels of interpretation, let us consider the most general and most controversial level of analysis. Here Eliade moves beyond even the general analysis of what the religious data reveal about the basic mode of being of *homo religiosus*. He formulates normative judgments about the human mode of being generally, about the human condition as such. On this greatest level of generality, Mircea Eliade is no longer within the domain of descriptive phenomenology. Indeed, many of his judgments are on the level of analysis of philosophical anthropology.

Now the crucial methodological point, as we interpret this level of generality, is the following: Mircea Eliade has gone beyond the limits of descriptive analysis and has formulated various ontological concepts, but *such an ontological move is founded on and informed by the primary symbolic structures*.

True, when Mircea Eliade claims that modern human beings cannot overcome their sense of alienation if they completely make themselves through history; that in the authentically human dimension of existence, Sartre is wrong and existence does not precede essence; his analysis reveals an ontological move. It reveals a normative 'leap' in the sense that analysis on such a level of generality is more speculative and less certain than the more descriptive levels of analysis. The more descriptive analyses are 'closer' to or more directly dependent on the primary symbolisms. The general normative claims are on the greatest level of generality and are many levels 'removed' from the fundamental symbolisms.

The special ontological status of archetypal symbolism, we would submit, is the following: they are the fundamental *expressions for an extralinguistic reality*; they reveal various places where *language does 'key in' with actual experience.*[38] Symbols serve as 'ciphers' of reality. We can decipher the meaning of such ciphers in an infinite variety of ways and on many planes of interpretation. The symbolisms express the enigmas and ambiguities of being and the inexhaustible possibilities for philosophical reflection.

Philosophical reflection — and we interpret Professor Eliade's most significant normative judgments as on the plane of philosophical anthropology — is many levels removed from the archetypal symbolisms. Thus, between describing a lunar structure and making an ontological judgment about one's true nature, there are many intervening stages of interpretation, which we have usually expressed as Eliade's analysis on greater and greater levels of generality.

But this does not mean that such ontological moves are completely arbitrary and subjective. If they are to express deep aspects of reality, they must be informed by and be consistent with the basic intentionality of the primary symbolisms.

In short, the levels of philosophical analysis arise out and go beyond the 'givenness' of the archetypal symbolisms and the fundamentally descriptive levels of analysis. But philosophical reflection must continually *return to its foundation*, not only to be enriched and renewed

---

38. Cf. Ricœur, 'The Problem of the Double-Sense as Hermeneutic Problem and as Semantic Problem', pp. 64–68; Don Ihde, 'Some Parallels Between Analysis and Phenomenology', *Philosophy and Phenomenological Research* 27, no. 4 (1967): 583–586.

through the realization of previously unseen creative possibilities, but also to check that its ontological analyses and judgments on this 'distant' level of generality have not distorted the basic intentionality which constitutes its philosophical foundation.[39]

Now how might Eliade *verify* such ontological moves? How can he be sure that, in 'moving' to levels of interpretation more removed from the archetypal symbolisms, his analysis still 'keys in' with aspects of reality?

One realizes that this process of verification, unlike some of the methodological 'checks' on the levels of descriptive hermeneutics, cannot be carried out exclusively on the plane of symbolic structures. Such ontological analyses are founded on the symbolic structures, but *use symbols to get beyond the symbolic plane*. For example, Eliade may analyze a specific shamanic or yogic phenomenon of 'mystical flight' as revealing a structure of 'freedom and transcendence'. He may check his interpretation by reintegrating that symbolic expression within its total coherent system of 'ascension symbolism'. But how does Eliade verify his ontological claim that this symbolic structure reveals something about 'the true nature of the human being' and is 'constitutive of man'?

It seems to us that implicit in much of Eliade's phenomenology is a sense of verification not unlike the proposals of Paul Ricœur and other existential phenomenologists. Ricœur distinguishes three different levels of interpreting symbols: descriptive phenomenology, where, as we have seen, he places Eliade's phenomenology of religion and discusses verification in terms of the 'horizontal' plane of internal coherence; the 'circle of hermeneutics'; and philosophical hermeneutics.[40]

Paul Ricœur describes the level of philosophical hermeneutics in

39. We would never maintain that all of Eliade's normative judgments can be viewed in this manner. Within his phenomenology of religion, one finds the insertion of various parenthetical remarks and highly subjective, personal feelings. But the above analysis expresses our general understanding of how Eliade arrives at his most significant ontological claims.

40. *The Symbolism of Evil*, pp. 351–357; 'The Symbol: Food for Thought', pp. 202–207. Our concern here is not with describing the methodological 'movement' from one level to the next, but only with the notion of verification on the 'third level' of philosophical hermeneutics, which 'is the properly philosophical stage'.

terms of a 'wager': 'I wager that I shall have a better understanding of man and of the bond between the being of man and the being of all beings if I follow the *indication* of symbolic thought.' Ricœur calls the task of *verifying* his wager a 'transcendental deduction' of symbols, 'in the Kantian sense' of 'justifying a concept by showing that it makes possible the construction of a domain of objectivity'. Ricœur's description of this task seems to reveal precisely what Eliade is doing: 'In fact, the symbol, used as a means of detecting and deciphering human reality, will have been verified by its power to raise up, to illuminate, to give order to that region of human experience . . . which we were too ready to reduce to error, habit, emotion, passivity — in short, to one or another of the dimensions of finitude that have no need of the symbols . . . to open them up and discover them.'[41]

The symbol is not 'a simple revealer of self-awareness', but has an 'ontological function' of speaking to us 'of the situation of the being of man in the being of the world'. Hence the task of philosophical phenomenology is 'starting from the symbols, to elaborate existential concepts — that is to say, not only structures of reflection but structures of existence, insofar as existence is the being of man'.[42]

We have selected Ricœur's formulation, in preference to other similar accounts in existential phenomenology, because it describes almost perfectly our understanding of Eliade's ontological analysis. Perhaps this is why we regard Eliade's approach to religious phenomena, at least on several levels of interpretation, as having more in common with various approaches in existential phenomenology than with most approaches of scholars in the History of Religions. We would submit that Mircea Eliade's occasional reluctance to be identified in any way with philosophical phenomenology usually is based on the

41. *The Symbolism of Evil*, p. 355. If this is precisely what Mircea Eliade is doing, the reader may wonder why Ricœur limits Eliade's phenomenology of religion to the 'first level' of comprehension. (One very brief exception is in 'The Symbol: Food for Thought', p. 202, where Ricœur states that Eliade goes beyond 'living the life of symbols to autonomous thinking'.) Mircea Eliade has accounted for this 'first level' interpretation by explaining that Ricœur had read only his *Patterns* and that what impressed Ricœur most was Eliade's descriptive and comparative analysis on the symbolic plane of internal coherence.

42. *Ibid.*, pp. 356–357.

very same criticisms which philosophical phenomenology has directed against traditional (normative, reductionist, etc.) philosophy.

As we have seen, Eliade conceives of religion as a total existential orientation; as the religious person's irreducible mode of being in the world. By reflecting on the archetypal symbolisms, those inexhaustible 'ciphers' of reality, Eliade creatively formulates those most general of existential concepts, which reveal the fundamental structures of the human condition, of our 'true' nature and our 'real' mode of being in the world.

What makes Eliade's verification of these existential concepts so controversial, what adds to the impression that he reads into the religious data all kinds of sophisticated meanings and provides us with completely subjective interpretations, is the fact that he seems almost obsessed with those phenomena which Ricœur describes in terms of 'error, habit, emotion, passivity'. In other words, Eliade frequently verifies his existential structures by their power 'to raise up, to illuminate, to give order to' those phenomena which traditional philosophy has usually deemed unworthy of investigation and which other disciplines have reduced to the most 'aberrant', 'infantile', 'superstitious', and lowest levels of manifestation.

Thus, one might empathize with the phenomenologist's endeavor to verify some structure of transcendence in the light of the most 'elevated' expressions of philosophical and mystical yoga. But Mircea Eliade will devote more of his time to verifying this same structure of transcendence by its power to illuminate the nature and reveal the ontological foundation of customs of peasants, of erotic forms of tantric yoga, of beliefs and practices of alchemy, etc. Eliade often verifies such ontological structures by showing how they render more intelligible so much of modern behavior which we consider completely secular: our dreams, nostalgias, and fantasies; our various games and athletic contests; our movies, science fiction, contemporary novels, sculpture, paintings, and other aesthetic creations; our national chauvinism, way of regarding foreign peoples, and attitude toward work; our 'secular' rituals and customs, such as getting drunk on New Year's Eve; etc.

In short, Mircea Eliade, by reflecting on those essential symbolisms which 'key in' with many layers of actual experience, is able to 'burst open' the 'limited' dimensions of experience in order to reveal the *most profound ontological structures*. Here we have Eliade's frequent image of the human being, not simply as a historical being, but as *'a living symbol'*, who unifies phenomena on different levels of experience, who renews her or himself by 'opening out' to the transcendent, and who succeeds in 'living the universal'.

We offered an earlier observation that Mircea Eliade's ontological move to greater and greater levels of generality appears to take him beyond his perspectival limitations. His ontological analysis often takes him beyond some evaluation of what *homo religiosus*, on the basis of one's religious scale, regards to be real. In disregarding such perspectival limitations, isn't Mircea Eliade violating his own antireductionist principles and being guilty of the same kind of methodological reductionism he has consistently attacked?

Our position is that Mircea Eliade, on his levels of greatest generality, is involved in a reductionistic analysis, which, if he upholds his previously elucidated methodological principles, probably pushes his phenomenology of religion beyond the proper domain of the History of Religions. But such an analysis arises out of and is informed by the religious perspective. Indeed, it is dependent on a certain *privileged status* of the religious reality.

On this level of ontological analysis, we understand Mircea Eliade as saying the following. On the basis of the religious perspective, especially in the light of the fundamental symbolic structures of the sacred, we shall frame general existential concepts. Our assumption is that the fundamental symbols, which point beyond themselves to 'extra-linguistic' reality, exhibit *their highest and deepest function when they reveal the sacred*. In this case of religious symbolism, the symbols point beyond themselves and reveal 'the universal'; they 'open out' to the most general structures of reality.

Now let us 'wager' that such ontological concepts, formulated from the religious perspective, will reveal the nature of the human being and of reality better than the existential concepts framed in terms of some nonreligious perspective. We shall *verify* such a wager by showing that the primary symbolic structures of religious experience have the power to illuminate the fundamental structures of the human consciousness and mode of being *generally*, of the human condition *as such*.

Indeed, such a level of ontological analysis will reveal that only by experiencing the symbolic structures of the sacred, only be renewing ourselves through new revalorizations of religious symbolisms, can modern Western human beings overcome their 'terror of history' and their existential anxiety and live a truly meaningful human existence.

NEW PHILOSOPHICAL ANTHROPOLOGIES

As we have seen, on the levels of greatest generality, Mircea Eliade is concerned with ontology. His general normative judgments reveal an ontological analysis which, as we have suggested, often functions on the plane of philosophical anthropology. We may conclude this study by relating two themes which appear throughout the works of Eliade and which suggest his quest for laying the foundation for new philosophical anthropologies.

The first theme concerns Eliade's persistent critique of the provincialism and impoverishment of our contemporary Western orientations. Here we find his negative judgments of our modern attempts to define the human mode of being and the human condition in purely historical, temporal, rational, scientific, or other secular ways.

Second, there is Mircea Eliade's almost obsession with the theme of *œuvres*. He even praises 'reductionists' such as Freud and Durkheim for these creative 'breakthroughs', which 'burst open' the prevailing and limiting conditionings and open us to new universes of meaning. Eliade frequently analyzes the function of religion and the dialectic of the sacred in terms of such 'openings'.

On the level of interpretation we have just examined, on the level of such general normative judgments, it would seem that Mircea Eliade is concerned with both of these themes and is suggesting the possibilities for new and creative philosophical anthropologies. He contends that we have severely limited our present and possible future *œuvres* by defining reality in terms of our conditioned and self-imposed historical, temporal, and other structures. And his judgments reveal his view that there are countless possibilities for 'breakthroughs' which we have excluded because of our narrow, impoverished, contemporary perspectives.

Throughout his works, Professor Eliade has not only been critical of much of our modern Western perspective, but he even maintains that our limiting views of the human mode of being in the world and the human condition have not allowed us to understand our own behavior. This has led to self-deception and impoverished sensitivity and creativity. We have seen his claim that an awareness of a religious perspective, especially the primary symbolic structures, would lead to a new understanding of our dreams and fantasies, our artistic creations, and many of our 'secular' customs and institutions.

Eliade tells us that everywhere in the religious universe we find 'the same fundamental conception of the necessity to live in an intelligible and meaningful world, and we find that this conception emerges ultimately from the experience of a sacred space'.

> Now one can ask in what sense such experiences of the sacred space of houses, cities, and lands are still significant for modern desacralized man. Certainly, we know that man has never lived in the space conceived by mathematicians and physicists as being isotropic, that is, space having the same properties in all directions. The space experienced by man is *oriented* and thus anisotropic, for each dimension and direction has a specific value. . . . The question is whether the experience of oriented space and other comparable experiences of intentionally structured spaces (for example, the different spaces of art and architecture) have something in common with the sacred space known by *Homo religiosus*.[43]

It is Eliade's view that such reflection on many of our fundamental modern phenomena will lead to creative breakthroughs, to the discovery of new universes of meaning, to new philosophical anthropologies.

By focusing on our recent illustrations of the Chinese and Vietnamese revolutionary experiences, we may be able to suggest the

43. Eliade, 'The World, the City, the House', *Occultism, Witchcraft, and Cultural Fashions*, p. 30. On p. 27, Eliade claims that our 'scientific understanding of cosmic space — a space which has no center and is infinite — has nothing to do with the existential experience of living in a familiar and meaningful world'. On p. 31, he submits that 'the cosmic symbolism of sacred space is so old and so familiar that many are not yet able to recognize it'.

possible relevance of Eliade's phenomenology for creative openings and new philosophical anthropologies, even though this is an area far removed from Eliade's specific values and concerns.

During the past few decades, millions of Westerners have been inspired by and have identified with the Chinese and Vietnamese anti-imperalist struggles. Such modern Westerners have often criticized contemporary perspectives as leading to meaninglessness, alienation, and dehumanization; as being provincial, reactionary, and outdated; and as not allowing us to cope with those phenomena we considered under 'the terror of history'. The Chinese and Vietnamese, it has frequently been maintained, have presented us with new views of the self and of human nature, of a harmonious and meaningful life-world; in short, with new philosophical anthropologies.

Now such Westerners, in interpreting the successes of the Chinese and the Vietnamese, have almost always emphasized the 'correct' economic and political analysis formulated by Mao Tse-tung, Ho Chi Minh, and other revolutionaries. And certainly the Vietnamese and Chinese struggles would not have been successful without such a correct analysis.

But to someone who is sensitive to the phenomenological analysis of an Eliade— and who is also sensitive to such economic and political factors, in a way that Eliade is not — the Vietnamese and Chinese experiences will reveal many other dimensions of reality. The correct economic and political analysis will be seen as necessary but not sufficient in accounting for such experiences. The interpreter will decipher profound mythic and symbolic structures in the thought of Mao Tse-tung and Ho Chi Minh; essential symbolisms which key in with the deepest levels of reality and allow the integration of the fragmentary, meaningless, and even terrifying aspects of existence into a coherent, meaningful, purposeful whole.

Just as Eliade would not call for us to return to some archaic mode of being, Mao and Ho did not call for a return to Buddhist, Confucianist, and other earlier Oriental modes of being. But those aware of the phenomenological foundation we have formulated would begin to grasp how Mao and Ho did not simply reject, but revalorized certain progressive aspects of those values, integrating them within a new Marxist framework; so that we are presented with new creations, new universes of meaning, possibilities for new philosophical anthropologies.

As a phenomenologist of religion, Eliade has uncovered profound universes of meaning by interpreting the past symbolic and mythic structures of the archaic and the Oriental life-worlds. He has also seen that religious symbolism provides inexhaustible possibilities for future cosmic and other symbolic revalorizations which we have excluded because of our narrow sensitivity and intellectual horizon.

We would propose that Mircea Eliade seems to be suggesting that modern human beings, by establishing a dialogue with those archaic and Oriental universes of meaning and by establishing a dialogue with those primary symbolic structures and their inexhaustible possibilities for revalorization on all planes of reality, will be able to burst open our present limiting structures, so that we shall be able to see new creative possibilities and experience new philosophical anthropologies.

Bibliography

SELECTED BOOKS

Adams, Charles J. (ed.), *A Reader's Guide to the Great Religions*, New York: Free Press, 1965.

Alston, William P., *Religious Belief and Philosophical Thought*, New York: Harcourt, Brace & World, 1963.

Altizer, Thomas J. J., *Mircea Eliade and the Dialectic of the Sacred*, Philadelphia: Westminster Press, 1963.

——, Beardslee, William A., and Young, Harvey J. (eds.), *Truth, Myth, and Symbol*, Englewood Cliffs, N.J.: Prentice-Hall, 1962.

Baaren, Th. P. van, and Drijvers, H. J. W. (eds.), *Religion, Culture and Methodology*, The Hague: Mouton & Co., 1973 (Series 'Religion and Reason', vol. 8).

Baird, Robert D., *Category Formation and the History of Religions*, The Hague: Mouton & Co., 1971 (Series 'Religion and Reason', vol. 1).

Banton, Michael (ed.), *Anthropological Approaches to the Study of Religion*, New York: Frederick A. Praeger, 1966.

Berndt, R. M., *Kunapipi*, Melbourne: F. W. Chesire, 1951.

——, and Berdnt, C. H., *The First Australians*, Sydney: U. Smith, 1952.

Bianchi, U., Bleeker, C. J., and Bausani, A. (eds.), *Problems and Methods of the History of Religions*, Leiden: E. J. Brill, 1972.

Bouquet, A. C., *Comparative Religion: A Short Outline*, London: Penguin Books, 1962.

Caillois, Roger, *Man and the Sacred* (translated by Meyer Barash), Glencoe, Illinois: Free Press, 1959.

Camus, Albert, *The Myth of Sisyphus and Other Essays* (translated by Justin O'Brien), New York: Random House, Vintage Books, 1959.

——, *The Rebel: An Essay on Man in Revolt*, New York: Random House, Vintage Books, 1956.

Cassirer, Ernst, *An Essay on Man*, New Haven: Yale University Press, 1966.

——, *Language and Myth* (translated by Susanne K. Langer), New York: Dover Publications, 1946.

——, *The Philosophy of the Enlightenment* (translated by Fritz C. A. Koelln and James P. Pettegrone), Boston: Beacon Press, 1961.

Codrington, R. H., *The Melanesians*, Oxford: Clarendon Press, 1891.

Durkheim, Émile, *The Elementary Forms of the Religious Life* (translated by Joseph Ward Swain), Glencoe, Illinois: Free Press, 1954.

——, and Mauss, Marcel, *Primitive Classification* (translated with an Introduction by Rodney Needham), Chicago: University of Chicago Press, 1963.

Eliade, Mircea, *Australian Religions: An Introduction*, Ithaca: Cornell University Press, 1973.

Eliade, Mircea, *Cosmos and History: The Myth of the Eternal Return* (translated by Willard R. Trask), New York: Harper & Row, Torchbooks, 1959.

——, *The Forge and the Crucible* (translated by Stephen Corrin), New York: Harper and Brothers, 1962.

——, *From Primitives to Zen: A Thematic Sourcebook of the History of Religions*, New York: Harper & Row, 1967.

——, *Images and Symbols: Studies in Religious Symbolism*, New York: Sheed and Ward, 1961.

——, *Mephistopheles and the Androgyne: Studies in Religious Myth and Symbol* (translated by J. M. Cohen), New York: Sheed and Ward, 1965.

——, *Myth and Reality* (translated by Willard R. Trask), New York: Harper & Row, 1963.

——, *The Myth of the Eternal Return* (translated by Willard R. Trask), New York: Pantheon Books, 1954.

——, *Myths, Dreams and Mysteries* (translated by Philip Mairet), New York: Harper and Brothers, 1960.

——, *Occultism, Witchcraft, and Cultural Fashions: Essays in Comparative Religions*, Chicago: University of Chicago Press, 1976.

——, *Patterns in Comparative Religion* (translated by Rosemary Sheed), New York: World Publishing Co., Meridian Books, 1963.

——, *The Quest: History and Meaning in Religion*, Chicago: University of Chicago Press, 1969.

——, *Rites and Symbols of Initiation* (translated by Willard R. Trask), New York: Harper & Row, Torchbooks, 1965.

——, *The Sacred and the Profane: The Nature of Religion* (translated by Willard R. Trask), Harper & Row, Torchbooks, 1961.

——, *Shamanism: Archaic Techniques of Ecstasy* (translated by Willard R. Trask), New York: Pantheon Books, 1964.

——, *Yoga: Immortality and Freedom* (translated by Willard R. Trask), New York: Pantheon Books, 1958.

——, *Zalmoxis: The Vanishing God* (translated by Willard R. Trask), Chicago: University of Chicago Press, 1972.

——, and Kitagawa, Joseph M. (eds.) *The History of Religions: Essays in Methodology*, Chicago: University of Chicago Press, 1959.

Evans-Pritchard, E. E., *Theories of Primitive Religion*, Oxford: Oxford University Press, 1966.

Frazer, James George, *The Golden Bough: A Study in Magic and Religion*, 1st ed., 1890. (3d ed., in 12 vols., London: Macmillan and Co., 1907–15.)

——, *Totemism and Exogamy*, Vol. 1, London: Macmillan and Co., 1910.

Freud, Sigmund, *The Future of an Illusion* (translated by W. D. Robson-Scott), New York: Liveright Co., 1961.

——, *Totem and Taboo* (translated by A. A. Brill), New York: Moffat, Yard and Co., 1918.

Fromm, Erich, *Psychoanalysis and Religion*, New Haven: Yale University Press, 1959.

Gilkey, Langdon, *Naming the Whirlwind: The Renewal of God-Language*, Indianapolis: Bobbs-Merrill Co., 1969.

Helfer, James S. (ed.), *On Method in the History of Religions* (Beiheft 8 of *History and Theory*), Middletown, Conn.: Wesleyan University Press, 1968.

Hook, Sidney (ed.), *Religious Experience and Truth*, New York: New York University Press, 1961.

Husserl, Edmund, *Ideas: General Introduction to Pure Phenomenology* (translated by W. R. Boyce Gibson), London: George Allen & Unwin, 1931.

——, *Phenomenology and the Crisis of Philosophy* (translated with an Introduction by Quentin Lauer), New York: Harper & Row, Torchbooks, 1965.

Kirk, G. S., *Myth: Its Meaning and Functions in Ancient and Other Cultures*, Cambridge: At the University Press; Berkeley and Los Angeles: University of California Press, 1970.

James, William, *The Varieties of Religious Experience*, New York: New American Library, Mentor Books, 1958.

Johnson, F. Ernest (ed.), *Religious Symbolism*, New York: Harper & Brothers, 1955.

Jung, C. G., *Psychological Reflections* (edited by Jolande Jacobi), New York: Harper & Row, Torchbooks, 1961.

——, *Psychology and Religion*, New Haven: Yale University Press, 1938.

King Winston L., *Introduction to Religion: A Phenomenological Approach*, New York: Harper & Row, 1968.

Kitagawa, Joseph M. (ed.), *The History of Religions: Essays on the Problem of Understanding* (Vol. 1 of *Essays in Divinity*, edited by Jerald C. Brauer), Chicago: University of Chicago Press, 1967.

——, and Long, Charles H. (eds.), *Myths and Symbols: Studies in Honor of Mircea Eliade*, Chicago: University of Chicago Press, 1969.

Kockelmans, Joseph J. (ed.), *Phenomenology: The Philosophy of Edmund Husserl and Its Interpretation*, Garden City, N.Y.: Doubleday & Co., Anchor Books, 1967.

Kraemer, Hendrik, *The Christian Message in a Non-Christian World*, London: James Clarke & Co., 1956.

——, *Religion and the Christian Faith*, Philadelphia: Westminster Press, 1956.

Kristensen, W. Brede, *The Meaning of Religion* (translated by John B. Carman, Introduction by Hendrik Kraemer), The Hague: Martinus Nijhoff, 1960.

Kroeber, A. L. (ed.), *Anthropology Today*, Chicago: University of Chicago Press, 1957.

Lang, Andrew, *The Making of Religion*, London: Longmans, Green and Co., 1898.

——, *Myth, Ritual and Religion*, Vol. 1. 4th ed., London: Longmans, Green and Co., 1913.

Lawrence, Nathaniel, and O'Connor, Daniel (eds.), *Readings in Existential Phenomenology*, Englewood Cliffs, N.J.: Prentice-Hall, 1967.

Leeuw, Gerardus van der, *Religion in Essence and Manifestation*, 2 vols. (translated by J. E. Turner), New York: Harper & Row, Torchbooks, 1963.

Lenski, Gerhard, *The Religious Factor*, New York: Doubleday & Co., Anchor Books, 1963.

Lessa, William A., and Vogt, Evon Z. (eds.), *Reader in Comparative Religion: An Anthropological Approach*, New York: Harper & Row, 1958.

Lévi-Strauss, Claude, *The Savage Mind* (translated from *La Pensée Sauvage*), Chicago: University of Chicago Press, 1966.

——, *Structural Anthropology* (translated by Claire Jacobson and Brooke Grundfest Schoepf), Garden City, N.Y.: Doubleday & Co., Anchor Books, 1967.

——, *Totemism* (translated by Rodney Needham), Boston: Beacon Press, 1963.

Lévy-Bruhl, Lucien, *Primitive Mentality*, London: George Allen & Unwin, 1923.

Long, Charles H., *Alpha: The Myths of Creation*, New York: George Braziller, 1963.

Lowie, Robert H., *The History of Ethnological Theory*, New York: Farrar and Rinehart, 1937.
——, *Primitive Religion*, New York: Boni and Liveright, 1924.
Malinowski, Bronisław, *Magic, Science and Religion*, Glencoe, Illinois: Free Press, 1948.
Marett, R. R., *The Threshold of Religion*, London: Methuen and Co., 1909.
Merleau-Ponty, Maurice, *Phenomenology of Perception* (translated by Colin Smith), New York: Humanities Press, 1962.
——, *The Primacy of Perception* (edited with an Introduction by James M. Edie), Evanston: Northwestern University Press, 1964.
——, *Signs* (translated with an Introduction by Richard C. McCleary), Evanston: Northwestern University Press, 1964.
Müller, F. Max, *Anthropological Religion*, London: Longmans & Co., 1892.
——, *Chips from a German Workshop*, Vol. 1, New York: Scribners, 1869.
——, *Contributions to the Science of Mythology*, Vol. 1, London: Longmans & Co., 1897.
——, *Lectures on the Science of Language*, 2d series, New York: Scribner, Armstrong, and Co., 1875.
——, *The Six Systems of Indian Philosophy*, 1919. (Reprint. Varanasi, India: Chowkhamba Sanskrit Studies, n.d.)
Otto, Rudolf, *The Idea of the Holy* (translated by John W. Harvey), New York: Oxford University Press, A Galaxy Book, 1958.
Pettazzoni, Raffaele, *The All-Knowing God* (translated by H. J. Rose), London: Methuen and Co., 1956.
——, *Essays on the History of Religions* (translated by H. J. Rose), Leiden: E. J. Brill, 1954.
Radcliffe-Brown, A. R., *Method in Social Anthropology* (edited by M. N. Srinivas), Chicago: University of Chicago Press, 1958.
Radhakrishnan, Sarvepalli, *Eastern Religions and Western Thought*, London: Oxford University Press, 1958.
——, *The Heart of Hindusthan*, Madras: G. A. Natesan & Co., 1936.
——, *The Hindu View of Life*, London: Unwin Books, 1963.
Ramsey, Paul (ed.), *Religion*, Englewood-Cliffs, N.J.: Prentice-Hall, 1965.
Ricœur, Paul, *Husserl: An Analysis of His Phenomenology* (translated by Edward G. Ballard and Lester E. Embree), Evanston: Northwestern University Press, 1967.
——, *The Symbolism of Evil* (translated by Emerson Buchanan), New York: Harper & Row, 1967.
Schilpp, Paul Arthur (ed.), *The Philosophy of Sarvepalli Radhakrishnan* (Vol. 8 of *The Library of Living Philosophers*), New York: Tudor Publishing Co., 1952.
Schmidt, Wilhelm, *The Culture Historical Method of Ethnology* (translated by S. A. Sieber), New York: Fortuny's, 1939.
——, *The Origin and Growth of Religion* (translated by H. J. Rose), London: Methuen and Co., 1931.
Sebeok, Thomas A. (ed.), *Myth: a Symposium*, Philadelphia: American Folklore Society, 1955.
Smith, Homer W., *Man and His Gods*, New York: Grosset's Universal Library, 1957.
Smith, Huston, *The Religions of Man*, New York: New American Library, Mentor Books, 1959.
Smith, John E., *Reason and God*, New Haven: Yale University Press, 1967.

Smith, Wilfred Cantwell, *The Meaning and End of Religion*, New York: Macmillan Co., 1963.

Stanner, W. E. H., *On Aboriginal Religion* (The Oceania Monograph No. 11), Sydney: Australian Medical Publishing Co., 1963.

Strasser, Stephan, *The Soul in Metaphysical and Empirical Psychology*, Pittsburgh: Duquesne University Press, 1962.

Tax, Sol, Eiseley, Loren C., Rouse, Irving, and Voegelin, Carl F. (eds.), *An Appraisal of Anthropology Today*, Chicago: University of Chicago Press, 1953.

Tillich, Paul, *Systematic Theology*, Vol. 1, Chicago: University of Chicago Press, 1951.

Tylor, Edward B., *Primitive Culture*, Vol. 1., 1st ed., 1871. (6th ed. in 2 vols. London: John Murray, 1920.)

Underhill, Evelyn, *Mysticism*, New York: E. P. Dutton and Co., 1961.

Vries, Jan de, *The Study of Religion: A Historical Approach* (translated with an Introduction by Kees W. Bolle), New York: Harcourt, Brace & World, 1967.

Wach, Joachim, *The Comparative Study of Religions* (edited with an Introduction by Joseph M. Kitagawa), New York: Columbia University Press, 1961.

——, *Sociology of Religion*, Chicago: University of Chicago Press, Phoenix Books, 1962.

——, *Types of Religious Experience: Christian and non-Christian*, Chicago: University of Chicago Press, 1951.

Weber, Max, *From Max Weber: Essays in Sociology* (translated by H. H. Gerth and C. Wright Mills), New York: Oxford University Press, 1946.

——, *Gesammelte Aufsätze zur Religionssosiologie*, Vol, 1, Tübingen: J. C. B. Mohr, 1922. Partly translated as *The Protestant Ethic and the Spirit of Capitalism* by Talcott Parsons, London: G. Allen & Unwin, 1930.

——, *The Protestant Ethic and the Spirit of Capitalism* (translated by Talcott Parsons), New York: Charles Scribner's Sons, 1958.

Zaehner, R. C., *The Comparison of Religions*, Boston: Beacon Press, 1962.

Zimmer, Heinrich, *Myths and Symbols in Indian Art and Civilization* (edited by Joseph Campbell), New York: Harper & Brothers, Torchbooks, 1962.

SELECTED ARTICLES

Adams, Charles J., 'The History of Religions and the Study of Islām', in: *The History of Religions: Essays on the Problem of Understanding*, edited by Joseph M. Kitagawa, Chicago: University of Chicago Press, 1967.

Altizer, Thomas J. J., 'Mircea Eliade and the Recovery of the Sacred', *The Christian Scholar* 45 (1962): 267–289.

——, 'The Religious Meaning of Myth and Symbol', in: *Truth, Myth, and Symbol*, edited by Thomas J. J. Altizer, William A. Beardslee, and J. Harvey Young, Englewood Cliffs, N.J.: Prentice-Hall, 1962.

Ashby, Philip H., 'The History of Religions', in: *Religion*, edited by Paul Ramsay, Englewood Cliffs, N.J.: Prentice-Hall, 1965.

——, 'The History of Religions and the Study of Hinduism', in: *The History of Religions: Essays on the Problem of Understanding*, edited by Joseph M. Kitagawa, Chicago: University of Chicago Press, 1967.

Baaren, Th. P. van, 'Science of Religion as a Systematic Discipline: Some Introductory Remarks', in: *Religion, Culture and Methodology*, edited by Th. P. van Baaren and H. J. W. Drijvers, The Hague: Mouton & Co., 1973.

Beardslee, William A., 'Truth in the Study of Religion', in: *Truth, Myth, and Symbol*, edited by Thomas J. J. Altizer, William A. Beardslee, and J. Harvey Young, Englewood Cliffs, N.J.: Prentice-Hall, 1962.

Bednarski, Jules, 'The Eidetic Reduction', *Philosophy Today* 6 (1962): 14–24.

Bianchi, Ugo, 'The Definition of Religion: On the Methodology of Historical-Comparative Research', in: *Problems and Methods of the History of Religions*, edited by U. Bianchi, C. J. Bleeker, and A. Bausani, Leiden: E. J. Brill, 1972.

Bidney, David, 'The Concept of Value in Modern Anthropology', in: *Anthropology Today*, edited by A. L. Kroeber, Chicago: University of Chicago Press, 1957.

——, 'Myth, Symbolism and Truth', in: *Myth: A Symposium*, edited by Thomas A. Sebeok, Philadelphia: American Folklore Society, 1955.

Bleeker, C. Jouco, 'The Contribution of the Phenomenology of Religion to the Study of the History of Religions', in: *Problems and Methods of the History of Religions*, edited by U. Bianchi, C. J. Bleeker, and A. Bausani, Leiden: E. J. Brill, 1972.

——, 'The Future Task of the History of Religions', *Numen* 7 (1960): 221–234.

——, 'The Phenomenological Method', *Numen* 6 (1959): 96–111.

Boas, Franz, 'Evolution or Diffusion?', *American Anthropologist* 26 (1924): 340–344.

——, 'The Origin of Totemism', *American Anthropologist* 18 (1916): 319–326.

Bolle, Kees W., Introduction to *The Study of Religion*, by Jan de Vries, New York: Harcourt, Brace & World, 1967.

Dorson, Richard M., 'The Eclipse of Solar Mythology', in: *Myth: A Symposium*, edited by Thomas A. Sebeok, Philadelphia: American Folklore Society, 1955.

Dumézil, Georges, Preface to *Traité d'histoire des religions*, by Mircea Eliade, Paris: Payot, 1949.

Eliade, Mircea, 'Archaic Myth and Historical Man', *McCormick Quarterly* (Special Supplement: *Myth and Modern Man*) 18 (1965): 23–36.

——, 'Australian Religions, Part I: An Introduction', *History of Religions* 6 (1966): 108–134.

——, 'Australian Religions, Part II: An Introduction', *History of Religions* 6 (1967): 208–235.

——, 'Australian Religions, Part III: Initiation Rites and Secret Cults', *History of Religions* 7 (1967): 61–90.

——, 'Australian Religions, Part IV: The Medicine Men and Their Supernatural Models', *History of Religions* 7 (1967): 159–183.

——, 'Australian Religions, Part V: Death, Eschatology, and Some Conclusions', *History of Religions* 7 (1968): 244–268.

——, 'Comparative Religion: Its Past and Future', in: *Knowledge and the Future of Man*, edited by Walter J. Ong, S. J., New York: Holt, Rinehart and Winston, 1968.

——, 'Cosmogonic Myth and "Sacred History" ', *Religious Studies* 2 (1967): 171–183.

——, 'Crisis and Renewal in History of Religions', *History of Religions* 5 (1965): 1–17.

——, 'Cultural Fashions and the History of Religions', in: *The History of Religions: Essays on the Problem of Understanding*, edited by Joseph M. Kitagawa, Chicago: University of Chicago Press, 1967.

——, 'Encounters at Ascona', in: *Spiritual Disciplines*. Papers from the *Eranos-Jahrbuch*, Bollington Series, Band 30, Vol. 4 (1959): xvii–xxi.

——, 'Historical Events and Structural Meaning in Tension', *Criterion* 6 (1967): 29–31.

——, 'History of Religions and a New Humanism', *History of Religions* 1 (1961): 1–8.

——, 'History of Religions in Retrospect: 1912–1962', *Journal of Bible and Religion* 31 (1963): 98–109.

——, 'Methodological Remarks on the Study of Religious Symbolism', in *The History of Religions: Essays in Methodology*, edited by Mircea Eliade and Joseph M. Kitagawa, Chicago: University of Chicago Press, 1959.

——, 'On Prehistoric Religions', *History of Religions* 14 (1974): 140–147.

——, 'On Understanding Primitive Religions', in *Glaube, Geist, Geschichte: Festschrift für Ernst Benz*, edited by Gerhard Müller and Winfried Zeller, Leiden: E. J. Brill, 1967.

——, 'The Quest for the "Origins" of Religion', *History of Religions* 4 (1964): 154–169.

——, 'Recent Works on Shamanism: A Review Article', *History of Religions* 1 (1962): 152–186.

——, 'The Sacred and the Modern Artist', *Criterion* 4 (1965): 22–24.

——, 'The Sacred in the Secular World', *Cultural Hermeneutics* 1 (1973): 101–113.

——, South American High Gods: Part I', *History of Religions* 8 (1969): 338–354.

——, 'Structure and Changes in the History of Religion' (translated by Kathryn Atwater), in: *City Invincible*, edited by Carl Kraeling, Chicago: University of Chicago Press, 1960.

——, 'The Yearning for Paradise in Primitive Tradition', *Daedalus* 88 (1959): 255–267.

Faruqi, Isma'il Ragi A. al, 'History of Religions: Its Nature and Significance for Christian Education and the Muslim-Christian Dialogue', *Numen* 12 (1965): 35–65.

Fenton, John Y., 'Reductionism in the Study of Religions', *Soundings* 53 (1970): 61–76.

Frye, Northrop, 'World Enough Without Time', *The Hudson Review* 12 (1959): 423–431.

Geertz, Clifford, 'Religion as a Cultural System', in: *Anthropological Approaches to the Study of Religion*, edited by Michael Banton, New York: Frederick A. Praeger, 1966.

Goldenweiser, Alexander, 'Religion and Society: A Critique of Émile Durkheim's Theory of the Origin and Nature of Religion', *Journal of Philosophy, Psychology, and Scientific Methods* 14 (1917): 113–124.

Goodenough, Edwin R., *'Religionswissenschaft'*, *Numen* 6 (1959): 77–95.

Grabau, Richard F., 'Existential Universals', in: *An Invitation to Phenomenology*, edited by James M. Edie, Chicago: Quadrangle Books, 1965.

Hamilton, Kenneth, *'Homo Religiosus* and Historical Faith', *Journal of Bible and Religion* 33 (1965): 213–222.

Hartland, E. S., 'The "High Gods" of Australia', *Folklore* 9 (1898): 290–329.

Heiler, Friedrich, 'The History of Religions as a Preparation for the Co-operation of Religions', in: *The History of Religions: Essays in Methodology*, edited by Mircea Eliade and Joseph M. Kitagawa, Chicago: University of Chicago Press, 1959.

Hocart, A. M., 'Mana', *Man* 14 (1914): 97–101.

Hogbin, H. Ian, 'Mana', *Oceania* 6 (1936): 247–274.

Hudson, Wilson M., 'Eliade's Contribution to the Study of Myth', in: *Tire Shrinker to Dragster*, edited by Wilson M. Hudson, Austin: The Encino Press, 1968.

Ihde, Don, 'Some Parallels Between Analysis and Phenomenology', *Philosophy and Phenomenological Research* 27 (1967): 577–586.

King, Winston L., Review of *The Quest: History and Meaning in Religion*, by Mircea Eliade, *Journal for the Scientific Study of Religion* 9 (1970): 70–72.

Kishimoto, Hideo, 'An Operational Definition of Religion', *Numen* 8 (1961): 236–240.

Kitagawa, Joseph M., 'The History of Religions in America', in: *The History of Religions: Essays in Methodology*, edited by Mircea Eliade and Joseph M. Kitagawa, Chicago: University of Chicago Press, 1959.

——, 'The Life and Thought of Joachim Wach', in: *The Comparative Study of Religions*, by Joachim Wach, New York: Columbia University Press, 1961.

——, 'The Nature and Program of the History of Religions Field', (University of Chicago) *Divinity School News* (November 1957): 13–25.

——, 'Primitive, Classical, and Modern Religions: A Perspective on Understanding the History of Religions', in: *The History of Religions: Essays on the Problem of Understanding*, edited by Joseph M. Kitagawa, Chicago: University of Chicago Press, 1967.

Kockelmans, Joseph J., 'On Myth and Its Relationship to Hermeneutics', *Cultural Hermeneutics* 1 (1973): 47–86.

Kraemer, Hendrik, Introduction to *The Meaning of Religion*, by W. Brede Kristensen, The Hague: Martinus Nijhoff, 1960.

Kroeber, Alfred L., 'Totem and Taboo: An Ethnologic Psychoanalysis', *American Anthropologist* 22 (1920): 48–55.

Kwant, Remy C., 'Merleau-Ponty's Criticism of Husserl's Eidetic Reduction', in: *Phenomenology: The Philosophy of Edmund Husserl and Its Interpretation*, edited by Joseph J. Kockelmans, Garden City, N.Y.: Doubleday & Co., 1967. This selection is taken from Kwant's *From Phenomenology to Metaphysics* (Pittsburgh: Duquesne University Press, 1966).

Leach, Edmund, 'Sermons by a Man on a Ladder', *New York Review of Books* (20 October 1966): 28–31.

Lévi-Strauss, Claude, 'Social Structure', in: *Anthropology Today*, edited by A. L. Kroeber, Chicago: University of Chicago Press, 1957.

Lewis, Oscar, 'Comparisons in Cultural Anthropology', in: *Yearbook of Anthropology, 1955*, edited by William L. Thomas, Jr., New York: Wenner-Gren Foundation for Anthropological Research, 1955.

Long, Charles H., 'Archaism and Hermeneutics', in: *The History of Religions: Essays on the Problem of Understanding*, edited by Joseph M. Kitagawa, Chicago: University of Chicago Press, 1967.

——, 'The Meaning of Religion in the Contemporary Study of Religions', *Criterion* 2 (1963): 23–26.

——, 'Primitive Religion', in: *A Reader's Guide to the Great Religions*, edited by Charles J. Adams, New York: Free Press, 1965.

——, 'Prolegomenon to a Religious Hermeneutic', *History of Religions* 6 (1967): 254–264.

——, 'Where is the History of Religions Leading Us?', *Criterion* 6 (1967): 19–21.

Luyster, Robert, 'The Study of Myth: Two Approaches', *Journal of Bible and Religion* 34 (1966): 235–243.

Marshak, Alexander, 'Cognitive Aspects of Upper Paleolithic Engraving', *Current Anthropology* 13 (1972): 445–477.

Miller, David L., '*Homo Religiosus* and the Death of God', *Journal of Bible and Religion* 34 (1966): 305–315.

Morgan, John Henry, 'Religious Myth and Symbol: A Convergence of Philosophy and Anthropology', *Philosophy Today* 18 (1974): 68–84.

———. 'Myths for Moderns', *Times Literary Supplement* (London), 10 February 1966: 102.

Natanson, Maurice, 'A Study in Philosophy and the Social Sciences', in: *Literature, Philosophy, and the Social Sciences*, The Hague: Martinus Nijhoff, 1962.

Pemberton, Prentiss L., 'Universalism and Particularity: A Review Article', *Journal of Bible and Religion* 20 (1952): 97–99.

Penner, Hans H., 'Myth and Ritual: A Wasteland or a Forest of Symbols?', in: *On Method in the History of Religions*, edited by James S. Helfer, Middletown, Conn.: Wesleyan University Press, 1968.

Pettazzoni, Raffaele, 'The Supreme Being: Phenomenological Structure and Historical Development', in: *The History of Religions: Essays in Methodology*, edited by Mircea Eliade and Joseph M. Kitagawa, Chicago: University of Chicago Press, 1959.

Progoff, Ira, 'Culture and Being: Mircea Eliade's Studies in Religion', *International Journal of Parapsychology* 2 (1960): 47–60.

———, 'The Man Who Transforms Consciousness', in: *Eranos-Jahrbuch 1966*, Band 35 (1967): 99–144.

Radcliffe-Brown, A. R., 'Historical Note on British Social Anthropology', *American Anthropologist* 54 (1952): 275–277.

Radin, Paul, 'Religion of the North American Indians', *Journal of American Folklore* 27 (1914): 335–373.

Rasmussen, David, 'Mircea Eliade: Structural Hermeneutics and Philosophy', *Philosophy Today* 12 (1968): 138–146.

Ricketts, Mac Linscott, 'Eliade and Altizer: Very Different Outlooks', *Christian Advocate*, October 1967: 11–12.

———, 'Mircea Eliade and the Death of God', *Religion in Life* 36 (1967): 40–52.

———, 'The Nature and Extent of Eliade's "Jungianism" ', *Union Seminary Quarterly Review* 25 (1970): 211–234.

Ricœur, Paul, 'The Hermeneutics of Symbols and Philosophical Reflection', *International Philosophical Quarterly* 2 (1962): 191–218.

———, 'The Problem of the Double-Sense as Hermeneutic Problem and as Semantic Problem', in: *Myths and Symbols: Studies in Honor of Mircea Eliade*, edited by Joseph M. Kitagawa and Charles H. Long, Chicago: University of Chicago Press, 1969.

———, 'The Symbol: Food for Thought', *Philosophy Today* 4 (1960): 196–207.

Saiving, Valerie, 'Androcentrism in Religious Studies', *Journal of Religion* 56 (1976): 177–197.

Schimmel, Annemarie, 'Summary of the Discussion', *Numen* 7 (1960): 235–239.

'Scientist of Symbols', *Time*, 11 February 1966: 68, 70.

Smith, John E., 'The Structure of Religion', *Religious Studies* 1 (1965): 63–73.

Smith, Wilfred Cantwell, 'Comparative Religion: Whither — and Why?', in: *The History of Religions: Essays in Methodology*, edited by Mircea Eliade and Joseph M. Kitagawa, Chicago: University of Chicago Press, 1959.

———, 'The Comparative Study of Religion: Reflections on the Possibility and Purpose of a Religious Science', *McGill University, Faculty of Divinity, Inaugural Lectures*, Montreal: McGill University Press, 1950.

Strasser, Stephan, 'Phenomenologies and Psychologies', *Review of Existential Psychology and Psychiatry* 5 (1965): 80–105.

Tillich, Paul, 'The Meaning and Justification of Religious Symbols', in: *Religious Experience and Truth*, edited by Sidney Hook, New York: New York University Press, 1961.

——, 'The Religious Symbol', in: *Religious Experience and Truth*, edited by Sidney Hook, New York: New York University Press, 1961.

——, 'Theology and Symbolism', in: *Religious Symbolism*, edited by F. Ernest Johnson, New York: Harper & Brothers, 1955.

Tylor, E. B., 'Limits of Savage Religion', *Journal of the Anthropological Institute* 21 (1891): 283–301.

Wach, Joachim, 'Introduction: The Meaning and Task of the History of Religions', in: *The History of Religions: Essays on the Problem of Understanding*, edited by Joseph M. Kitagawa, (translated by Karl W. Luckert with the help of Alan L. Miller), Chicago: University of Chicago Press, 1967.

——, 'Radhakrishnan and the Comparative Study of Religion', in: *The Philosophy of Sarvepalli Radhakrishnan*, edited by Paul Arthur Schilpp, New York: Tudor Publishing Co., 1952.

——, 'Sociology of Religion', in: *Twentieth Century Sociology*, edited by G. Gurvitch and W. E. Moore, New York: Philosophical Library, 1945.

Watson, Goodwin, 'A Psychologist's View of Religious Symbols', in: *Religious Symbolism*, edited by F. Ernest Johnson, New York: Harper & Brothers, 1955.

Welbon, G. Richard, 'Some Remarks on the Work of Mircea Eliade', *Acta Philosophica et Theologica* 2 (1964): 465–492.

Index

Religion and Reason
Method and Theory in the Study and Interpretation of Religion

7. *Logique et Religion.*
L'Atomisme logique de L. Wittgenstein et la possibilité des proposi-
tions religieuses.
Including 'Logic and Religion', a shortened and adapted English
version of the text,
par Jacques Poulain (Université de Montréal, Canada)
1973, 228 pages. Clothbound
ISBN: 90-279-7284-2

8. *Religion, Culture and Methodology.*
Papers of the Groningen Working-group for the Study of Fundamental Problems and Methods of Science of Religion,
ed. by Th. P. van Baaren and H. J. W. Drijvers (University of
Groningen)
1973, 172 pages. Clothbound
ISBN: 90-279-7249-4

9. *Religion and Primitive Cultures.*
A Study in Ethnophilosophy,
by Wilhelm Dupré (University of Nijmegen)
1975, X + 356 pages. Clothbound
ISBN: 90-279-7531-0

10. *Christologies and Cultures.*
Toward a Typology of Religious Worldviews,
by George Rupp (Harvard University)
1974, XIV + 270 pages. Clothbound
ISBN: 90-279-7641-4

11. *The Biographical Process.*
Studies in the History and Psychology of Religion,
ed. by Frank E. Reynolds (University of Chicago) and Donald Capps
(University of North Carolina at Charlotte)
1976, XII + 436 pages. Clothbound
ISBN: 90-279-7522-1

12. *The Study of Religion and Its Meaning.*
New Explorations in Light of Karl Popper and Emile Durkheim,
by J. E. Barnhart (North Texas State University)
1977, XIV + 216 pages. Clothbound
ISBN: 90-279-7762-3

13. *Studies in the Methodology of the Science of Religion,*
     ed. by Lauri Honko (University of Turku, Finland)
     1978, approx. 600 pages. Clothbound
     ISBN: 90–279–7854–9

14. *Structure and Creativity in Religion.*
     Hermeneutics in Mircea Eliade's Phenomenology and New Direc-
     tions, by Douglas Allen (University of Maine)
     1978, XVIII + 266 pages. Clothbound
     ISBN: 90–279–7594–9

15. *Reflections on the Study of Religion.*
     Including an Essay on the Work of Gerardus van der Leeuw,
     by Jacques Waardenburg (University of Utrecht)
     1978, XII + 284 pages. Clothbound
     ISBN: 90–279–7604–X

16. *Interpretation and Dionysos.*
     Method in the Study of a God,
     by Park McGinty (Leigh University)
     1978, VIII + 258 pages. Clothbound
     ISBN: 90–279–7844–1

17. *Principles of Integral Science of Religion.*
     by Georg Schmid (Teachers College, Chur, Switzerland)
     1978, approx. 200 pages. Clothbound
     ISBN: 90–279–7864–6

Other volumes are in preparation

Mouton Publishers · The Hague · Paris · New York

DM 49.—